Paternalism

WARSAW STUDIES IN PHILOSOPHY AND SOCIAL SCIENCES

Edited by
Tadeusz Szawiel and Jakub Kloc-Konkołowicz

VOLUME 5

PETER LANG
EDITION

Antal Szerletics

Paternalism

Moral Theory and Legal Practice

PETER LANG
EDITION

Bibliographic Information published by the Deutsche Nationalbibliothek
The Deutsche Nationalbibliothek lists this publication in the Deutsche Nationalbibliografie; detailed bibliographic data is available in the internet at http://dnb.d-nb.de.

Library of Congress Cataloging-in-Publication Data
Szerletics, Antal, 1981-
Paternalism : moral theory and legal practice / Antal Szerletics. — 1 [edition].
pages cm. — (Warsaw studies in philosophy and social sciences, ISSN 2196-0143 ; Volume 5)
Includes bibliographical references.
ISBN 978-3-631-66800-9
1. Paternalism—Moral and ethical aspects. 2. Liberty. 3. Liberalism. I. Title.
JC571.S99 2015
170—dc23

2015033305

This publication was financially supported
by the National University of Public Service in Budapest.

ISSN 2196-0143
ISBN 978-3-631-66800-9 (Print)
E-ISBN 978-3-653-05924-3 (E-Book)
DOI 10.3726/978-3-653-05924-3

Peter Lang – Frankfurt am Main · Bern · Bruxelles · New York ·
Oxford · Warszawa · Wien

This publication has been peer reviewed.

www.peterlang.com

Contents

1. Introduction

A strange form of entertainment appeared among the French youth in the beginning of the 1990s. Local discotheques started to organize 'dwarf tossing' events, in which a dwarf, wearing suitable protective gear, would allow himself to be thrown short distances onto an air bed by the clients. French authorities soon prohibited these events, on the basis that the practice violated the principle of human dignity. In a series of appeals, the case was brought before the French *Conseil d'Etat* and the UN Human Rights Committee.[1] The applicant, Mr. Wackenheim, one of dwarf employees in question, claimed that banning him from his work had an adverse effect on his life and represented an affront to his dignity, since human dignity consists in having a job. Although his petition was rejected by both forums, Mr. Wackenheim's reasoning is also understandable to a certain degree. The case raises an interesting question for legal theorists. What are the acceptable limits of state intervention to protect competent individuals from their own self-harming conduct? Put it more directly, what are the rules and limits of legal paternalism?

Beginning with the age of the Enlightenment, paternalism came increasingly to the forefront of philosophical attention. Ever since this period, the dilemma of regulating self-harming behaviour has occupied the mind of many moral and legal philosophers. For the past two centuries, the discourse has been dominated by the harm principle of John Stuart Mill. The principle, when stating that "[...] the *only* purpose for which power can be rightfully exercised over any member of a civilized community, against his will, is to prevent harm to others", provides a clear-cut rule in relation to paternalism: it plainly excludes paternalism from the sphere of legitimate state interventions.[2] Taking Mill seriously, paternalism would not be an overly interesting question, either from a legal or an ethical perspective, because the harm principle regulates the question in a comprehensive manner. How come then that paternalism still raises so many theoretical controversies and generates so much debate in public discourse?

Obviously, the harm principle is far from being an uncontested formula. It is an essentially liberal precept that has been subjected to numerous criticisms,

---

1 *Wackenheim v France*, CCPR/C/75/D/854/1999; *Conseil d'Etat*, 27 Octobre 1995, N° 136727, *Commune de Morsang-sur-Orge*.

2 Mill, John Stuart: *On Liberty*. Norton: New York 1975, p. 10. This statement will be refined in chapter 3.2.

mainly because its radical prohibition of paternalism seems untenable in modern societies. There are several cases when paternalism seems unobjectionable and for some people, even expressly necessary. In principle, it is possible to agree with Feinberg that "[...] the [main] problem is to reconcile somehow our general repugnance for paternalism with the apparent necessity, or at least reasonableness, of some paternalistic regulations".[3] There are a lot of different justificatory theories of paternalism, and one can rightfully ask which theory handles self-harming actions most 'successfully'. The existence of these competing approaches partly explains the controversial character of paternalism, especially when considering that the debates over this question are heavily laden with moral and political presuppositions. These often preclude the possibility of rational discussion. However, there is a deeper problem that contributes to the controversial nature of paternalism, independent of political orientation or personal moral convictions. It seems to be related to any theory that strives to give a comprehensive rule for paternalism. Apparently, paternalism is such a complex and delicate issue that it is impossible to devise one overarching principle that could adequately 'govern' all of its dealings.

To demonstrate this complexity, consider some typical examples of paternalism. 'Classical' examples include regulations requiring motorcyclists to wear crash helmets or drivers to fasten their seat belts; prescribing safety equipment for construction workers; restricting the sale of alcoholic beverages or tobacco; establishing special rules for dangerous sports (e.g. high altitude mountaineering, white-water rafting, motor racing, etc.) or simply prohibiting potentially harmful activities (e.g. base jumping, the consumption of dangerous food).[4] More fundamental issues involve the prohibition of euthanasia, the criminalization of drug use or the introduction of compulsory public education. Paternalism often comes up in a non-legal context. The doctor who lies to a terminally ill woman on her deathbed (telling her that her son is doing well, although he has just lost his life in a car accident) definitely acts paternalistically. Parents offering extra pocket money to their children for earning good grades in school also act in a paternalistic way. It seems that the real significance of the question becomes evident when paternalism affects fundamental life choices (e.g. euthanasia).

3 Feinberg, Joel: *Harm to Self.* (= The Moral Limits of the Criminal Law) Oxford University Press: New York 1989, p. 111.

4 Certain parts of the Japanese blowfish *fugu* contain lethal amounts of poison. While licensed chefs are allowed to prepare the fish in Japan, the EU categorically prohibits its sale in Europe. Base jumping is similar to skydiving, except that base jumpers jump off fixed structures or cliffs instead of airplanes.

As long as paternalism deals with merely instrumental problems (e.g. safety belts or crash-helmets), it might 'feed' interesting theoretical debates but it has much less practical relevance.

1.1 The relevance of the topic

Paternalism has been a favourite 'playground' of moral philosophers for the last forty years. It has generated an immense amount of literature and articles still keep popping up regularly until this day. Although Hart already touches on the issue of paternalism in *Law, Liberty and Morality* (1963), the beginning of the intense debate can be attributed to the publication of Joel Feinberg's and Gerald Dworkin's seminal papers in 1971 and 1972.[5] An important stage in the theoretical development was the appearance of Feinberg's comprehensive book on paternalism published as the third part of his four-volume *magnum opus* entitled *The Moral Limits of the Criminal Law* (1989). The theoretical discourse continues with changing intensity. New scientific trends put the topic in new perspectives. For example, the recent idea of libertarian paternalism, based on the findings of cognitive psychology and behavioural economics, focuses on the application of non-coercive forms of paternalism. Newly emerging ethical theories, such as the ethics of care, demand the re-examination of previous models of paternalism based on traditional ethical approaches.

The protection from self-harming behaviour is not only a persistent theoretical question but also a fact of life that emerges in new forms with the increasing complexity and pluralism of modern societies. Technological advancement also creates new moral dilemmas with paternalistic implications (e.g. euthanasia). Consequently, paternalism often becomes the 'battlefield' of conflicting worldviews and remains a highly relevant issue nowadays. Paternalism permeates private and public relations as well. In the latter case, the question arises to what extent a 'paternalistic' welfare state should provide help to its citizens. This seems particularly relevant in post-socialist Central and Eastern Europe where people often feel nostalgic about the 'old times' when the state used to take 'better care' of its citizens.

5 These articles have been reprinted several times. For the original publications, see Feinberg, Joel: "Legal Paternalism". *Canadian Journal of Philosophy* 1 (1) (1971), pp. 105–124; Dworkin, Gerald: "Paternalism". *The Monist* 56 (1) (1972), pp. 64–84.

1.2 The method and scope of the research

The approach of this book is predominantly theoretical. There is a huge variety of philosophical arguments and theories related to paternalism and one of the objectives here is to try and 'clean up the conceptual mess' that characterizes this field. The book's method is 'meta-theoretical' to a certain extent, in the sense that it is a discourse on paternalistic discourses: it presents, evaluates and critically reflects on different justificatory theories of paternalism.

I primarily conceive paternalism as an ethical dilemma. Although it often becomes a legal issue in the form of paternalistic regulations and subsequent judicial decisions, there are questions of paternalism that never enter the field of law. Additionally, it seems that paternalistic state interventions are often backed up by ethical arguments. Paternalism at the level of constitutional adjudication can be conceived as the collision of certain fundamental rights and/or constitutional interests, typically with the right to privacy in focus. Despite the fact that there are established constitutional tests in the jurisprudence of high courts to resolve these collisions, it can be convincingly argued that the balancing procedure often reflects ethical arguments and the outcome of cases is determined by ethical considerations.

There are three possible methods to decide an ethical dilemma such as paternalism.[6] (1) The top-down approach follows the traditional syllogism-model of applying pre-existing rules to specific situations.[7] It works by subsuming a particular case under a general norm or abstract principle. This deductivist model seems to function well in 'simple' cases that can be brought directly and unambiguously under one specific moral principle. Unfortunately, most paternalistic cases are not so easy to decide because the abstract rules regulating paternalism are often indeterminate and there might be conflicting principles that require balancing as well. Let us take a simple autonomy-based rule for paternalism, for example that 'paternalistic interventions are justified as long as they do not violate the autonomy of the paternalised person'. Two problems seem to render the top-down model inoperable here. The first one is related to the abstract character of the rule, most notably that it does not specify the exact meaning of the term 'autonomy'. The second problem is that a 'rival' principle potentially applicable to paternalistic situations, namely the principle of benevolence might prescribe different actions than the principle of autonomy. (2) The bottom-up strategy of

---

6 Beauchamp, Tom L. / Childress, James F.: *Principles of Biomedical Ethics*. 6th edition. Oxford University Press: New York 2009, p. 195.

7 Van Hoecke, Mark: *Law as Communication*. Hart Publishing: Oxford 2002, p. 172.

justification is an inductivist method which claims that paradigmatic cases and particular judgments allow us to draw moral conclusions independently of general norms. Such 'casuistic' model is comparable to the precedent-system of the common law. New cases are decided on the basis of previous cases that show similar features and present similar problems as the case in question. Chapter 4 will examine the possibility of a 'contextual' and 'case-sensitive' approach to the justification of paternalistic interventions. However, this approach does not necessarily imply casuistry. With virtue ethics in centre, the question is not how to derive right actions from previous paradigmatic decisions, but how to derive right actions from virtuous character. (3) It is possible to argue that there is a 'middle way' between the top-down and the bottom-up approaches in which general rules and individual cases seem to mutually influence each other in a 'reflective equilibrium'. Neither principles, nor paradigmatic cases are given priority here. It is the coherence of these elements that matters. The way this book makes use of certain hard cases of paternalism seems to reflect a 'reflective equilibrium' approach since the discussed cases aim to demonstrate how moral intuitions might influence abstract principles in concrete situations.

The method of my theoretical investigation is mainly analytical which might be explained by the fact that the discourse on paternalism is dominated by the works of English and American authors. The scope of legal research is limited to the analysis of selected cases and problems. A comprehensive empirical overview of paternalistic legal regulations will not be provided, partly because it is irrelevant from a theoretical perspective, and partly because it seems impossible to examine all laws and judicial decisions related to this issue. The notion of paternalism is extremely wide, especially when benefit-promoting forms are taken into account. With a slight exaggeration, most forms of welfare regulations and institutions, from public education to health insurance policies, can be considered as having paternalistic implications.

1.3 The structure of the book

This book consists of four main chapters. The theoretical investigations of the first three chapters (chapters 2, 3 and 4) make up the larger part of the work, while the last chapter (chapter 5) discusses practical legal issues. **Chapter 2** deals with the definitional and justificatory questions of paternalism. Although it might seem easy at first sight to give an account of paternalism, there is a large variety of substantially different definitions in the philosophical literature. The aim of this chapter is to identify the definitional elements that seem necessary to construct an 'adequately wide' notion of paternalism. The analysis will show that most definitions make reference to the violation of the subject's liberty or autonomy (i.e. the 'element of interference') and to the harm-preventing or benefit-promoting character of paternalism (i.e. the 'element of benevolence'). The chapter also demonstrates how definitions gradually extend the 'element of interference' in order to cover most diverse forms of paternalism. Since completely self-regarding actions are extremely rare and almost any action can be interpreted as 'interfering' with someone else's autonomy, the question arises whether 'interference' is a necessary conceptual element of paternalism at all. It is possible to argue that paternalism is best defined by its motive which, on a rudimentary level, implies benevolence, i.e. the benevolent desire to take care of someone in need. After the analysis of possible definitional elements, the 'external' and the 'internal' aspects of paternalism are examined. Since paternalism often overlaps with other liberty-limiting principles, conceptual clarity requires that it is separated from other principles used to justify intervention to someone's liberty. With respect to the 'internal' aspects of paternalism, distinctions are made *within* the concept and different 'subtypes' of paternalism are identified.

The second part of the chapter presents the most commonly employed justificatory models of paternalism. It seems possible to distinguish between three basic approaches of justification, corresponding to the three main trends of normative ethics. Emphasis will be placed on the examination of autonomy-based justifications due to their apparent predominance in the scientific discourse. Two main trends are distinguished within this category: voluntariness-based justifications focus on the voluntariness of self-harming actions, while consent-based theories require the paternalised person's consent to justify paternalistic interventions. The voluntariness-model is presented through a critical examination of Joel Feinberg's theory. Certain weaknesses of Feinberg's theory are pointed out, including the problem of 'evaluative' self-harming decisions. These decisions are fully voluntary, but they might seem irrational or unreasonable to others because they represent unusual and essentially subjective preferences. Feinberg's theory seems unable to give a conclusive answer to paternalism when it comes to such self-harming choices. On a more fundamental level, it is possible to object to the 'fetishization' of voluntary choice on the basis that Feinberg connects voluntariness too 'intimately' to the notion of autonomy. Equating voluntariness with autonomy is problematic because voluntariness seems to be only one element of autonomous decision-making and acting voluntarily does not necessarily lead to an autonomous life based on truly authentic preferences. Proceeding to consent-based theories, five types of consent will be examined with respect to their justificatory potential related to paternalism (contemporaneous, prior, subsequent, anticipated and hypothetical consent).

Chapter 3 is an attempt to point out some of the weaknesses of the autonomy-based approaches. The first section contains a detailed examination of the notion of autonomy. Autonomy is a complex concept that can be understood in many different ways. Consequently, an autonomy-based approach to paternalism first seems to presuppose the adoption of a specific theory of autonomy. Personal autonomy is constituted by external and internal components that can be oppositely affected by different interventions. Paternalistic manipulation, for example, interferes with the internal conditions of autonomy (e.g. by affecting the process of preference formation) but it does not necessarily take away options from someone. Moreover, the value and the normative character of autonomy seem to be 'contingent' on social-historical circumstances. People attribute a distinguished value to autonomy in the modern age but with the failure of the 'Enlightenment-project', the 'myth' of autonomy is gradually dissolved. As emphasis shifts from the individual to the community, the approach to paternalism also seems to change from rejection to (limited) acceptance.

The second section examines the problems associated with the harm principle of John Stuart Mill. The principle, in its original form, sets a blanket prohibition to legal paternalism and moralism which is justified by Mill's utilitarian reasoning. However, there is a tension between Mill's commitment to utilitarianism and his categorical approach towards liberty. This tension is resolved by 'replacing' the utilitarian justification of the harm principle with a deontological framework. It will be demonstrated that this 'interpretational change' is already implicit in *On Liberty* and it is fulfilled in the theories of modern liberal authors such as Joel Feinberg. Taking into account this interpretational shift, a strange paradox appears: while the absolute character of Mill's prohibition is gradually abandoned through different methods of 'softening' the harm principle, the utilitarian justification is replaced by a deontological background, which seems more suitable for justifying categorical prohibitions.

The aim of the third section is to present some hard cases that illustrate the practical difficulties with respect to the harm principle's strict deontological reading. The discussed cases can be considered 'hard' because there seems to be an apparent tension between one's moral intuitions and the way the harm principle instructs us to resolve these examples of paternalism. The cases in this section are related to physical protection (e.g. crash helmet and safety-belt regulations), dangerous substances (e.g. cigarette and alcohol consumption), active euthanasia and certain aspects of protection of human dignity.

The last section of the third chapter 'elevates' the discussion on paternalism to the level of political philosophy. The requirement of state neutrality seems to fit well with autonomy-based approaches. This is hardly a coincidence considering the common theoretical background of the harm principle and liberal neutrality. The basic idea here is that citizens in modern pluralistic societies hold different views about what constitutes a 'good' life to them. Thus, the state should be neutral towards the competing conceptions of the moral good and should not interfere with the autonomous choices of competent individuals, even if these are self-harming or morally despicable. This section presents the ideas of John Rawls and Ronald Dworkin related to paternalism and demonstrates how the liberal separation between the 'right' and the 'good' is criticized by communitarian authors.

Chapter 4 presents 'alternative approaches' to paternalism. I will briefly discuss virtue ethics and the ethics of care and show that just as these theories bring along a new perspective compared to Kantianism and utilitarianism in general, they are capable of changing one's approach towards paternalism as well. It is possible to argue that virtue ethics can provide more practical and case-sensitive (but less comprehensive) guidelines for the justification of paternalism than deontology or consequentialism. Paternalism that exhibits the virtue of care can hardly be conceived as a violation of personal autonomy, especially if autonomy is reinterpreted as a relational concept that exists and develops *within* social relations.

Chapter 5 contains an analysis of the jurisprudence of the Hungarian Constitutional Court and the European Court of Human Rights. The examination of the Hungarian case law focuses on the constitutionality of 'traditional' harm-preventing forms of paternalism, such as the regulation of drugs, euthanasia, medical sterilization and the compulsory vaccination of children. Some centrally important judgments on homosexuality (e.g. age of consent, registered partnership) are also discussed. The objective of this part is to explore the relevant constitutional doctrine and the political or moral presuppositions that determine the Court's approach related to self-harming cases. Although the Hungarian Court generally tries to avoid references to 'substantive' values in its reasoning, deciding hard cases of paternalism necessarily implies taking sides in controversial moral debates. The question seems to be how the Court manages to reconcile this 'inevitable impartiality' with its professed value neutrality.[8] The next part of

8 Sólyom, László: *Az alkotmánybíráskodás kezdetei Magyarországon*. Osiris: Budapest 2001, p. 689.

the chapter focuses on the issue of 'moral paternalism' in the jurisprudence of the European Court of Human Rights. It starts with a short overview of legal moralism, touching mainly on the Hart-Devlin debate and its theoretical repercussions in order to show that questions of moralism and paternalism often overlap. The European Court of Human Rights had to examine in a number of cases whether moralistic restrictions affecting the right to privacy (e.g. homosexuality) or the right to freedom of expression (e.g. obscenity, blasphemy) are in line with the European Convention; the aim is to uncover any paternalistic or moralistic rationale behind the restrictive regulations of member states in these cases.

2. Definitional and justificatory questions

2.1 Defining paternalism

I will give an overview of the concept of paternalism in this chapter. First, I am going to discuss the etymological questions related to the expression. In order to conduct an impartial examination, it seems necessary to reveal any negative connotation that has become attached to the concept during its historical development. In the second part, I analyse different definitions of paternalism and critically examine core conceptual elements that might be considered as constitutive for an 'adequate' definition. Particular emphasis will be placed on the questions of autonomy and benevolence because paternalism seems inseparable from these concepts in most cases. Since paternalism often overlaps with other liberty-limiting principles, conceptual clarity requires that we separate it from other 'external' principles commonly used to justify intervention to someone's liberty (cf. the third part of this chapter). Finally, I will make distinctions within the concept itself and give an overview of the different types of paternalism that have been identified.

2.1.1 The origins of the expression

The presumption that paternalism is rooted in fundamental human characteristics such as empathy and benevolence implies that paternalistic behaviour has been present in social interactions from a very early age. The expression, however, seems relatively new. Kleinig claims that the word 'paternalism' appeared only in the late 19th century reflecting the proliferation of '-isms' in this period.[9] Accordingly, the first illustration of the word in the Oxford English Dictionary dates back to 1873, mentioning it in the context of international relations, i.e. as a policy that England adapts toward Ireland.[10]

---

9 Kleinig, John: *Paternalism*. Manchester University Press: Manchester 1983, p. 3. See also Thompson, Lindsay: *Paternalism*. Encyclopedia Britannica Online (2015) (http://www.britannica.com/topic/paternalism) (06.01.2015).

10 Paternalism, Oxford English Dictionary (Oxford University Press: June 2015) (http://www.oed.com/) (07.05.2015). Kultgen mentions 1881 as the year of the expression's first evidenced use. Kultgen, John: *Autonomy and Intervention: Parentalism in the Caring Life*. Oxford University Press: New York 1995, p. 249.

It seems that the conceptual origins of paternalism can be traced back to the early modern age.[11] Paternalistic practices were relatively uncontroversial in ancient and medieval times; the birth of the concept can partly be attributed to the emergence of a 'modern' dilemma, i.e. the separation between private and public and the question whether protective paternal power considered permissible in private relations is also acceptable in the public sphere. Apparently, the notion of paternalism was forged during the historical process of the Enlightenment and it is closely connected to the birth of modern liberalism.

John Locke draws a distinction between paternal and political power and argues that while paternal power is natural, political power is given to 'governors' for the benefit of their subjects by voluntary agreement.[12] He holds parental paternalism necessary in the case of minors because they lack sufficient reason to act independently. He writes:

> "First, then, Paternal or parental power is nothing but that which parents have over their children, to govern them for the children's good, till they come to the use of reason, or a state of knowledge, wherein they may be supposed capable to understand that rule, whether it be the law of nature, or the municipal law of their country [...] The affection and tenderness which God hath planted in the breast of parents towards their children, makes it evident, that this is not intended to be a severe arbitrary government, but only for the help, instruction, and preservation of their offspring."[13]

Locke argues for the acceptability of 'soft paternalism' within family relationships: coercion seems primarily justified because children are not yet able to make responsible choices. Parents have 'temporary jurisdiction' over them but the 'bonds of this subjection' are loosened by 'age and reason' as they grow.[14] Moreover, arbitrariness is limited by the affection of parents towards their children. For Locke, political power is different from paternal power in three important ways – if these differences exist, the claim that we need to relate differently to public than

11 Apparently, the concept of paternalism appeared earlier than the expression. Locke, for example, seems to be preoccupied with certain questions of paternalism without mentioning the word in the Two Treatises of Government.

12 "Nature gives the first of these, viz. paternal power to parents for the benefit of their children during their minority, to supply their want of ability, and understanding how to manage their property. [...] Voluntary agreement gives the second, viz. political power to governors for the benefit of their subjects, to secure them in the possession and use of their properties." Locke, John: *Second Treatise of Government*. Hackett Publishing: Indianapolis, Ind. 1980, p. 90. (section 173).

13 Ibid. 88 (section 173).

14 Locke 1980, p. 31 (section 55).

to private paternalism seems defensible. Firstly, the subjects of political power are mostly competent adults so this form of power does not have a natural source but must be based on a 'compact'. Secondly, the impersonal relations of the public sphere imply that guarantees other than parental affection are be necessary to prevent arbitrary exercise of political power. Thirdly, and somewhat relatedly to the previous point, there is a difference with respect to the underlying motives behind public and private 'parentalism'. Parental paternalism seems to be motivated by altruistic behaviour, driven by the desire to provide the best, or at least what is thought to be best, for someone's offspring. State paternalism might have different, much less altruistic motives.[15]

The word 'paternalism' has negative connotations attached to it. Such negative overtones are commonly attributed to the coercive character of paternalistic interventions or to the impermissible intentions behind paternalism (i.e. the intention to benefit someone against his or her will).[16] Paternalism is not, however, an 'inherently' immoral concept; rather, it seems to have acquired its bad connotations throughout the course of history.[17] Going just one historical step before Locke, paternalism can also be associated with the medieval concept of *patriarchalism*, which used the paternal analogy to justify the privileges of the feudal ruling elite over the common people.[18] The main 'ideologist' of this approach, Sir Robert Filmer, argued that the Sovereign has power over his people just as father has power over his children. In his book *Patriarcha*, Filmer made great efforts to trace back the lineage of kings to Adam and the Biblical patriarchs in order to prove that rulers are in a certain way parents of their people (since they are descendants of Adam, the father of all people), and therefore have natural paternal rights over them.

---

15 Isaiah Berlin distinguished three reasons why people want to curtail the liberties of other people: either (a) because they wish to impose their power on others; or (b) because they want conformity; or (c) because they believe that that there is one true answer of how people should lead their lives. Isaiah Berlin, *John Stuart Mill and the Ends of Life,* in Matravers, Derek / Pike, Jonathan / Warburton, Nigel: *Reading Political Philosophy: Machiavelli to Mill.* Routledge in association with the Open University: London 2000, p. 336.

16 Cornell, Nicholas: "A Third Theory of Paternalism". *Michigan Law Review* 113 (2015), p. 3.

17 Kleinig explains that moral condemnation is not inherent in the word 'paternalism', unlike, for example, in the word 'murder'. Kleinig 1983, p. 4.

18 Ibid. See also Kultgen 1995, p. 132.

> "It may seem absurd to maintain, that Kings now are the Fathers of their People, since Experience shews the contrary. It is true, all Kings be not the Natural Parents of their Subjects, yet they all either are, or are to be reputed the next Heirs to those first Progenitors, who were at first the Natural Parents of the whole People."[19]

With the coming of the Enlightenment, such natural law explanations were gradually replaced by contractarian models of sovereignty. Locke provides an extensive critique of Filmer's *Patriarcha* in his *First Treatise of Government*, rejecting the analogy between parental power and political sovereignty. As discussed earlier, the *Second Treatise* also rejects the idea of building political power on 'natural' grounds and emphasizes the role of consent in the formation of political community.

It might be that the term paternalism was originally coined to combat the *patriarchalist* ideology of the former ruling elite,[20] but in the process of conceptualization, paternalism acquired the same negative connotations. Paternalism was not welcomed in a time that started to prize individuality and autonomy over traditional medieval values. The term might have still reminded people of the despotism of the 'Patriarchs', but the main problem, it seems, was its incompatibility with the new liberal order of modern age. Paternalism implies unjustified authority and suggests that the state stands to its citizens as a father stands to his children, treating competent adults as if they were children.[21] This goes against the fundamental principles of modernity. To quote a well-known passage from Kant:

> "Enlightenment is man's emergence from his self-imposed immaturity. Immaturity is the inability to use one's understanding without guidance from another. This immaturity is self-imposed when its cause lies not in lack of understanding, but in lack of resolve and courage to use it without guidance from another."[22]

If adults are treated as children, it is fearful that they will never emerge from their 'self-imposed immaturity' and easily fall prey to the oppression of tyrannical political regimes. Kant echoes this concern in the following way: "If a government were founded on the principle of benevolence toward the people as a father's toward his children – in other words if it were a paternalistic government

---

19 Filmer, Robert: *Patriarcha and Other Writings*. Cambridge University Press: Cambridge 1991, p. 10 (chapter 1, section 8).

20 Kultgen 1995, p. 209.

21 Feinberg 1989, p. 22.

22 Kant, Immanuel: *An Answer to the Question: What is Enlightenment?*, in *Kant Selections*. Macmillan: New York, London 1988, p. 462.

(*imperium paternale*) [...] – such a government would be the worst conceivable despotism."[23]

Given the troubled history of the concept, it is no wonder that paternalism has become, if not a curse word, a 'preposterous doctrine' for liberal philosophers.[24] However, paternalism has not always been associated with pejorative connotations. Aristotle thought that the *polis* does not only have the right to act paternalistically but often has a duty to do so, especially when it comes to promoting the moral character of its citizens. "But those who are concerned with good government give careful attention to political virtue and vice. Hence it is quite evident that the city-state (at any rate, the one truly so called and not just for the sake of argument) must be concerned with virtue."[25] Following this tradition, most perfectionist moral and political theories do not perceive paternalism as inherently wrong but reinterpret it as an intervention that is potentially conducive to human welfare and flourishing.

It seems essential to keep in mind the value-laden character of the expression in order to conduct an impartial and objective examination in the following chapters. John Kultgen, for similar reasons, proposes to replace paternalism with the word 'parentalism'.[26] It is tempting to follow this option, not only because of the new expression's gender neutral character, but also because it avoids the negative connotations paternalism carries. Nevertheless, for the sake of convenience, this book will use the word 'paternalism' from now on.

---

23 Kant, Immanuel: *On the Old Saw: That May be Right in Theory But It Won't Work in Practice*. University of Pennsylvania Press: Philadelphia 1974, pp. 58–59.

24 Feinberg 1989, p. 24.

25 Aristotle: *Politics*. Hackett Publishing: Indianapolis 1998, Book III. 1280b. Robert P. George quotes Ernest Barker's translation: "Any *polis* which is truly so called, and is not merely one in name, must devote itself to the end of encouraging goodness. [...] What constitutes a *polis* is an association of households and clans in a good life, for the sake of attaining a perfect and self-sufficing existence." George, Robert P.: *Making Men Moral – Civil Liberties and Public Morality*. Clarendon Press: Oxford 1995, p. 21.

26 Kultgen 1995, p. 61. John Locke has already raised a similar point concerning paternal power: "[a]nd yet possibly it may not be amiss to offer new ones [i.e. words and names], when the old are apt to lead men into mistakes, as this of *paternal power* probably has done, which seems so to place the power of parents over their children wholly in the father, as if the mother had no share in it [...]" Locke, John: *Second Treatise of Government*. Hackett Publishing: Indianapolis 1980, p. 30 (section 52).

2.1.2 The concept of paternalism

Definitions, by determining our understanding of reality, affect the scope of scientific examination. Although it is important to keep conceptual (descriptive) and justificatory (normative) issues separated, it seems that the definition of paternalism might have normative relevance inasmuch as it determines the range of phenomena that require justification *as* paternalism. Without touching on any of the justificatory questions for the time being, a broad definition of paternalism seems desirable in order to keep the scope of the initial investigation as wide as possible.[27]

There have been many attempts to define paternalism. Paternalism is not a 'natural kind'[28] and – seeing the huge amount of complex and often conflicting definitions – one is tempted to give a stipulative definition of the concept.[29] Presumably, this would preclude possible debates over the definition's correctness because stipulative definitions are arbitrary in the sense that they assign a meaning to a word for the first time.[30] However, the word 'paternalism' has acquired a meaning in ordinary language use and it seems plausible to test the different definitions against the colloquial meaning of the word – even if it is quite vague and uncertain. This correspondence is important but an 'adequate' definition will have to satisfy a number of other expectations as well; a definition will be judged

---

27 The importance of separating justificatory and definitional elements is articulated by Donald VanDeVeer. "Our ultimate focus [...] concerns the justifiability of paternalistic acts. We want to evaluate them. But when is an act correctly described as a 'paternalistic act'? The latter is a conceptual issue; the former is an evaluative one. In familiar discussions these two questions often get confused and, as a result, the inquiry or dispute gets muddled." VanDeVeer, Donald: *Paternalistic Intervention: The Moral Bounds of Benevolence*. Princeton University Press: Princeton, NJ 1986, p. 6. See also Pope, Thaddeus Mason: "Counting the Dragon's Teeth and Claws: The Definition of Hard Paternalism". *Georgia State University Law Review* 20 (3) (2004), pp. 659–722, p. 681.

28 Gerald Dworkin, *Defining Paternalism*, in Coons, Christian / Weber, Michael (eds.): *Paternalism: Theory and Practice*. Cambridge University Press: Cambridge 2013, p. 38. According to the Stanford Encyclopedia of Philosophy, a 'kind is *natural* if it corresponds to a grouping or ordering that does not depend on humans.' Bird, Alexander / Tobin, Emma: "Natural Kinds". In: Zalta, Edward N. (ed.): *The Stanford Encyclopedia of Philosophy*. 2012 Winter (http://plato.stanford.edu/entries/natural-kinds/) (01.03.2015).

29 Gerald Dworkin, *Defining Paternalism*, in Coons / Weber 2013, p. 31.

30 Hurley, Patrick J.: *A Concise Introduction to Logic*. 9th ed. Thomson/Wadsworth: Belmont, CA 2006, p. 88.

according to e.g. its consistency, its context and the set of problems it is used to clarify and resolve.[31]

In colloquial English, paternalism can be understood as "the policy or practice of restricting the freedoms and responsibilities of subordinates or dependants in what is considered or claimed to be their best interests".[32] Despite the imprecision of this definition, it is already possible to discern two 'candidates' that might constitute the basic conceptual elements of paternalism: the restriction of freedom and the element of best interests (benevolent aims).

There is a huge variety of definitions readily available for paternalism in the philosophical literature.[33] Most authors focus on notions such as freedom, liberty, autonomy, consent or voluntariness in their definitions. This 'clamorous cacophony' is increased by the confusion of definitional and justificatory elements. Some elements, like voluntariness and consent seem to affect justificatory questions but not the concept itself.[34]

Paternalism, in its crudest form, can be defined as coercive intervention to the behaviour of a person in order to prevent the individual from causing harm to his or her self.[35] This definition has three basic components: (1) intervention, (2) coercion and (3) the aim of preventing self-harm. In order to create a sufficiently wide and precise definition, each of these elements needs further explanation.

---

31 Gerald Dworkin, *Defining Paternalism*, in Coons / Weber 2013, p. 25.

32 Paternalism, Oxford English Dictionary, June 2015. Oxford University Press: 2015.

33 A recent definition given by Gerald Dworkin looks the following: 'X acts paternalistically towards Y by doing (or omitting) Z if and only if: (1) Z (or its omission) interferes with the liberty or autonomy of Y; (2) X does so without the consent of Y; (3) X does so just because doing Z will improve the welfare of Y, or in some way promote the interests, values, or good of Y.' Gerald Dworkin, *Defining Paternalism*, in Coons / Weber 2013, p. 29. The following is a non-exhaustive list of other possible definitions. Dworkin 1972, p. 70. Feinberg 1971, p. 105. Murphy, Jeffrie G.: "Incompetence and Paternalism". *Archiv für Rechts- und Sozialphilosophie* 60 (4) (1974), pp. 465–486, p. 465; Gert, Bernard / Culver, Charles M.: "Paternalistic Behavior". *Philosophy & Public Affairs* 6 (1) (1976), pp. 45–57, p. 49; Hospers, John: "Libertarianism and Legal Paternalism". *Journal of Libertarian Studies* 4 (3) (1980), pp. 255–265, p. 255. Archard, David: "Paternalism Defined". *Analysis* 50 (1) (1990), pp. 36–42, p. 36. Valdés, Ernesto Garzón: "On Justifying Legal Paternalism". *Ratio Juris* 3 (1990), pp. 173–184, p. 173; Grill, Kalle: "The Normative Core Of Paternalism". *Res Publica* 13 (4) (2007), pp. 441–458, p. 442; Scoccia, Danny: "In Defense of Hard Paternalism". *Law and Philosophy* 27 (4) (2008), pp. 351–381, p. 353.

34 Garren, David J.: "Paternalism, Part I". *Philosophical Books* 47 (4) (2006), pp. 334–341, p. 340.

35 Valdés 1990, p. 173.

(1) Paternalism is not necessarily active behaviour. It can manifest itself in omission as well (e.g. in withholding information). Consequently, it seems more appropriate to use the word 'conduct' or 'behaviour' instead of 'intervention'. Paternalistic conduct is essentially in regard to others; it is directed towards an external subject (or group of subjects) but it can also affect third parties and, through its relational character, the actor himself.[36] It also implies, in many cases, a hierarchical relation between the paternalistic actor and the subject of paternalism.

(2) Paternalistic conduct is not always coercive and does not always interfere with the explicit will of the subject. Gert and Culver argue that the concept of paternalism does not presuppose coercion or interference with the subject's liberty of action.[37] Consider, for example, the cases of deception, misinformation or withholding information. A doctor who lies to a mother on her deathbed about her son (telling her that he is doing well, although he has just lost his life in a car accident) definitely acts paternalistically.[38] Paternalism does not necessarily involve an attempt to control the behaviour of the person. Giving blood transfusion to the unconscious victim of a traffic accident, while knowing of his religious objections to transfusion, is paternalistic, yet it does not coerce or attempt to control the subject's behaviour.[39] Thus, Archard proposes to cash out this element in terms of diminishing or denying choices. The mentioned examples are not coercive but seem to deny or diminish the paternalised person's possibility to choose.[40]

(3) The aims of paternalism are not only prevention from self-harm but also the promotion of the welfare and interests of its subjects. Compulsory primary education or compulsory social security membership does not directly prevent self-harm but aims to create long-term benefits for citizens. Consequently, we have to distinguish between benefit-promoting and harm-preventing paternalism (cf. chapter 2.1.4.)

---

36 I shall understand the word 'conduct' in a broad sense, including not only physical actions but also legislative acts and judicial decisions.

37 Gert / Culver 1976, p. 49.

38 Ibid. 46.

39 Ibid. See also Archard 1990, p. 36. Häyry mentions that in some countries e.g. in Finland, it is actually the policy of physicians to wait until the patient has lost consciousness and then proceed to administer the blood transfusion. Häyry, Heta: *The Limits of Medical Paternalism*. Routledge: London, New York 1991, p. 159.

40 Archard 1990, p. 36.

Based on these considerations, a more suitable definition would emphasize that paternalism (1) primarily regards the conduct or behaviour of others, (2) interferes with the liberty of the subject, either by going explicitly against his or her will or by not seeking prior consent, and (3) aims to prevent self-harm or to promote the subject's best interests.[41]

At this point, it seems useful to discuss separately the second and the third element of this revised definition. In fact, these two elements (i.e. interference and benevolent aim) seem to form the core of the concept of paternalism. It is fascinating to see how these components constantly 'pop up' in various forms as authors constantly rephrase their definitions. Kalle Grill understands paternalism as an 'action-reason compound'. An action-reason compound is paternalistic "if and only if the reason is one referring to the *good of a person* and the action is an *interference with the same person*".[42] Tom Beauchamp defines paternalism "as the *intentional overriding of one person's known preferences or actions by another person*, where the person who overrides justifies the action by the *goal of benefiting or avoiding harm to the person* whose preferences or actions are overridden".[43]

2.1.2.1 The element of interference

A dominant element in the discourse on definitions is the requirement of 'some sort' of interference with the subject of paternalism. This is phrased in various ways: 'interference with a person's liberty of action', 'against one's will', 'coercion', 'overriding of one person's known preferences or actions'. There seem to be many candidates as to what exactly needs to be interfered with, the two most prominent ones being the subject's liberty and autonomy.

The relation of liberty and autonomy is a very complex one. In general, autonomy seems a broader concept that incorporates both internal and external elements while liberty is more focused on the external conditions of freedom (e.g. lack of constraints) and less on the authenticity of internal preferences. The aim of this chapter is to show how definitions gradually extend the element of interference in order to cover a wide range of paternalistic practices. Finally, the

41 Pfordten, Dietmar Von der: "Paternalismus und die Berücksichtigung des Anderen". In: Anderheiden, Michael et al. (eds.): *Paternalismus und Recht: in memoriam Angela Augustin (1968–2004)*. Mohr Siebeck: Tübingen 2006, p. 94.

42 Grill 2007, p. 442. Emphasis added.

43 Beauchamp, Tom: "The Principle of Beneficence in Applied Ethics". In: Zalta, Edward N. (ed.): *The Stanford Encyclopedia of Philosophy*. Winter 2013. (http://plato.stanford.edu/archives/win2013/entries/principle-beneficence/) (12.05.2015). Emphasis added.

question arises whether the infringement of autonomy is a necessary conceptual element for paternalism at all. It is possible to argue that paternalism, on a rudimentary level, implies beneficent motives and can also appear in caring relations where hierarchy and autonomy is not of prime importance.

2.1.2.1.1 Negative liberty

Liberty in the negative sense demarcates the area within which the subject should left to do what he is able to do without interference by others.[44] Accordingly, definitions in the early discourse on paternalism emphasize the coercive nature of paternalism. Gerald Dworkin, in his seminal paper, defines paternalism as "[…] the *interference with a person's liberty of action* justified by reasons referring exclusively to the welfare, good, happiness, needs, interests or values of the person being *coerced* ".[45] According to Feinberg, "[…] the principle of legal paternalism justifies state *coercion* to protect individuals from self-inflicted harm, or in its extreme version, to guide them, whether they like it or not, toward their own good".[46] Murphy states that "[…] paternalism is the *coercing* of people primarily for what is believed to be their own good".[47] It has been already discussed previously that such definitions seem overly restrictive because there are non-coercive forms of paternalism as well. A professor, for example, may refuse to recommend his student to a certain university because he knows that the student will be 'out of his league'.[48] It is hard to see how such a paternalistic 'omission' would affect the negative liberty of the student.

Even though I have asserted previously that liberty mainly focuses on the lack of external constraints and the existence of an 'adequate' range of options, there are certain conceptions of freedom that seem to incorporate internal elements as well. Feinberg distinguishes between two types of freedom, 'dispositional' and 'actually occurrent' freedom.[49] If someone is locked in a room, but does not know about it and never wants to leave the room, he is free to do whatever he wants: he is 'actually' free. However, there is no dispositional freedom, since *if* he were to choose to leave the room, *then* he would be blocked. Arguably, it seems that

---

44 Berlin, Isaiah: "Two Concepts of Liberty". In: *Four Essays on Liberty*. Oxford University Press: Oxford 1969, p. 121.

45 Dworkin 1972, p. 64. Emphasis added.

46 Feinberg 1971, p. 110. Emphasis added.

47 Murphy 1974, p. 465. Emphasis added.

48 Dworkin, Gerald: *The Theory and Practice of Autonomy*. Cambridge University Press: Cambridge 1988, p. 122.

49 Feinberg, Joel: *Social Philosophy*. Prentice-Hall: Englewood Cliffs 1973, p. 5.

'dispositional' freedom is just as important from the perspective of paternalism as 'actually occurrent' freedom because paternalism can appear as a limitation of 'dispositional' freedom as well. Let us consider two hypothetical examples here.

Suppose that someone called Bart can do one thousand things at a certain moment, but not the one thing he wants most to do. Contrary to Bart, Bram can only do one thing, but it happens to be the thing he wants the most.[50] Somewhat paradoxically, the ancient Stoics concentrating on internal aspects of freedom would have argued that Bram is more free than Bart, because he is free of any frustration and his desires correspond to his possibilities. This argument does not seem particularly convincing. Bart seems more free, because he has a wider range of choices, despite the fact that the one thing he wants to do the most is not available to him. As a second example, let us imagine a utopian 'cigarette-free world', where – out of pure coincidence – nobody wants to smoke cigarettes. Cigarettes are readily available in the stores but there is no consumption at all. A statute prohibiting the sale of cigarettes would still look paternalistic, although it does not go against the desires of people, simply because nobody wants to smoke. We can see that restrictions on smoking in this case still interfere with 'dispositional liberty' although not with 'actually occurrent' freedom.

2.1.2.1.2 Positive liberty

It might be that paternalistic conduct interferes with the positive liberty of individuals: the freedom to self-fulfilment and the possibility to take control of one's life and realize one's fundamental purposes.[51] Positive liberty does not only imply non-interference and the absence of external obstacles but also requires the presence of adequate options and internal skills necessary for self-determination.[52] It demands that someone is supplied with positive goods, such as basic and critical skills and an adequate range of choices, so that he or she can lead an *autonomous* life.[53] Autonomy and positive liberty seem to be very close to each other and some conceptions of positive liberty can probably be equated with personal

50 For Feinberg's original example, see ibid. 7.

51 Carter, Ian: "Positive and Negative Liberty". In: Zalta, Edward N. (ed.): *The Stanford Encyclopedia of Philosophy*. Spring 2012. (http://plato.stanford.edu/entries/liberty-positive-negative/) (06.01.2015).

52 To demonstrate the difference between positive and negative liberty, consider the example of someone who is unable travel to an exotic, far-away destination because he cannot afford the plane ticket. He seems to be free in the negative sense of the word (i.e. he is not constrained, not in prison, etc.) but not 'positively' free.

53 Gaus, Gerald F.: *Social Philosophy*. M.E. Sharpe Inc.: Armonk, NY 1999, p. 132.

autonomy.[54] The difference, however, seems to be that autonomy mainly focuses on the authenticity of desires that move people to act, while liberty emphasizes the ability to act without external or internal constraints.[55]

If the infringement of positive liberty and/or autonomy is taken as a necessary condition for paternalism, it is possible to cover both coercive and non-coercive and harm-preventing and benefit-promoting forms of paternalism. Many definitions indeed make use of the concept of autonomy. Gerald Dworkin, for example, argues that "[…] there must be a violation of person's autonomy for one to treat another paternalistically".[56] A potential problem with autonomy-based definitions is that the relation between positive liberty, negative liberty and autonomy is not entirely clear.[57] These concepts are interconnected but not necessarily in a 'hierarchical' manner: interference with liberty does not always imply interference with autonomy and *vice-versa*. Let us consider three conceptual relations at this point. (1) It is possible that autonomy and liberty overlap and that the limitation of liberty limits autonomy at the same time. Obliging someone to undergo medical treatment against his or her religious convictions (e.g. to receive blood transfusion) is one such example. (2) Paternalism can restrict negative liberty while promoting or leaving positive liberty (or autonomy) unaffected. A problem may arise from the tension between one's short term and long term preferences. Take, for example, the mythological story of Odysseus and the Sirens. Odysseus knew that the Sirens could enchant men with their songs. Determined to listen to their song, he commanded his crew to tie him to the ship's mast and not to let him go, no matter how much he would ask for it later.[58] Tying Odysseus to the mast was a limitation of his liberty of action but not his autonomy, since the limitation corresponded to his long term preferences. (3) Non-coercive methods

54 Christman, John: "Autonomy in Moral and Political Philosophy". In: Zalta, Edward N. (ed.): *The Stanford Encyclopedia of Philosophy*. Spring 2015. (http://plato.stanford.edu/entries/autonomy-moral/) (04.06.2015).

55 Ibid.

56 Dworkin 1988, p. 123.

57 Kleinig, somewhat differently, separates three elements of freedom: liberty, autonomy and the capacity for rational choice. He claims that paternalism may violate any of these three. "In so far as paternalistic impositions involve a constraint on freedom, any one or all of these freedoms may be intended. Liberty may be curtailed; the capacity for rational choice may be ignored; autonomy may be overridden or undermined." Kleinig 1983, p. 21.

58 Dworkin 1972, p. 77.

of paternalism might be able to limit positive liberty without violating negative liberty (deception, misinformation, restriction of available options etc.).

2.1.2.1.3 Paternalism without interference?

This chapter examines instances of non-coercive paternalism that interfere with personal autonomy only to a 'minimal extent'. The potentially paternalistic character of incentives and information giving will be discussed, followed by a brief overview of the newly emerging theory of libertarian paternalism. Interference with autonomy seems 'so small' in some of these cases that it naturally raises the question whether interference is really a necessary definitional element of paternalism or it is possible to create an adequate definition without it.

There are many examples of paternalism that are non-coercive but still seem to interfere with personal autonomy. *Incentives* often expand rather than limit the number of available options, thus they cannot be seen as violating liberty in the traditional sense. However, the father who offers his teenage son monetary rewards for earning good grades in school treats his son paternalistically;[59] the violation of autonomy being manifested in the father's 'tampering' with the child's autonomous preference-formation.

Mere *provision of information* does not seem to affect individual liberty. The primary aim of information giving in relation to paternalism is to ensure the 'informed' character of self-harming choices. However, provision of information can also target emotions in a non-neutral and manipulative way. Consider, for example, television commercials using graphic images to draw attention to the harmful character of drugs or warnings on cigarette boxes combined with gruesome photos depicting health problems smoking can cause. Authority attributed to the source of information seems to matter as well: the advice of the surgeon general is supposed to have more deterrent effect than a simple warning that lacks medical authority. Cass Sunstein argues that even seemingly 'innocent' cases of information giving can have manipulative character. Fuel economy labels designed to inform people of the fuel consumption of particular cars can be taken as a form of paternalism "insofar as government is singling out the

59 Scoccia 2008, p. 353. As Kultgen explains, 'rewards' can violate personal autonomy because they alter the conditions of choice. A highly paternalistic society based on positive reinforcements disregards autonomy, just as a coercive dictatorship does. Kultgen 1995, p. 70.

particular variable of fuel economy and attempting to focus people's attention on that variable, as opposed to numerous other variables that remain ungraded."[60]

Another form of non-coercive paternalism, known as 'libertarian paternalism', operates by modifying choice-architecture. Changing the default rule from non-enrolment to automatic enrolment for an otherwise non-compulsory training course will increase the participation of employees, since most of them will probably not opt-out after being enrolled. Putting the apples and oranges before the snacks at a school cafeteria will probably increase the consumption of fruits and decrease the consumption of snacks.[61]

Proponents of libertarian paternalism start off from the premise that people, even when they possess sufficient cognitive skills, do not always act in their own best interests. They draw on the empirical findings of cognitive psychology and adopt a model of 'bounded rationality' that stands in opposition to the previously dominant 'rational choice' model of neoclassical economics. Libertarian paternalists do not perceive humans as infallible economic choosers; rather, they focus on the factors that distort people's ability to make rational decisions.

People tend to rely on established patterns of thinking when deciding in complex or uncertain situations. Such 'rules of thumb' facilitate easier decision-making but they can also lead to systematic cognitive biases.[62] *Mental anchoring*, for example, is a natural tendency to place cognitive focus on a single reference (e.g. past events, numbers, ideas or explanations) which can often result in biased thinking and the neglect of new information. In an experiment conducted by Amos Tversky and Daniel Kahneman, people were asked to guess the percentage of African countries in the United Nations.[63] Those who were first asked 'Was it more or less than 10 percent?' came up with significantly lower estimates than those who had been asked if it was more or less than 65 percent.[64] This example shows how the changing of the *mental anchor* can change people's estimates, expectations or decisions. A different cognitive bias, the so-called *framing bias*

---

60 Sunstein, Cass R.: *Why Nudge? – The Politics of Libertarian Paternalism*. Yale University Press: New Haven 2014, p. 66.

61 Sunstein, Cass R. / Thaler, Richard H.: "Libertarian Paternalism is not an Oxymoron". *University of Chicago Law Review* 70 (2003), p. 1159, p. 1166. For more examples of libertarian paternalism, see Thaler, Richard H. / Sunstein, Cass R.: *Nudge: Improving Decisions About Health, Wealth, and Happiness*. Penguin Books: New York 2009.

62 Thaler / Sunstein 2009, p. 25.

63 Tversky, Amos / Kahneman, Daniel: "Judgment under Uncertainty: Heuristics and Biases". *Science* 185 (1974), pp. 1124–1131, p. 1128.

64 25 and 45 percent on average, respectively.

builds on the observation that the way different options are presented to the decision-maker can influence the choice being made.[65] From the perspective of patient consent, it makes a huge difference if the patient is told that nine out of ten people survive the operation than if told that one out of ten dies during the surgery. The *status quo bias* is based on people's inertia not to opt out of certain situations and can be used to modify people's choices by modifying the default option. Behavioural scientists have identified many other cognitive biases which libertarian paternalism aims to 'exploit'. The mentioned examples were meant to illustrate how people's choices can be influenced by non-coercive 'nudging', simply by changing the mental anchor, the default option or the terming of certain questions.

Libertarian paternalism is a relatively weak and non-intrusive type of paternalism so far as it is understood as imposing only trivial costs on those who seek to depart from the planner's preferred option.[66] It almost exclusively operates by modifying choice-architecture, either by changing the default option (as in the case of organ donation or automatic enrolments), changing the physical environment (e.g. removing sweets from supermarket checkouts) or through the provision of information (e.g. providing nutritional information on the labelling of food products).[67] Fiscal incentives (e.g. taxation), the restriction of available options (e.g. by means of legal prohibition) and direct persuasion do not fall within the ambit of libertarian paternalism.

One of the central objections against libertarian paternalism is that it imposes a certain value choice on individuals and fails to remain neutral when interfering with people's choice architecture.[68] As a response, Sunstein and Thaler argue that it is simply impossible to remain neutral in such situations: if the policy maker does not intervene, it implicitly adopts the present choice architecture. If it is necessary to choose a certain architecture, why not choose the one which benefits people the most? Why not arrange the food in the school cafeteria in a way that makes students better off instead of arranging it randomly, or, even worse, in a way that maximizes profit irrespective of harmful health consequences? An additional moral concern besides non-neutrality is that nudges manipulate

---

65 Ménard, Jean-Frédérick: "A "Nudge" for Public Health Ethics: Libertarian Paternalism as a Framework for Ethical Analysis of Public Health Interventions?" *Public Health Ethics* 3 (3) (2010), pp. 229–238, p. 231.

66 Sunstein / Thaler 2003, p. 1162.

67 *Report on Behaviour Change*. Science and Technology Select Committee, House of Lords: London 2011, p. 10.

68 Thaler / Sunstein 2009, pp. 246–248.

through mechanisms of which people are not obviously aware.[69] To avoid this accusation, proponents of libertarian paternalism require that the regulator should be transparent about the implementation of nudges – not necessarily telling directly about them, but ensuring that a 'perceptive person' could discern for himself that an intervention had been implemented.[70] Other objections against libertarian paternalism invoke the 'slippery slope' argument and claim that once we accept modest paternalism, it is possible that highly intrusive interventions will follow.[71] The question is whether there are sufficient guarantees which ensure that libertarian paternalists will stop at the relatively harmless interventions and that they will not use methods of behaviour change for furthering their own agenda. Despite all these concerns, the idea of 'nudge paternalism' (probably due to its non-invasive character and presumed cost-effectiveness[72]) has received considerable public attention and has been endorsed in official government politics both in Britain and the United States.[73]

Some examples of libertarian paternalism already suggest that there might be interventions that do not interfere with a person's autonomy while they still retain their paternalistic character. Sunstein and Thaler insist that modifying choice architecture does not limit freedom of choice, because people remain free to opt out of undesirable arrangements. Consequently, libertarian paternalism has the effect of preserving liberty in the long run.[74] A few authors indeed contend that the violation of personal autonomy is not a necessary definitional element of paternalism.[75] Consider the following 'hard case' from Heta Häyry.

---

69 *Report on Behaviour Change*. Science and Technology Select Committee, House of Lords: London 2011, p. 12.

70 Ibid. 13, 108–109 (referring to the evidence given by Luc Bovens). See also Thaler / Sunstein 2009, pp. 243–246.

71 Ibid. 235–240.

72 Nudges are considered to be relatively inexpensive methods but their effectiveness can also be questioned. See, for example, House of Lords Report on Behaviour Change (2011), especially chapters 6 and 7.

73 The Behavioural Insights Team was set up in 2010 in the UK with the aim to 'help Government departments think about non-regulatory means of achieving behaviour change' (House of Lords Report citing the evidence of Oliver Letwin, p. 33). The Office of Information and Regulatory Affairs (OIRA), headed by Cass Sunstein, has similar functions in the US administration when reviewing draft regulations and overseeing the implementation of government-wide policies.

74 Thaler / Sunstein 2009, p. 5.

75 Häyry 1991, p. 61. Shiffrin, Seana: "Paternalism, Unconscionability Doctrine, and Accommodation". *Philosophy & Public Affairs* 29 (3) (2000), pp. 205–250, p. 218.

"Dr. Smiley is a dentist and in the waiting room of her office there are magazines for the patients. Now, if Dr. Smiley decides to add to the reading selection some pamphlets propagating the importance of dental hygiene, her behaviour will hardly constitute violations of the patient's autonomy or other transgressions of major moral rules. Nevertheless [...] it might well go against the common usage of language to say that her behaviour cannot be described as paternalistic unless there are violations of some sort present."[76]

Of course, it is possible to argue that a 'seed' of interference with autonomy is still present in these cases. As mentioned earlier, the authority of the information-provider or the hierarchical relation between the provider and the receiver might influence individual behaviour. Even if there is no hierarchical relation present, by communicating an advice, the advice-giver tries to force the other person to face facts that he or she might otherwise disregard or suppress for psychological reasons. People often feel that unnecessary 'preaching' violates their autonomy: rational people do not always welcome rational arguments.[77]

The definition of paternalism proposed by Seana Shiffrin avoids reference to the concept of autonomy.[78] She argues that paternalism does not necessarily imply the violation of someone's autonomy but rather involves the substitution of the paternalistic actor's judgment or agency for the subject's. Consider, for example, the case where the husband hides his sleeping pills from his depressed, suicidal wife: such an action does not violate a distinct autonomy right because the wife has no right to access her husband's sleeping pills.[79] However, paternalism can still manifest an "attitude of disrespect toward highly salient qualities of the autonomous agent" and aim to "take over what is properly within the agent's own legitimate domain of judgment or action".[80] It seems that the substitution of one's judgment for someone else's can involve a violation of autonomy but it does not necessarily have to. Thus, one might possibly conclude that an action can be

76 Häyry 1991, p. 61.

77 Kultgen 1995, p. 71.

78 Shiffrin gives the following definition. Paternalism by A toward B may be characterized as behavior (whether through action or through omission) (a) aimed to have (or to avoid) an effect on B or her sphere of legitimate agency; (b) that involves the substitution of A's judgment or agency for B's; (c) directed at B's own interests or matters that legitimately lie within B's control; (d) undertaken on the grounds that compared to B's judgment or agency with respect to those interests or other matters, A regards her judgment or agency to be (or as likely to be), in some respect, superior to B's. Shiffrin 2000, p. 218.

79 Gerald Dworkin: *Defining Paternalism* in Coons / Weber 2013, p. 27.

80 Shiffrin 2000, p. 216, 220.

considered paternalism even if it 'does not contain coercive, liberty-restricting, autonomy-violating or otherwise prima-facie immoral elements.'[81]

2.1.2.2 The element of benevolence

The other, often underemphasized component of the definition of paternalism is related to its benevolent character. This element requires that the paternalistic intervention (1) be aimed at (2) preventing self-harm and/or (3) promoting the benefit of the subject. The first constituent ('be aimed at') stresses the importance of the motives and intentions of the paternalistic actor. Although subject to disagreement, it seems plausible to claim that the paternalistic agent does not necessarily have to be successful in achieving good for the subject.[82] Consider, for example, the case of an overprotective mother whose over-caring distorts her child's psychological development. Her behaviour is paternalistic even though not actually beneficent. Conversely, an actually beneficent intervention that lacks benevolent motives does not qualify as paternalism. One may protect others from self-harm for non-paternalistic reasons. For example, a slaveholder may prevent his slave from killing or disfiguring herself in order to use her as a prostitute.[83] Definitional and justificatory issues seem to get mixed at this point. Obviously, a paternalistic intervention that has beneficial consequences is much easier to justify. Thus, it is important to keep in mind that intended or unintended positive consequences, even though probably irrelevant from the perspective of a definition, can still affect the justification of paternalism.

It is not easy to determine the 'genuinely benevolent' character of paternalistic motives – especially not in an institutional (i.e. regulatory and legislative) context.[84] A *prima facie* paternalistic legislation can have very different underlying rationales. For example, an appeal to paternalistic considerations can make

81 Häyry 1991, p. 64.

82 "The definition of paternalism does not require that the paternalistic agent be successful in achieving good for the subject." Kleinig 1983, p. 76. 'It is not essential that it achieve that end.' Archard 1990, p. 37. See also Pope 2004, p. 697.

83 Kultgen 1995, p. 62.

84 Scoccia claims that reference made to the benevolent character of paternalism is sufficient for justification, even if the 'real' underlying motive is different. Legislators who vote for a ban on recreational marijuana use may be motivated by their political expectations to get reelected. The law counts as paternalistic, however, if the majority of those who support it refer to the the need to protect marijuana users from self-inflicted harm. Driven by the same dilemma, Feinberg argues that since it is impossible to identify the original intent of the legislator, it is a form of 'reconstructed intent' that should be

the moralistic character of a policy less obtrusive. Also, seemingly benevolent motives may turn out to hide "selfish motives behind a façade of concern for others".[85] In fact, it is possible to argue that paternalism is never purely altruistic even if performed in loving or caring relations due to the 'intersubjective unity' between the 'self' and the 'other' in these cases. The 'self' can be motivated to act paternalistically by the fact that it suffers the pain of the 'other'.[86]

The second and third constituents of the element of benevolence are (2) the prevention of self-harm and (3) the promotion of benefit. Harm can be defined in various ways (cf. chapter 2.1.3). Arguably, harm-preventing and benefit-promoting paternalism can be thought of as the two sides of the same coin, since protection from harm is a type of benefit promotion and unrealized benefits can be conceived as a form of harm. However, it seems that the endorsement of benefit promotion extends the scope of paternalism to a wider – and often more controversial – range of issues, including debates on the meaning of a 'good life' or the 'best interests' of individuals.

Shiffrin's definition of paternalism, besides avoiding the concept of autonomy, is also unconventional in the sense that reference to the subject's welfare is no longer a necessary condition of paternalism.[87] This significantly changes the sort of actions that may be referred to as being 'paternalistic'. Consider the example of the park ranger who prohibits a hiker to take a dangerous mountain path not out of concern for the welfare of the hiker but in order to protect the hiker's wife from the grief and emotional suffering caused by a potentially fatal accident. Shiffrin claims that such prohibition is an instance of paternalism even though it is not intended to promote the welfare of the subject of paternalism. In fact, a paternalist motive need not concern any person's welfare at all.[88]

Two practices are frequently confused with paternalism in colloquial speech. The first type of practice has the benevolent character of paternalism but it is not connected to self-harm. There are regulations that aim to protect children

taken into account when determining benevolent motivations. Scoccia 2008, p. 352. Pope 2004, p. 706.

85 Kennedy, Duncan: "Distributive and Paternalist Motives in Contract and Tort Law, with Special Reference to Compulsory Terms and Unequal Bargaining Power". *Maryland Law Review* 41 (1982), pp. 563–658, p. 641.

86 Ibid. 639.

87 Shiffrin 2000, p. 219; Gerald Dworkin: *Defining Paternalism* in Coons / Weber 2013, p. 34.

88 Shiffrin 2000, p. 217.

or other vulnerable groups from harm caused by others.[89] When the state creates special crimes against child abuse, it acts in this 'paternalistic' way for example. Even though benevolent, these regulations are not paternalistic because they do not aim to protect from self-harm but from harm caused by others.

The second category confused with paternalism contains practices that are not even remotely benevolent.[90] Take the example of the management of a factory, which, for greater profit and production, treats employees as if they were school children (keeping a constant close watch on them, requiring them to ask permission to go to the toilet, etc.). Such rules are not paternalistic but they are sometimes confused because their authority reminds us of parental authority.

Arguably, the so-called 'good' and 'bad Samaritan laws' can also qualify as instances of legal paternalism. Bad Samaritan laws require third parties, under the pain of criminal punishment, to provide help to victims of accidents, natural catastrophes, crimes, etc. Good Samaritan laws provide protection against liability for persons who cause harm in the course of providing aid.[91] Although usually unknown as statutory regulations in common law, most civil law systems have such regulations. The Hungarian Criminal Code, for example, states that "[any] person who fails to offer aid or assistance as it may be expected of him to an injured person, or to a person whose life or bodily integrity is in imminent danger, is guilty of a misdemeanour punishable by imprisonment not exceeding two years."[92] As for 'good Samaritanism', the Civil Code prescribes that "[i]n the event of danger (emergency) constituting a direct threat to the life, safety or property of another person [...], an owner shall tolerate his thing to be used, utilized or damaged to the extent necessary for abolishing the emergency situation".[93]

89 Feinberg calls this category 'presumptively nonblamable paternalism'. It consists of defending relatively helpless or vulnerable people from external dangers, including harm from other people when the protected parties have not voluntarily consented to the risk. Feinberg 1989, p. 5.

90 Feinberg calls this category 'blamably nonbenevolent paternalism'. Although Feinberg refers to these practices as paternalism, he is convinced that they fall outside the scope of a proper definition. Ibid.

91 For the distinction between good and bad Samaritan laws and for an in-depth analysis of the moral justifiability of these regulations, see Malm, Heidi M.: "Malm – Liberalism, Bad Samaritan Law and Legal Paternalism". *Ethics* 106 (1) (1995), pp. 4–31; Malm, Heidi M.: "Bad Samaritan Laws: Harm, Help, or Hype?". *Law and Philosophy* (2000), pp. 707–750.

92 The Criminal Code of Hungary (Act C/2012), section 166 (1).

93 The Civil Code of Hungary (Act V/2013), book 5, section 26 (1). The English translations of the statutes are available at www.legislationline.org (12.11.2014).

Consequently, the 'good Samaritan' who causes necessary harm during help is not liable for the damages.

Samaritan laws can be enacted out of paternalistic considerations. Some argue that these laws are instances of moral paternalism, in the sense that they aim to foster the moral character of the paternalistic actor: by helping others in need, he becomes a better person himself.[94] From a different perspective, bad Samaritan laws might be indirectly paternalistic if they prescribe compulsory help in the case of self-harm (i.e. to provide help in the case of attempted suicide). However, Samaritan laws seem to be conceptually different from paternalistic regulations.[95] While the former laws require people to help others, the latter require them to refrain from self-harm. Bad Samaritan laws are morally problematic because they force people to act in ways they might not want to act (and it is in their freedom not to act because there seems to be no general moral obligation to help others). A consequent liberal will have a hard time explaining why he or she believes that bad Samaritan laws are acceptable while rejecting paternalism at the same time.[96]

2.1.3 The external aspects of paternalism: the system of liberty-limiting principles

Self-harm is not the only reason that might justify intervention with individual liberty. Reference to harm caused to others, for example, is a common argument to support criminal legislation. Generally, four main liberty-limiting principles are distinguished: the harm principle, the offense principle, paternalism and moralism.[97] Even though these principles are 'relevant reasons' for legal coercion, they are neither jointly necessary nor sufficient conditions in themselves.[98] They are insufficient because these principles might not always outweigh the value attributed to liberty. They are neither jointly necessary since it is possible to justify a legal regulation by referring only to one liberty-limiting principle. The principles, however, frequently overlap and a legal intervention can have several justificatory rationales at the same time.

94 Feinberg, Joel: *Harmless Wrongdoing.* (= The Moral Limits of the Criminal Law) Oxford University Press: New York 1990, p. 29.

95 Hospers 1980, p. 255.

96 Malm 1995, p. 8.

97 For a more elaborate system of liberty-limiting principles, see Feinberg 1989, p. xix.

98 Feinberg, Joel: *Harm to Others.* (= The Moral Limits of the Criminal Law) Oxford University Press: New York 1984, p. 10.

Paternalism is often confused with moralism. Legal moralism is the possibility of states to interfere with a person's liberty on the sole ground that the conduct is inherently immoral.[99] Since self-harming conduct is often considered as immoral (at least in the Judeo-Christian tradition), moralistic and paternalistic reasoning tend to go hand in hand.[100] Consider, for example, the morally heated debate over euthanasia.[101] In the philosophical literature, the distinction between paternalism and moralism is more precise. When a law restricts the individual's choices for his moral good, it represents 'moral paternalism',[102] which is a form of benefit-promoting paternalism. When a law restricts the individual's choices in order to enforce social morality, it is possible to speak of 'legal moralism'. This distinction fits well with a 'motivational approach' to paternalism. What separates moral paternalism from strict moralism is the paternalistic concern to improve the character of individuals. However, individual moral good seems to be strongly connected to positive social morality. Thus, moral paternalism has a strong moralistic character. I will come back to the issue of moralism and its relation to paternalism in chapter 5.2.

Feinberg's formulation of the harm principle states that "[…] it is always a good reason in support of penal legislation that it would be effective in preventing (eliminating, reducing) harm to persons other than the actor (the one prohibited from acting) and that there is probably no other means that is equally

---

99 According to Feinberg's definition, legal moralism means that "[i]t can be morally legitimate to prohibit conduct on the ground that it is inherently immoral, even though it causes neither harm nor offense to the actor or to others". Feinberg 1989, p. xix.

100 Consider the following excerpt from the Bible: 'Do you not know that your bodies are temples of the Holy Spirit, who is in you, whom you have received from God? You are not your own; you were bought at a price. Therefore honor God with your bodies.' 1 Corinthians 6: 19–20.

101 In the Pretty v UK case, for example, the Catholic Bishop's Conference of England and Wales, as an intervening third party, submitted that euthanasia is "outside the range of *morally* acceptable options in dealing with human suffering and dying". The European Court of Human Rights in the Open Door and Dublin Well Woman v Ireland case held that the Irish prohibition of abortion pursued a legitimate aim, namely "the protection of *morals* of which the protection in Ireland of the right to life of the unborn is one aspect". Pretty v United Kingdom, Judgment of 29 April 2002, para. 29; Open Door and Dublin Well Woman v Ireland, Judgment of 29 October 1992, para. 63.

102 Dworkin, Gerald: "Moral Paternalism". *Law and Philosophy* 24 (3) (2005), pp. 305–319.

effective at no greater cost to other values."[103] As we will see, Mill's approach is much stricter than Feinberg's. For Mill, harm to others is the *sole* reason for coercion. It excludes all other liberty-limiting principles from the sphere of acceptable interventions. Mill's principle unifies self-harm and harm caused to others in a controversial way. Its positive side accepts the harm-to-others principle, while its negative side excludes paternalism and moralism (cf. chapter 3.2).

The scope of the harm principle depends on how we understand the concept of harm. In Feinberg's framework, harm refers to "those states of *set-back to the interests of an individual* that are the consequence of acts or omissions by others".[104] Harm must be distinguished from actions that cause feelings that people do not like. One such category of actions is the category of offense.[105] Offense is the production of a non-painful, unpleasant or uncomfortable 'universally disliked mental state'. This includes, for example, unpleasant or loud sounds and shocking or disturbing public behaviour. Consequently, the offense principle is defined by Feinberg as "it is always a good reason in support of a proposed criminal prohibition that it is necessary to prevent serious offense to persons other than the actor".[106] The offense principle is an 'auxiliary' principle to the harm principle: it is not only the prevention of physical harm but also offensive behaviour that can justify legal coercion.[107]

---

103 Feinberg 1989, p. xvi.

104 Feinberg 1984, p. 35. An additional question is the relation of harms and wrongs in Feinberg's theory. It seems that intervention requires that the harmful conduct be committed wrongfully (i.e. typically without the subject's consent) as well. For a detailed examination, see Duff, Antony: "Harms and Wrongs". *Buffalo Criminal Law Review* 5 (1) (2001), pp. 13–45; Stewart, Hamish: "Harms, Wrongs, and Set-Backs in Feinberg's Moral Limits of the Criminal Law". *Buffalo Criminal Law Review* 5 (1) (2001), pp. 47–67.

105 Another category, according to Feinberg, is the category of 'hurts'. Hurts can be defined as non-harmful physical and mental pains (e.g. twinges, aches, 'heartache', grief, despair, etc.) or physical discomforts (nausea, dizziness, tension, etc.). In addition to hurts and offenses, there are 'other kinds of unpleasant experiences' that are neither offensive nor hurtful such as anxiety or boredom. Feinberg 1984, p. 47.

106 Ibid. xvii.

107 Hart demonstrates the offense principle with the example of bigamy. It is a criminal offence for a married person to enter into a second marriage, while a married man can live with a woman other than his wife without risking any criminal charges. Hart explains the difference with the state's willingness to protect religious sensibilities from outrage caused by a public act (i.e. the public marriage ceremony that is missing in cases of cohabitation). However, it seems that cohabitation of adulterous couples may be just as offensive for morally conservative people as bigamy. Hart's example is

The offense principle can overlap with other principles, becoming a tool of legal moralism and paternalism. Prohibiting alcohol consumption in public places is paternalistic but the original aim of such regulations is to safeguard the tranquillity of the neighbourhood. Self-harming acts, if performed publicly, may provoke anger, disgust or sadness in others. Certain 'immoral' behaviours can also be banned under the offense principle. Sexual intercourse in private is not the state's business but it is prohibited if performed publicly due to its offensive character. Begging on the street is not harmful, but it can be considered offensive.

Most liberals accept the harm and the offense principles as legitimate liberty-limiting principles. Feinberg claims that "[...] liberalism is the view that the harm and offense principles, and only these, state good and relevant reasons for state coercion by means of the criminal law."[108] On the other hand, the original formulation of the harm principle excludes moralism, paternalism and the offense principle from the field of legitimate state coercion.[109] What seems common between liberal authors, including Mill, Feinberg, Hart and Raz, is the rejection of legal moralism.

2.1.4 The internal aspects of paternalism: identifying subcategories

Paternalism has different types. The most important distinction is probably made between soft and hard paternalism, which is based on the voluntariness of the subject. Since it plays an important role in the justification of paternalism, I am going to discuss this category separately in the next chapter.

In the case of direct paternalism, the class of persons whose autonomy is restricted is identical with the class of persons whose benefit is intended to be promoted by such restrictions.[110] Laws prohibiting suicide or requiring passengers

---

more plausible if we replace cohabitation with a secretly conducted adulterous affair. Hart, H.L.A.: *Law, Liberty and Morality*. Stanford University Press: Stanford 1963, p. 39.

108 Feinberg 1989, p. 3.

109 Stanton-Ife, John: "The Limits of Law". In: Zalta, Edward N. (ed.): *The Stanford Encyclopedia of Philosophy*. Winter 2014. (http://plato.stanford.edu/entries/law-limits/).

110 Gerald Dworkin uses the words pure and impure for direct and indirect paternalism. It can be easily mistaken with Feinberg's category of mixed and unmixed paternalism which is referred to as pure and impure paternalism in John Kleinig's terminology. Feinberg's distinction between single and two-party cases of paternalism seems also similar to direct and indirect paternalism. Gerald Dworkin, *Paternalism*, in Dworkin, Gerald (ed.): *Mill's On Liberty: Critical Essays*. Rowman & Littlefield Publishers: Lanham, Md. 1997, p. 65; Feinberg 1989, p. 9; Kleinig 1983, p. 12.

in automobiles to wear seat-belts are typical examples. Indirect paternalism involves the restriction of other persons besides those who are benefited. Consider, for example, consumer protection laws or licensing requirements for doctors or lawyers. A ban on the sale of cigarettes is indirect paternalism because it directly limits cigarette manufacturers and only indirectly affects the autonomy of smokers, whose benefit was intended to be promoted by the prohibition. Gerald Dworkin argues that indirect paternalism requires stronger justification, because it involves third-parties "who are losing a portion of their liberty and they do not even have the solace of having it done in their own interest".[111] Others claim that indirect paternalism is not genuinely paternalistic because such limitations can be justified under the harm-to-others principle (i.e. indirect paternalism is subsumable under the harm principle): by preventing cigarette manufacturers to sell cigarettes, we prevent them from causing illness to others in the same way we prevent factories from releasing pollutants into the air.[112]

It is possible to distinguish between mixed and unmixed paternalism, which is, in a certain respect, the 'flipside' of the distinction between direct and indirect paternalism.[113] While the direct-indirect category focuses on the subject's limitation of liberty, the mixed-unmixed distinction emphasizes the motives of paternalistic intervention. In practice, paternalistic regulations are not exclusively motivated by protection from self-harm. Other considerations, such as the protection of others, public order, morals, etc. are also taken into account. There are very few unmixed cases of paternalism. Even in a seemingly 'pure' case (e.g. prescribing motorcyclists to wear crash helmets), one can refer to the indirect harm caused to society by the additional social security expenses. This issue is closely related to the distinction of self-regarding and other-regarding acts (cf. chapter 3.2).

The distinction between harm-preventing and benefit-promoting paternalism can be expressed in various ways.[114] Most definitions try to encompass both aspects. They use phrases such as: 'benefiting or avoiding harm to the person'; 'benefiting them or not act in ways that will harm them'; 'the welfare, good,

111 Gerald Dworkin, *Paternalism*, in Dworkin 1997, p. 66.

112 Michael Bayles, *Criminal Paternalism,* in Pennock, J. Roland / Chapman, John W. (eds.): *Nomos XV: The Limits of Law*. Lieber-Atherton: New York 1974, pp. 174–188.

113 Using the combination of the two categories, Pope identifies four possible cases: unmixed-direct, unmixed-indirect, mixed-direct and mixed-indirect forms of paternalism. Pope 2004, p. 699.

114 This category is also called as promotive/preservative, negative/positive, beneficent/protective paternalism. Kleinig 1983, p. 13; Kultgen 1995, p. 66.

happiness, needs, interests or values of the person'.[115] A notable exception is Feinberg, who focuses only on the harm-preventing element of paternalism.[116] He considers benefit-promoting paternalism an 'extreme' form of paternalism and formulates a separate liberty-limiting principle for it, independent from the principle of legal paternalism.

Active paternalism requires action, while passive paternalism requires the subject to refrain from a certain type of action.[117] Laws prescribing passengers to wear seat belts or motorcyclists to wear crash-helmets belong to the active category. The prohibition of suicide, for example, is passive paternalism.

A final distinction must be made between coercive and non-coercive forms of paternalism.[118] Mill's harm principle prohibits only coercive interferences with liberty (cf. chapter 3.2.1). Generally, authors pertaining to the 'Millian' tradition emphasize the coercive nature of paternalism. They focus on criminal law issues. As Feinberg admits, "[...] it is the latter [i.e. prohibitive pronouncements backed up by criminal sanctions] with which we are primarily, though not exclusively, concerned here".[119] However, there are many examples of non-coercive paternalism as well, just consider the previously mentioned cases of paternalistic deception and manipulation. Libertarian paternalism also operates with non-coercive methods. Structuring someone's options, e.g. by changing the default rule from non-enrolment to enrolment, imposes very minimal costs on the subject and can hardly be seen as coercion.

2.1.5 State paternalism

The term 'paternalism' can be predicated of many different things.[120] It is possible to talk of paternalistic people, acts, policies, institutions and so on. An important distinction is to be made between 'private' and 'public' paternalism because

---

115 Scoccia 2008, p. 352.; Dworkin 1997, p. 62, respectively.

116 Feinberg 1989, p. 8.

117 For the distinction, see Pope 2004, p. 688; Feinberg 1984, p. 8; Kultgen 1995, p. 158 or Kleinig 1983, p. 14.

118 A somewhat similar distinction is made between compulsive and coercive paternalism. Pope, following Feinberg, explains their difference as "[w]hile compulsive paternalism definitively closes the subject's chosen options, coercive paternalism merely destroys the appeal of some options by making them difficult, by making them inconvenient, or – to employ the metaphor of a price tag – by increasing their cost". In this sense, criminal law is coercive but not compulsive. Pope 2004, p. 691.

119 Feinberg 1989, p. 8.

120 Gerald Dworkin, *Defining Paternalism*, in Coons / Weber 2013, p. 26.

different standards of justification seem to apply to state interventions than to private ones. John Kultgen warns us that justified forms of public paternalism might not exactly parallel justified cases of personal paternalism.[121] Abstract legal regulations treat people in a standardized way and they are less responsive to individual circumstances. Thus, it seems that the justification of paternalistic public policies and legal regulations requires 'more' than a single act of private paternalism e.g. from the perspective of democratic accountability. On the other hand, there are certain factors that make the state a 'better' decision-maker than the individual.

Bill New examines the justification of paternalistic public policies from a consequentialist perspective.[122] He argues that contrary to the Millian assumption, the state may be a better judge of personal preferences than the individual himself because there are certain failures in human reasoning that the state is not necessarily subject to. New distinguishes four such failures. First, individuals might make sub-optimal choices because the amount of information needed is so great or because the "causal connections between choice and outcome are difficult to make".[123] Human intellect is limited and this leads to a 'technical inability' to make good decisions in complex situations. Secondly, people neglect to act in accordance with their long term interests due to weakness of will (*akrasia*). Thirdly, humans are often prone to emotional decision-making, for example "becoming attached to making certain choices, such as following a habitual route to work, even if it is longer or less attractive than an alternative one".[124] Finally, people sometimes lack first-hand experience with respect to the consequences of their potentially self-harming decisions. Even though most smokers have an 'abstract' knowledge of the harmful consequences of cigarettes, they do not have experience of all the pain that smoking-related illnesses will potentially cause to them.

New argues that the state is less susceptible to such failures in reasoning and a paternalistic state policy can be justified provided that it produces a better outcome than individual choice and that the increase in welfare is sufficient to compensate for the loss of autonomy that the intervention entails.[125] The state can be considered to be more impartial ('phlegmatic') than the individual and

121 Kultgen 1995, p. 161.

122 New, Bill: "Paternalism and Public Policy". *Economics and Philosophy* 15 (1) (1999), pp. 63–83.

123 Ibid. 70.

124 Ibid.

125 Ibid. 76.

therefore more resistant to temptation, weakness of will and emotional decision-making: choosing 'wisely' between a luxurious holiday in the present and saving for retirement in the future is obviously less difficult for the 'impartial' state than for the person concerned. New claims that the state and its employees also have a wider perspective when it comes to experiences related to possibly self-harming activities. Although public employees (e.g. doctors, nurses, etc.) do not experience directly the negative effects of potentially self-harming choices (e.g. not wearing a crash helmet), they are still in a better position to make a judgment on the harmful consequences of accidents than ordinary drivers. Finally, relating to the technical inability of individuals to make decisions in complex situations, the state has the advantage to employ experts who can fully devote themselves to solving these problems. With the help of experts, the state has better knowledge of complex situations than ordinary citizens.

Thomas and Buckmaster argue that an appropriate paternalistic policy should always 'discriminate between those for whom paternalism is deemed necessary and those for whom it is not'.[126] This practically means that paternalism should be limited as much as possible to those who are benefited by the restriction: instances of 'impure' paternalism involving the restriction of others besides those who are benefited should be kept to a minimum (cf. chapter 2.1.4). Proportionality, accountability and efficacy are also important principles when evaluating paternalistic policies. Accountability means that paternalistic interventions shall be transparent to the person subjected to the intervention. This is particularly important in cases of 'libertarian paternalism' that operate by modifying choice-architecture often in a way that is not obvious to the paternalised person. Efficacy implies that the paternalistic intervention is efficient in producing the intended outcomes. Although there seems to be a general consensus that social policies must be evidence-based, it is not entirely clear what evidence shall be considered when determining the efficacy of paternalistic policies.[127]

2.2 Justifying paternalism

A comprehensive moral rule regulating the issue of paternalism will likely draw inspiration from one of the three major theories of normative ethics. The scientific discourse on paternalism seems to be dominated by autonomy-based approaches grounded in deontological ethics, and to a smaller extent, by

126 Thomas, Matthew / Buckmaster, Luke: *Paternalism in Social Policy – When It Is Justifiable?*. Parliament of Australia, Department of Parliamentary Services: 2010, p. 18.

127 Ibid. 22–25.

consequentialism. Justifications based on virtue ethics are less common. This chapter gives a brief overview of each justificatory approach, focusing primarily on the characteristics of autonomy-based justifications.

2.2.1 Autonomy-based justifications

The notion of autonomy is not only relevant for the definition of paternalism but also plays a central role in justifications inspired by Kantian ethics. These views tend to be absolutistic in their objections to (hard) paternalism and command an absolute respect for the autonomy of the individual. To deny an adult the right to make his own decisions is wrong because it treats the person as simply means to his own good, rather than as ends in himself. Isaiah Berlin writes:

> "For if the essence of men is that they are autonomous beings – authors of values, of ends in themselves, the ultimate authority of which consists precisely in the fact that they are willed freely – then nothing is worse than to treat them as if they were not-autonomous, but natural objects [...]"[128]

Paternalism, especially hard paternalism, seems to deny individual autonomy. The question is what kind of paternalistic interferences violate autonomy. It is possible to distinguish two main forms of autonomy-based justifications, the central concern of both being the preservation of individual autonomy. These might be referred to as 'voluntariness' and 'consent-based' approaches.

Autonomy, though centrally important, is not the only relevant value when determining the justifiability of paternalism. Consequently, strict autonomy-based anti-paternalistic theories gradually 'open up' and give way to certain forms of paternalism. Besides the principle of autonomy, the principle of beneficence is also an important element of the justification of paternalism. These principles often conflict and balancing between them seems inevitable, even in the deontological framework. There are three possibilities, namely, that (1) autonomy always trumps beneficence, (2) beneficence always overrides autonomy and (3) sometimes autonomy and sometimes beneficence trumps the other one.[129] Intuitively, the third category seems to be the case, but for now, I will focus only on the principle of autonomy and come back to the question of balancing and the principle of beneficence a little later.

---

128 Berlin 1969, p. 136.

129 Scoccia 2008, p. 362.

2.2.1.1 Voluntariness-based justifications

From the viewpoint of justification, the most significant distinction is between soft (weak) and hard (strong) paternalism.[130] This distinction is based on the voluntariness of the subject. Hard paternalism advocates coercion to protect competent adults against their voluntary self-harming choices. Soft paternalism allows protection from self-regarding harmful conduct, if "the conduct is substantially nonvoluntary, or when temporary intervention is necessary to establish if it is voluntary or not".[131] Soft paternalism seems acceptable for many because it does not impose external goals on competent individuals, while hard paternalism is discredited because it forces competent adults to act against their wishes.

Moving away from voluntariness, some try to grasp the essence of the soft-hard distinction in the dichotomy of autonomy and liberty. In this framework, soft paternalism can be defined as the limitation of a subject's liberty where the subject does not act substantially autonomously.[132] In contrast, hard paternalism interferes with the liberty of someone who is capable of making autonomous decisions. Consider the physical coercion of drunken or mentally ill people in order to protect them from self-inflicted harm. It qualifies as soft paternalism that limits liberty of action but does not infringe autonomy. Punishing competent adults for the use of light drugs in order to prevent them from harm is hard paternalism, because it limits liberty and autonomy at the same time. Connecting hard and soft paternalism to the concepts of autonomy and liberty seems intuitively appealing but it also presupposes clarifying what autonomy and liberty exactly mean – this is a task that is probably easier said than done.

Some argue that soft paternalism is not even paternalism because the harm is not self-inflicted but comes from external factors to the subject's will (incapacity, lack of information, etc.). As Beauchamp notes "[...] weak paternalism is not paternalism in any interesting sense since it is not a liberty-limiting principle independent of the harm-to-others principle".[133] However, soft paternalism can only be brought under the harm-to-others principle in two-party cases, when

130 Cass Sunstein uses the hard-soft distinction in a different sense. Hard paternalism, in his interpretation, imposes material costs on individuals, while soft paternalism influences people's choices without imposing material costs. Sunstein 2014, pp. 55–59.

131 Feinberg, Joel: "Legal Paternalism". In: *Rights, Justice and the Bounds of Liberty*. Princeton University Press: Princeton, NJ 1980, p. 118.

132 Pope 2004, p. 662.

133 Beauchamp, Tom L.: "Paternalism and Bio-Behavioral Control". *The Monist* 62 (1976), p. 67. See also Feinberg 1989, p. 13. Kleinig 1983, p. 8.

the subject agrees to harm caused by the other party on a non-voluntary basis.[134] In single-party cases, there is no other person actually present in the situation. Strictly speaking, the non-autonomous subject still inflicts the harm on himself, so the harm-to-others principle cannot apply. Consequently, it does not seem wrong to refer to soft paternalism as paternalism; justification, of course, is another matter.

2.2.1.1.1 Feinberg's theory on voluntariness

Feinberg qualifies as a soft anti-paternalist.[135] He rejects "the views both that the protection of a person from himself is *always* a valid ground for interference in his affairs, and that it is *never* a valid ground".[136] He accomplishes this by rejecting hard paternalism but allowing certain forms of soft paternalism. Therefore, Feinberg's central concern is how to decide if an act is substantially voluntary or not. With a little exaggeration, his whole book on paternalism can be considered as a treatise on the question of voluntariness.

The importance of voluntariness stems from Feinberg's absolute respect for autonomy: "[…] respect for a person's autonomy is respect for his unfettered voluntary choice as the sole rightful determinant of his actions except where the interests of others need protection from him".[137] He seems to equate autonomy with voluntariness and opposes hard paternalism on the ground that the hard paternalist wrongly subordinates the agent's right to his good.

Although it is impossible to deal with all aspects of Feinberg's theory, I will try to give a short overview on his account of voluntariness here. Feinberg considers the following factors to establish the voluntariness of an action. There is direct harm and there are cases when only a risk of harm is present. A person who knowingly swallows a lethal dose of arsenic or chops his left hand off with an axe directly causes harm to himself.[138] On the other hand, to smoke cigarettes or to drive at an excessive speed is not directly harmful. It increases the risk of harm. We also have to distinguish between reasonable and unreasonable risks. This distinction is quite vague and Feinberg admits that "[…] there is no simple mathematical formula to guide one […] for judging [a particular case]

134 Feinberg 1989, pp. 13–14.
135 From a different angle, but with the same meaning, Feinberg's paternalism can be qualified as 'absolutist anti-hard paternalism'. Scoccia 2008, p. 352.
136 Feinberg 1980, p. 111.
137 Feinberg 1989, p. 68.
138 Ibid. 101.

reasonable or unreasonable".[139] It is not necessarily more reasonable for someone with serious heart condition to increase his life expectancy by living a quiet life than to continue working hard in the hope of achieving something important even at the risk of a heart attack. Five considerations help us to determine the reasonability of risk: (1) the probability of self-harm, (2) the probability of the desired goal, (3) the magnitude of the harm, (4) the magnitude of the desired goal ('the value or importance of achieving the goal') and (5) the existence or absence of an alternative, less risky means to the desired goal. The first, second, third and fifth considerations are more or less objective, but the fourth one seems essentially subjective. People can attribute different preferences to different desires and it is, at least, unsure if it is possible to measure preferences by a common understanding of reasonableness. Nevertheless, Feinberg claims that there are manifestly unreasonable decisions. "It is certainly unreasonable to cut off one's arm with a power saw, and risk bleeding to death, in order to cure an infected finger".[140] This example is plausible, but does it, due to its unreasonableness, qualify as involuntary also? Voluntariness is clearly ruled out by irrationality (e.g. mental derangement, drunkenness, childhood, etc.) but unreasonableness does not always mean involuntariness. Of course, unreasonable decisions resulting from calculative errors (i.e. erroneous judgment of preferences) are "less than fully voluntary".[141] Still, there are conducts that are fully voluntary but still seem unreasonable to most people. Some unreasonable choices are made by competent persons; they only seem unreasonable, because they reflect different value preferences from the majority. According to Feinberg, paternalism is acceptable for irrational choices, but not for unreasonable ones. Choices reflecting specific value preferences should be respected. Feinberg's conclusion here is quite similar to Gerald Dworkin's in his hypothetical rational consent model (cf. chapter 2.2.1). It seems that the problem with Feinberg's and Dworkin's theories is that they are unable to handle seemingly unreasonable, but fully voluntary and rational 'evaluative' decisions.

One can easily agree with Feinberg that voluntariness, even though legal regulations tend to reduce it to an all or nothing category, is a matter of degree. Most choices fall somewhere between the extremes of perfect voluntariness and

139 Ibid. 102.

140 Ibid. Another example Feinberg quotes is that "[i]t is unreasonable to drive at sixty miles an hour through a twenty-mile-an-hour zone to arrive at a party on time, but it may be reasonable to drive fifty miles an hour to get a pregnant wife to the maternity ward."

141 Ibid. 112.

complete involuntariness.[142] But what is the amount of voluntariness needed for an act to qualify as 'substantially' voluntary from the viewpoint of non-intervention? Feinberg, in his early paper on legal paternalism, required full voluntariness.[143] Later, he introduced a 'sliding scale' which treats voluntariness as a variable concept: some choices require higher standards of voluntariness than others. He gives some rules that influence this sliding scale, but his list of rules is not an exhaustive one. One such rule, for example, is associated with the magnitude and the risk of self-harm: the more serious consequences a conduct has, the greater degree of voluntariness is required in general. If we see someone putting salt instead of sugar into his coffee, we do not have a right or duty to intervene (though the person would be probably grateful for a warning). On the other hand, if someone puts arsenic in his coffee, we must stop him to verify if he is acting substantially voluntarily (i.e. a presumption of non-voluntariness seems to come along with an increase in the magnitude of self-harm).[144] Also, a greater degree of voluntariness is required if the self-harm is irrevocable. Decisions about physician assisted suicide or euthanasia, for example, are determined by strict standards of voluntariness (cf. chapters 3.3.3 and 5.1.5).

So how is Feinberg's voluntariness theory applicable in practice? The three main factors of voluntariness should be considered together. The existence of direct harm or unreasonable risk is always a good reason to presume the lack of voluntariness. Take, for instance, Feinberg's hypothetical situation, where 'Richard Roe' requests 'Dr. Doe' to prescribe him a dangerous drug.[145] The following three discussions may take place:

> *Dr. Doe:* I cannot prescribe the requested drug to you because it will do you physical harm.
> *Mr. Roe:* But you are mistaken. It will not cause me physical harm.

142 Feinberg tries to establish the model of perfectly voluntary choice. There are five main elements of the model: (1) the chooser is competent (not infant, not insane, not retarded, etc.); (2) he does not choose under coercion or duress; (3) he does not choose because of more subtle manipulation (subliminal or post-hypnotic suggestion); (4) he does not choose because of ignorance or mistaken belief; (5) he does not choose in circumstances that are temporarily distorting (not while fatigued, not while excessively nervous, not under the influence of a powerful passion, not in pain, not under the influence of drugs or alcohol, etc.). Ibid. 115.

143 Feinberg 1971.

144 Feinberg 1989, p. 118.

145 Ibid.127 See also Feinberg 1971, p. 114.

Roe's decision here is based on mistaken factual belief, namely that the drug causes no harm to him. In a case like this, paternalism is justified because the state backs the doctor, who (presumably) has expertise in medical questions. Roe is not the best judge of his own interests and his choice cannot be considered fully voluntary. Of course, if he manages to prove that drugs are not harmful, he shall not be restricted to use them (hence the debate on the harmful effects of marijuana consumption). Suppose now that that the conversation goes as follows:

> *Dr. Doe:* I cannot prescribe the requested drug to you because it will do you physical harm.
> *Mr. Roe:* Exactly. That's just what I want. I want to harm myself.

There is no factual mistake in the second case. Yet, Roe's reasoning is so 'manifestly unreasonable' that we can presume that his decision is not fully voluntary. Thus, paternalism is justified here as well, as long as Roe does not show that his choice was voluntarily made. Now let us consider the third possibility:

> *Dr. Doe:* I cannot prescribe this drug to you because it is very likely to do you physical harm.
> *Mr. Roe:* I don't care if it causes me physical harm. I'll get a lot of pleasure first, so much pleasure in fact, that it is well worth running the risk of physical harm. If I must pay a price for my pleasure I am willing to do so.

This is the most difficult case because Roe's choice seems neither irrational nor totally unreasonable. Roe argues that the magnitude of the desired goal overcomes the risk and magnitude of physical harm. As mentioned before, the magnitude of the desired goal is subjective: individuals attach different values to different life goals. These choices might seem unreasonable or bizarre for the majority, but they still deserve protection, for they are autonomously made.

2.2.1.1.2 Critique of the voluntariness standard

The distinction between soft and hard paternalism is not as unproblematic as it seems. It is difficult, if not impossible to devise a coherent theory that can objectively determine the voluntariness of actions. Feinberg's sliding-scale of voluntariness is contingent on individual evaluations and on the specific situation (i.e. the gravity of harm, the magnitude of the desired goal, etc.). The list of rules he gives that determine this sliding-scale is non-exhaustive. Feinberg tries to justify instances of hard paternalism that seem 'reasonable' to him by disguising them as soft paternalism. He calls this 'the soft paternalistic strategy' and uses it to reconcile cases of inevitable hard paternalism with his autonomy-based theory.

For critics, it is nothing else than "ad hoc tinkering [...] to ensure that all justified paternalism can be seen as restraining only involuntary actions".[146]

On a more fundamental level, it is possible to object to the fetishization of voluntary choice on the basis that Feinberg connects voluntariness too 'intimately' to the notion of autonomy. Equating voluntariness with autonomy is problematic because voluntariness is only one element of autonomous decision-making and, as Arneson points out, acting voluntarily does not necessarily lead to an autonomous life based on truly authentic preferences. Those 'soft antipaternalists' who decide about self-harming choices on the basis of voluntariness "only defend personal sovereignty lite".[147] It is impossible to judge the moral rightness of paternalism by examining simply the voluntariness of the restricted act. We may reasonably doubt that "[...] the idea of individual voluntary choice can bear the enormous weight that the soft paternalist has to place on it".[148] Certain acts of paternalism do not seem morally objectionable, although they limit voluntary choices, for example the prohibition of slavery contracts mentioned in *On Liberty*.

Finally, Feinberg's theory must face criticisms that follow a consequentialist rationale. Utilitarian considerations may sometimes outweigh the value of autonomy. Approaching from the distributional consequences of enforcing an absolute right to autonomy, "anti-paternalism [...] looks to be an ideology of the good choosers, a doctrine that would operate to the advantage of the already better off at the expense of the worse off, the needy and vulnerable."[149] Good choosers do not benefit from paternalistic laws because they tend to make better choices from the range of options available to them. Paternalism is more beneficial to those who frequently make bad choices. Bad decisions are often made involuntarily but there are also voluntary decisions that are 'unwise' and do not serve the person's life prospects in the long run. Feinberg's theory of paternalism, based on the idea of voluntariness, does not protect from the latter category of bad choices. Arneson suggests that the capacity to make good choices are often

146 Pope quotes Goldman and Goldman in Pope, Thaddeus Mason: "Balancing Public Health Against Individual Liberty: the Ethics of Smoking Regulations". *University of Pittsburgh Law Review* 61 (2) (2000), p. 489. See also Pope, Thaddeus Mason: "Is Public Health Paternalism Really Never Justified? A Response to Joel Feinberg". *Oklahoma City University Law Review* 30 (1) (2005) (a), pp. 121–207.

147 Arneson, Richard: "Joel Feinberg and the Justification of Hard Paternalism". *Legal Theory* 11 (03) (2005), pp. 259–284, p. 269.

148 Ibid.

149 Ibid. 274.

the result of 'genetic endowment' or 'variously favorable early childhood circumstances' that do not lie within the agent's control.[150] Thus, it seems *unfair* to 'deny' paternalism from those who could potentially benefit from benevolent protective interventions.

2.2.1.2 Consent-based justifications

Consent-based justifications of paternalism are also related to the concept of autonomy. The idea behind this approach is that the protected person authorizes paternalism through an act of valid consent,[151] while still 'retaining the essence' of autonomous choice in the voluntariness of the consent which seems to establish a connection between consent-based theories and the hard-soft justificatory scheme. While soft paternalism is justifiable because the self-harming decision is not made voluntarily, consent based justifications emphasize the autonomy-preserving character of paternalism. The subject agrees to paternalism because he believes that, at the end of the day, he will be 'better off' with paternalistic intervention than without.

Before discussing the different types of consent-based justifications, a distinction must be made between consent to harm and consent to paternalistic intervention. Consenting to harm caused by a 'third party' seems to transform the harm-to-others to a harm-to-self issue because the voluntariness of the consent 'replaces' the voluntariness of the self-harming action. While single-party cases of paternalism focus on the voluntariness of the subject's action, two-party cases focus on the voluntariness of the subject's consent. It is hard paternalism to limit the infliction of harm to someone who has fully voluntarily consented to it. This is expressed in the doctrine of *volenti non fit iniuria* ('to a willing person, no injury is done'). Still, hard paternalism is thriving in this field: examples include active euthanasia, voluntary surgical mutilation, duelling, drug sales, usury and prostitution.[152] The question as to which forms of harm it is possible to consent to raises many questions (e.g. the possibility of waiving certain basic rights). Legal systems treat consent to harm quite differently but one thing is sure: there

---

150 Arneson, Richard: "Paternalism, Utility and Fairness". In: Dworkin, Gerald (ed.): *Mill's On Liberty: Critical Essays*. Rowman & Littlefield Publishers: Lanham, Md. 1997, p. 96.

151 Pope, Thaddeus Mason: "Monstrous Impersonation: A Critique of Consent-based Justifications for Hard Paternalism". *University of Missouri-Kansas City Law Review* 73 (2005) (b), pp. 681–713, p. 682.

152 Feinberg 1989, p. 173.

are certain limits to the *volenti non fit iniuria* principle.[153] Criminal liability is not necessarily eliminated by consent. The infamous German 'cannibal case' involved the killing of a 'volunteer' who replied to the internet advertisement of Armin Meiwes who sought people to be 'killed and eaten'. Even though the killing took place with the victim's consent, Meiwes was convicted for murder in the appeal procedure and sentenced to life imprisonment. The *Bundesgerichtshof* did not accept Meiwes' defence based on the victim's consent and requalified the act as murder (*Mord*) rather than manslaughter (*Totschlag*).[154] Another case where consent was refused as a means of defence was the *Laskey, Jaggard and Brown v United Kingdom* case involving sadomasochistic sexual activities (cf. chapter 5.2.2). Without entering deeper the 'consent-to-harm' question here, we can conclude that the *volenti non fit iniuria* principle is not absolute (it can be overridden by other considerations, e.g. public order, the rights of others) but it is generally considered as a mitigating factor during the judicial procedure.[155]

Consenting to paternalism is a different issue. Based on their temporality, it is possible to distinguish between five different types of consent in this respect: contemporaneous, prior, subsequent, anticipated and hypothetical consent.

In the case of contemporaneous consent, the subject consents to the agent's paternalistic restriction at the time of restriction.[156] The lack of interference with autonomy leads some commentators to conclude that such cases are not cases of paternalism at all.[157] Consenting to paternalism is valid if it is informed and free of coercion or manipulation, which again brings back the problem of voluntariness. Contemporaneous (and, in fact, prior and subsequent) consent can be given explicitly (by words or by conduct) or tacitly: the form of consent is irrelevant for its justificatory power. It is the 'content' of the consent what matters from this perspective.

Prior consent to paternalism is generally exemplified in cases of weakness of will (*akrasia*). Odysseus, for example, 'consented' to paternalistic treatment when commanding his crew to tie him to the mast of his ship and not let him go under the spell of the Sirens; the same rationale makes a drug addict agree to a medical

153 For an overview of the problem in common law, see Bergelson, Vera: "The Right to Be Hurt: Testing the Boundaries of Consent". *The George Washington Law Review* 75 (2007), p. 165.

154 BGH, Urteil vom 22. April 2005, 2 StR 310/04.

155 Feinberg gives a thorough overview of this issue in *Harm to Self*. Feinberg 1989, pp. 172–269.

156 Kultgen calls this type of consent 'current consent'. Kultgen 1995, p. 115.

157 Pope 2005b, p. 685.

treatment in advance that involves the limitation of his or her liberty. Prior consent is thought to justify paternalistic intervention because it represents the subject's long-term or settled preferences in contrast to his short-term, episodic ones. Paternalism based on prior consent does not only respect the subject's 'real' preferences but also contributes to their promotion.

There seems to be a dividing line between prior and contemporaneous consent, on the one hand, and subsequent, anticipated and hypothetical consent, on the other. Paternalism 'backed up' by prior or contemporaneous consent seems better justifiable because these restrictions are actually accepted by the subject, while in the rest of cases he does not participate in the decision on restriction.[158]

The typical example of subsequent consent is the case of children whose liberty is restricted by parents, with an appeal to the children's best interests.[159] Such paternalistic interventions are often said to be justified by the subsequent consent of children once they have grown up. Recourse to justifications by subsequent consent, however, seems a 'hazardous business'.[160] How can we know that the consent will be actually given? What if the paternalistic intervention turns out to be useless or harmful? Or what if the child dies before he could have acknowledged the things his parents had done for him?[161] There is also the threat of manipulation to structure the child's preferences during the upbringing in a way that he will acknowledge paternalistic interventions that were not truly beneficial to him.

The anticipated consent argument comes up in cases when the subject did not have the opportunity to consent to the paternalistic intervention but consent can be inferred from the circumstances.[162] It is similar to the subsequent or the hypothetical rational consent argument in that the element of consent is missing at the time of intervention. Stopping someone to cross an unsafe bridge or giving medical treatment to an unconscious victim of an accident are possible examples here.[163] However, these examples are also examples of soft paternalism because the lack of contemporaneous consent can be attributed to the subject's

158 Kultgen 1995, p. 235.

159 Feinberg 1989, p. 183; Kleinig 1983, p. 61; Kultgen 1995, p. 119; Pope 2005b, p. 693.

160 Feinberg 1989, p. 182.

161 Husak, Douglas N.: "Paternalism and autonomy". *Philosophy & Public Affairs* 10 (1981), pp. 27–46, p. 33.

162 Kleinig 1983, p. 59.

163 Cserne, Péter: *Freedom of Contract and Paternalism: Prospects and Limits of an Economic Approach*. Palgrave Macmillan: New York 2012, p. 25.

involuntariness. It seems that the anticipated consent argument collapses into a question of soft/hard paternalism.

It is also possible to use a 'hypothetical consent' scheme to determine the acceptability of hard paternalism. According to Gerald Dworkin, a paternalistic act is permissible if a fully rational individual would consent to having the restriction imposed upon him.[164] The underlying logic here is very similar to the contractarian reasoning adopted by John Rawls to justify the acceptance of the two principles of justice in the hypothetical situation of the 'original position'. Rawls himself applies this scheme to the question of paternalism. He argues that "[o]thers are authorized and sometimes required to act on our behalf and to do what we would do for ourselves if we were rational, this authorization coming into effect only when we cannot look after our own good."[165]

Hypothetical consent raises the question of rationality. Gerald Dworkin claims that there are two types of situations in which people act in a non-rational way.[166] In one case they attach allegedly 'incorrect' weights to some of their values. In the other case they neglect to act in accordance with their actual preferences (for example, due to *akrasia*). It is easier to justify paternalism in the latter case because it does not impose a distinct conception of good on the subject. The smoker, who is aware of the harmful character of smoking but is unable to stop because he lacks sufficient willpower, may be treated paternalistically in this respect (e.g. providing medical assistance to fight addiction). Intervention does not seem to interfere with his autonomy because it helps him to realize his 'long term' preferences. The former category contains 'evaluative' decisions of competing values. Competing values might be differently weighed. Dworkin implies that there is a distinct standard of rationality. This standard can be established by equating the goals of the subject with the life-plan of an 'average' person and assuming that any difference in the weighting of values is a result of incorrect, irrational calculation. He argues that if people who don't fasten their seat belts (or wear crash-helmets) were to be involved in an accident and severely injured, they would admit later that the inconvenience of using the seat belt or the helmet wasn't as bad as they originally thought.[167] Dworkin is probably right in this case but not all evaluative decisions are so clear. The Jehovah's Witnesses reject blood transfusions for religious reasons. They attach different values to bodily integrity

164 Gerald Dworkin, *Paternalism*, in Dworkin 1997, p. 76.

165 Rawls, John: *A Theory of Justice*. Revised edition. Belknap Press of Harvard University Press: Cambridge, Mass. 1999, p. 219. See also Pope 2005b, p. 700.

166 Dworkin 1997, p. 77.

167 Feinberg 1989, p. 135.

and religious rules than the majority but it is hard to say if their choice is irrational or not. An English court had to deal with a 'modified' version of the crash helmet example.[168] A religious Sikh man refused to wear a crash helmet because it prevented him to wear his turban, which is a religious duty for Sikhs. The value of wearing the turban seems to be greater for this person than the protection the helmet provides from injuries. It is possible to disagree with his choice, but it is probably an overstatement to call it irrational. Although Dworkin argues for the existence of irrational value choices, he is well aware of the incommensurability of values and the problematic nature of evaluative decisions. This is perhaps why he states that "[…] whatever the difference between facts and values […] we are genuinely more reluctant to consent to interferences when evaluative differences are the issue".[169]

Besides the 'content' of a person's value preferences and convictions, it is necessary to take into account the decision's character to determine if hypothetical consent is to be given or not. The similarity between Dworkin's and Feinberg's approach becomes evident here. In the case of irreversible, far-reaching or potentially dangerous decisions (cf. Feinberg's magnitude of harm, risk of harm, etc.), it is possible to think of paternalism as an insurance against non-voluntary decisions. Paternalistic interventions are more easily justified here.[170] The nature of prohibition is also important for the justification. Regulations that only limit a specific conduct (e.g. the prescription of protective equipment for sports-car drivers) are more easily accepted than total prohibitions (e.g. the full prohibition of car racing).[171]

So what is the weak point of hypothetical rational consent? Similarly to Feinberg's model, it is unable to handle the rationality of evaluative decisions. Certain choices of competent adults may seem unwise (taking drugs, smoking cigarettes, not fastening seat-belts, etc.) but to say that these choices are the result of irrational balancing and therefore they are not made voluntarily (Feinberg) or can never be hypothetically consented to (Dworkin) is an exaggeration. The 'reasonable person' standard does not take into account the individual differences

---

168 *R v Crown Court at Aylesbury, ex parte Chahal* [1976] RTR 489. See also the same case before the European Commission of Human Rights, *X v United Kingdom,* Decision of 12 July 1978, application no. 7992/77.

169 Dworkin 1997, p. 78.

170 Dworkin recommends to prescribe cooling-off periods or to set up 'Suicide Boards' to determine the voluntariness of suicide. Ibid. 79.

171 Choosing the 'least restrictive alternative' seems an obvious suggestion. Ibid. 82. See also Kleinig 1983, p. 74.

between people and drives the whole approach in a perfectionist direction.[172] In his subsequent work, Dworkin admits that he sought to show in his first article that persons who do not fasten their seat-belts act irrationally, because he 'felt' that intervention was legitimate in such case.[173]

Hypothetical consent theory can be criticized on similar grounds as Rawls' hypothetical contract scheme. As it was pointed out to Rawls, a contract to have binding force must actually be accepted; a contract only hypothetically approved is not a valid contract at all. To enforce a contract on the basis that 'it would have been certainly agreed to' seems far-fetched. Similarly, it is dubious if one can justify paternalism with a consent that is not actually given but merely 'anticipated', 'subsequent' or 'hypothetical'. There is another fundamental problem that consent-based theories cannot escape. Critics argue that consent has an ideological role to maintain the illusion that autonomy is being respected while it is quite evident that the 'voluntary' or 'informed' consent of the subject can be acquired by manipulation or by other 'malicious' means.[174] Consent seems to hide other standards, such as rationality or voluntariness which, as I have tried to demonstrate, are far from being non-problematic.

2.2.2 Consequentialist justifications

Autonomy, though centrally important, might not be the only relevant consideration when determining the justifiability of paternalism. Consequentialist

172 To avoid the problems of objective standards determined by the concept of 'reasonableness', it is possible to replace it with individualized standards. The subject's consent is still hypothetical here but "[r]ather than supposing that the subject would have consented to the paternalistic intervention because that is what an ideal or rational subject (as defined by the agent) would do, instead, [...] the agent determines the subject's consent by reference to the subject's own well-established life plans". Pope 2005b, p. 703.

173 Dworkin decides to go around this problem in his later theory. He admits that hypothetical consent does not work for evaluative decisions and wants to face these cases more 'squarely', i.e. by justifying them with nonpaternalistic reasons. In 'safety cases' (regulations requiring motorists to wear crash helmets, drivers to wear seat-belts, etc.), for example, he refers to the additional costs imposed on society by the accident. Dworkin 1988, p. 125.

174 Pope 2005b, p. 710. Pope quotes Douglas Husak to demonstrate his point: "The notion of consent is retained in the criteria to create the impression that a concern for moral autonomy is preserved. In reality, however, consent plays only a token role in the criteria [...] [T]he central focus is on the reasonableness of the interference". Husak 1981, pp.34–35.

justifications focus on the outcome of paternalistic interventions. Proponents of this approach argue that the value associated with the respect for personal autonomy must be assessed against the backdrop of beneficent consequences that might result from paternalistic interventions. Very simply put, paternalism is morally justifiable if it leads to 'good' or 'desirable' consequences. Obviously, much depends on how one understands these notions. Classical utilitarianism, for example, has a hedonistic character: pleasure is the ultimate good that measures the morality of all actions. Ever since Bentham, there have been many different approaches as to how the concept of good shall be construed. At the two extremes, consequentialist theories can adopt a desire or an ideal theory of the good.[175] Desire theories focus on the satisfaction of individual preferences (as determined by the subject) to the maximum extent possible. Ideal theories claim that some states of affairs are objective components of the person's good independently of what the person desires. One such value-theory is called perfectionism, a central tenet of which asserts that certain states make a person's life good without necessarily increasing his or her welfare, understood in terms of pleasurable experience or desire satisfaction.[176] Perfectionism is explored in more details in chapter 4.3. The capability approach, particularly its version developed by Martha Nussbaum, can also be seen as endorsing an ideal theory of the good. Nussbaum claims that there is a list of universal capabilities that are essential to human flourishing and shall be protected in every political community. Such basic capabilities include being able to live to the end of a human life of normal length, being able to have good health, being able to move freely or being able to participate effectively in political choices.[177]

From the perspective of paternalism, much depends on which value-theory we decide to subscribe to. If promoting one's well-being consists exclusively in satisfying one's actual preferences, then paternalism can hardly be justified under

175 Dan Brock, Paternalism and Promoting the Good, in Sartorius, Rolf E.: *Paternalism*. University of Minnesota Press: 1983, p. 250.

176 Sinnott-Armstrong, Walter: "Consequentialism". In: Zalta, Edward N. (ed.): *The Stanford Encyclopedia of Philosophy*. Spring 2014. (http://plato.stanford.edu/entries/consequentialism) (12.06.2015).

177 The list of basic capabilities is the following: (1) life; (2) bodily health; (3) bodily integrity; (4) senses, imagination and thought; (5) emotions; (6) practical reason; (7) affiliation; (8) other species; (9) play; and (10) control over one's environment. Nussbaum, Martha C.: *Women and Human Development: The Capabilities Approach*. Cambridge University Press: Cambridge 2000.

any circumstances.[178] If one accepts the existence of a well-defined set of objective goods, interventions that promote these goods become justifiable (even desirable), no matter how harsh they interfere with personal autonomy. To be sure, perfectionist political theories tend to allow for more paternalism and they are less concerned about adopting value neutral policies and regulations. In practice, desire and ideal theories often seem to be mixed: the question is how to create an adequate theory of the good that respects individual autonomy but at the same time resists criticisms directed at ethical relativism.

So what kind of observations can we make about the relation of paternalism and consequentialism in general? Firstly, one can plausibly argue that consequentialism does not command principled anti-paternalism. Although it *might* be argued that Mill's traditional anti-paternalism is based on utilitarian grounds, the epistemic presupposition that informs Mill's approach (namely that people are always the best judges of their own interests) can be seen as being fairly naïve and outdated.[179] As Douglas Husak aptly formulated: "It also is fair to say that most critics of paternalism have abandoned the attempt to formulate utilitarian objections to paternalism. It seems beyond dispute that many paternalistic interferences promote the good or welfare of the agent who is coerced, and do so without introducing disadvantages that outweigh the benefits."[180]

Secondly, it shall be emphasized that consequentialist theories are not necessarily hostile to autonomy. Autonomy can be a component of well-being; it can even hold a central place amongst the goods constituting welfare. However, trade-offs between freedom and other values might still be possible. In fact, a common criticism of consequentialism is that it might justify 'too much' coercion if autonomy-based side constraints are disregarded. As Gert and Culver warn us, "in discussing the justification of paternalism, it is very easy to fall into the error of supposing that all that we need do is compare the evils prevented

178 Zamir, Eyal: "The Efficiency of Paternalism". *Virginia Law Review* 84 (2) (1998), pp. 229–286, p. 240. As Zamir notes, it is possible to reconcile paternalism with the actual preferences theory by referring to people's second-order preferences. People have preferences with regard to their own preferences and these second-order preferences can be paternalistically promoted to overcome first-order ones.

179 Similarly to Mill's utilitarian argument, a long-time presupposition of neoclassical economics was that the market based on perfectly rational actors always produces the best (i.e. most efficient) result and that economic efficiency and paternalistic interventions are incompatible with each other. This presupposition has increasingly been questioned by recent economic theory. Ibid. 237.

180 Husak 1981, p. 27.

with the evils caused and always decided in favour of the lesser evil."[181] Consider the case of a mother who had lost her two children in a car accident, but was also seriously injured in the crash. She is in a critical condition and telling her the truth about her children would significantly decrease her chances of survival. Would paternalism, in the form of a white lie, be justified in this case? Benevolent deception would help the survival of the mother without causing significant harm to anyone, thus the case seems nonproblematic from a utilitarian perspective. Nevertheless, following Kantian rationale, it is possible to argue that mere utilitarian calculation might not be enough to justify hard paternalism. If an act is a violation of a moral rule (i.e. Do not lie!), "we must consider the hypothetical consequences of universally allowing this kind of violation".[182]

The argument from freedom maximization also rests on consequentialist grounds.[183] In short, this argument claims that paternalism can be justified if it increases someone's freedom in the future, even if it restricts actual freedom in the present. Freedom maximization might directly manifest itself in 'freedom protection' as in the case of Mill and the nonrecognition of voluntary slavery contracts, but it can also take the form of 'freedom promotion' or 'freedom enhancement'. The idea behind public education, supposedly, is not only to increase material welfare but also to develop character and foster capacities that help making autonomous decisions in the long run. The reason why freedom shall be maximized, at the same time, depends on the value one attributes to autonomy: autonomy can be thought of as being a constitutive element of well-being but also as an instrument that helps someone to attain higher order preferences. However, if we perceive autonomy in an instrumental way, an argument can be made in support of anti-paternalism as well, according to which the ability to make 'good' decisions is something we are not born with but it must be learnt in practice. In order to master the 'art of choosing', people must be allowed to make bad decisions, no matter how wrong or harmful they are.

2.2.3 Virtue ethics

Virtue ethics, (re)appearing as a reaction to the disillusionment from the 'Enlightenment-project' and the failure of traditional ethical theories, may provide an alternative justification to paternalism. Virtue ethics focuses on moral virtues

---

181 Gert, Bernard / Culver, Charles M.: "The Justification of Paternalism". 89 (2) (1979), pp. 199–210, p. 204.

182 Ibid. 205.

183 Kleinig 1983, p. 53.

and moral character instead of rules and principles. It specifies 'right' action as the action that a virtuous agent would take in the given situation. Although there is a rough correspondence between some virtues and moral norms, many virtues do not correspond to specific norms (e.g. caring, concern, compassion, sympathy, courage, modesty, etc.).[184] They require different actions in different situations, especially if we take into account that virtues themselves can conflict with each other (e.g. friendship with honesty, respect for autonomy with benevolence, etc.). Virtue ethicists seem to admit that their approach cannot provide a comprehensive theory to resolve all moral dilemmas. Rather than relying on abstract rules, they believe that the best way to 'preserve morality' is to develop moral character which makes people better equipped to make right choices. Morality is not simply following moral norms: if a friend performs an act of friendship, we expect that he does not only act out of a sense of obligation, but rather because he desires to be friendly, feels friendly and values friendship.[185]

Thus, the main question is how a virtuous person would relate to dilemmas concerning self-harming activities. As a first step, it is necessary to identify the virtues relevant in such situations. Chapter 4 goes into a detailed examination of virtue ethics, the ethics of care and the implications of these theories with respect to the justification of paternalism. However, before turning to these issues, I will discuss some possible problems and challenges that autonomy-based approaches of paternalism might face. The next chapter starts by examining the notion of autonomy in more details.

184 Beauchamp / Childress 2009, p. 46.

185 Ibid. 32.

3. Autonomy-based approaches

3.1 Autonomy and paternalism

Chapter 2.1 demonstrated the great diversity of definitions of paternalism. While many definitions emphasize the violation of the subject's autonomy, it can be asserted that paternalism in a wider sense does not necessarily involve interference with autonomy. If it was only a matter of definition, an examination of the concept of autonomy would hardly be necessary. However, it was shown in chapter 2.2 that autonomy also has a crucial role in the justification of paternalism. Some key questions naturally arise at this point. Who qualifies as an autonomous person? Is there a universal standard of autonomy or is it contingent on external factors (e.g. social circumstances, historical development)? What gives the prioritized value of autonomy when assessing the question of paternalism? Can autonomy, as a single concept, serve as the 'final arbiter' with respect to the justification of paternalism or do we need to consider other factors as well (e.g. consequences, paternalistic motives, conflicting values, etc.)?

In order to answer these questions, a deeper understanding of the concept of autonomy is needed. Autonomy is a complex notion that has been extensively researched both from a practical and a theoretical perspective. Its complexity can be partly attributed to the fact that it is embedded in a sociohistorical context and any examination of the concept shall take into account its distinctly modern origins. As John Christman explains, "[...] putting moral weight on an individual's ability to govern herself, independent of her place in a metaphysical order or her role in social structures and political institutions is very much the product of the Enlightenment humanism of which contemporary liberal political philosophy is an offshoot."[186] Another source of confusion is that the word 'autonomy' can be used in a normative and a non-normative sense. When people talk about the right to autonomy or claim that autonomy is a value to be respected, they use it in the normative sense. The non-normative sense of the word describes facts that determine whether autonomy has actually been achieved.[187] The two

186 Christman, John: "Autonomy in Moral and Political Philosophy". In: Zalta, Edward N. (ed.) *The Stanford Encyclopedia of Philosophy.* Spring 2015. (http://plato.stanford.edu/entries/autonomy-moral/) (04.06.2015).

187 O'Shea, Tom: *Critics of Autonomy.* (= Essex Autonomy Project Green Paper Report) University of Essex: 2012. (http://autonomy.essex.ac.uk/critics-of-autonomy) (07.06.2015).

senses do not always overlap: it is possible to argue that someone has a right to autonomy, even though he or she is actually non-autonomous at a given moment or in a given situation. This chapter examines the question of autonomy along the following lines: (1) the components of an autonomous life; (2) the difference between moral and personal autonomy; (3) the value of autonomy; (4) critiques directed against the concept.

3.1.1 The complex character of personal autonomy

Personal autonomy is commonly understood as self-governance. It implies that the subject is the author of his own life, freely determining its rules and taking actions to control his own destiny. This common understanding of the concept is fairly vague. Autonomy necessarily calls for a certain degree of self-awareness, but is it only self-awareness that constitutes autonomy? There is certainly an internal, psychological component in personal autonomy but it seems that both internal factors (i.e. those that stem directly or under external influence from the subject's psyche) and external circumstances, independent of the subject, play a role in constituting the concept of autonomous agency.

Personal autonomy can neither be equated with full self-awareness, nor with rational decision-making. An adequate concept, for instance, will accommodate decisions that may seem unreasonable but still belong to the sphere of self-governance (cf. unreasonable voluntary choices in Feinberg's theory). Moreover, certain actions motivated by strong emotions or desires might seem unreasonable but it does not necessarily mean that the agent lacks proper introspective capacity or that the action is made unconsciously.[188] Personal autonomy does not only cover freedom of action and it is not identical with the concept of negative liberty. It seems to include an individual's overall orientation towards life (i.e. the different conceptions of the 'good life'), no matter how crude, simple or unsophisticated it is. As long as one does not subscribe to a 'strongly substantive' account of autonomy, it implies that the 'shallow' and 'idle' lifestyles, e.g. the lifestyle of a television-watching, beer-drinking citizen, deserve the same respect as

---

188 Actions motivated by emotions do not necessarily lack rational self-reflection. As Harry Frankfurt describes this in relation to love: "Love is not an elementary psychic datum, which in itself implies no particular evaluative or practical attitude on the part of the lover toward its motivational tendency. To be sure, a person may regret loving what he loves. He may have attempted to avoid loving it; and he may try to extinguish his love." Frankfurt, Harry G.: *Necessity, Volition, and Love*. Cambridge University Press: Cambridge 1999, p. 137.

a scholarly life full of contemplation.[189] As Raz puts it, "[...] the ideal of personal autonomy is meant to be wider and compatible with other styles of life, including those which are very unintellectual".[190]

Joseph Raz proposes three minimum conditions of personal autonomy. First of all, to be autonomous, a person "must have the mental abilities to form intentions of a sufficiently complex kind".[191] These include minimum rationality, the ability to comprehend the means required to realize his goals and the mental faculties necessary to plan actions. The second condition of autonomy is independence – being free from coercion and manipulation by others.[192] Thirdly, there must be an adequate range of options available to the agent. Somewhat arguably, the third requirement can be considered as external, the first and the second as internal conditions of autonomy.[193] Internal factors originate from the subject's psyche, either 'inherently' (mental capacities) or under 'external stimuli' (manipulation and coercion).[194] The availability of options, as an external factor, is 'objectively' given for the individual.

Depending on the degree a theory focuses on the internal or the external conditions of self-determination, it is possible to distinguish between internalist and externalist conceptions of autonomy.[195] Purely externalist theories are rare

---

189 Jeremy Waldron, *Moral Autonomy and Personal Autonomy*, in Christman, John / Anderson, Joel (eds.): *Autonomy and the Challenges to Liberalism: New Essays*. Cambridge University Press: Cambridge 2005, p. 315. The example comes originally from Ronald Dworkin.

190 Raz, Joseph: *The Morality of Freedom*. Clarendon Press: Oxford 1986, p. 371.

191 Raz 1986, p. 372.

192 Coercion and manipulation are different from external circumstances that limit the number of options available to the agent. Coercion diminishes a person's options but it need not reduce them below adequacy; manipulation does not interfere with the number of available choices.

193 Trebilcock and Elliott make a somewhat similar distinction between internal and external autonomy. Internal autonomy, in their framework, involves constraints on free action internal to the person (e.g. cognitive incapacities). External autonomy is the freedom of the actor to do things in the world without impediment (such impediments may come from, e.g. the lack of capital and information, legal constraints or private coercion). Michael J. Trebilcock, Steven Elliott, *The Scope and Limits of Legal Paternalism,* in Benson, Peter (ed.): *The Theory of Contract Law: New Essays*. Cambridge University Press: Cambridge 2001, p. 55–56.

194 Since manipulation and coercion have external sources, the lack of these factors can be seen as an external condition of personal autonomy as well.

195 Ashley, Viv: *Philosophical Models of Autonomy*. (=Essex Autonomy Project Green Paper Report) 2012. (http://autonomy.essex.ac.uk/philosophical-models-of-autonomy) (03.04.2014).

because it seems implausible to equate autonomy with external conditions irrespective of the subject's reflective and evaluative capacities. Conversely, only very few people would claim that 'autonomy is all in the head' and it is possible to be autonomous in a coercive environment that limits available options to an unacceptably low level. The following chapters examine the external and internal conditions of autonomy in more details.

3.1.1.1 The external conditions of personal autonomy

To be called autonomous, a person must be able to choose from a 'sufficiently' wide range of options. To have only one or only a few options runs contrary to autonomy because it predetermines the life of the individual. A person who falls down a pit and has just enough food and drink to stay alive, but cannot do much more besides eating, drinking and sleeping, can hardly be called autonomous. "His choices are confined to whether to eat now or a little later, whether to sleep now or a little later, whether to scratch his left ear or not."[196] The availability of options presupposes freedom from coercion but also requires 'positive' elements of liberty (e.g. adequate financial possibilities).

It seems difficult to specify the exact number of options necessary for autonomy, partly because autonomy is a matter of degree, and partly because the number of options is not directly proportional to the degree of autonomy. It is a false presupposition to connect autonomy directly to the number of available options for two reasons.

The first reason is that expanding the number of available options does not always increase the person's autonomy. There seems to be a 'diminishing marginal utility' in this respect: adding one additional option to a large number of options will increase autonomy less than if it were added to just a few. There are cases when additional choice can even decrease autonomy and/or utility. The costs of acquiring the necessary information to make informed and reasonable decisions grow as the number of available options grows.[197] The more choices we have, the more time and effort we need to make a decision. Technological improvements may force us to face new moral dilemmas and make choices that people previously did not have to make (e.g. in the case of euthanasia).

---

196 Raz 1986, p. 374.

197 Dworkin, Gerald: *The Theory and Practice of Autonomy*. Cambridge University Press: Cambridge 1988, p. 62.

There are also strategic reasons for not wanting certain choices to be available. If a bank employee does not know the combination of the safe, he cannot be threatened into opening it.[198] Game theory demonstrates that restricting choices can sometimes be beneficial to both parties. Take, for example, the so-called 'chicken-game'.[199] The game is about two drivers, both headed for a single lane bridge from opposite directions. If neither driver swerves, the result is a fatal head-on collision. It is presumed that the best thing for each driver is to stay straight while the other swerves (since the other is the 'chicken' while the crash is avoided). Additionally, a crash is presumed to be the worst outcome for both players. The following payoff matrix illustrates the results of the game.[200]

	Driver 2 swerves	Driver 2 stays
Driver 1 swerves	0, 0	-1, +1
Driver 1 stays	+1, -1	-100, -100

Unlike in the prisoner's dilemma, there is no dominant strategy in this case. There are two positions of Nash equilibrium (+1, -1; -1, +1), which make the outcome of the game unpredictable. However, if one of the players voluntarily limited his or her options in the game, for example, by disabling the steering wheel and making it impossible to swerve, it would significantly improve the chances of winning *if* it was communicated to the other player before the match. Although a convincing 'bluff' might be also sufficient to make the other party swerve, this example shows that, in some circumstances, voluntarily reducing one's own options can be more beneficial than having more options.[201]

To understand that more choices do not necessarily increase personal autonomy, one should also consider the 'quality' of options available to the subject. Marina Oshana argues that people living under conditions of severe social constraint (e.g. serfdom or slavery) have limited autonomy, irrespective of their subjective

198 Ibid. 71.

199 Shor, Mikhael: "Game of Chicken". In: *Dictionary of Game Theory Terms.* (http:// www.gametheory.net/ Dictionary/Games/GameofChicken.html) (03.12.2014).

200 Ibid.

201 It should be emphasized that the arguments in this paragraph are essentially utilitarian. Having more choices is capable of decreasing utility but it is unsure if it affects autonomy in a similar way. In the 'chicken game' example, getting rid of certain choices definitely increases autonomy because it contributes to the realization of long-term preferences over short-term ones.

endorsement of the situation.[202] Her approach is externalist and strongly substantive, in the sense that it evaluates and specifies the options that people need to have in order to qualify as autonomous beings. Not all options contribute equally to autonomy; a decrease in purely instrumental or 'substantively wrong' options will not necessarily decrease autonomy. An instrumental option, such as the number of available clothing brands in the supermarket, is not important for the realization of one's long-term preferences and life goals. Of course, it is possible to argue that there are certain fundamental options that everybody wants to have and increasing these options should increase personal autonomy as well.

3.1.1.2 The internal conditions of personal autonomy

Internalist theories emphasize the role of internal psychological capacities and conditions in the process of autonomous decision-making. These conditions can be grouped into two broad categories, the so-called authenticity and competency conditions.[203] Competency is related to cognitive skills, rational thinking and unimpaired decision-making capacity. Cognitive mental health disorders (e.g. dementia) and developmental disabilities seem to primarily affect competency conditions of autonomy. Authenticity conditions aim to ensure that a person's values are really 'his own' and that higher-order preferences and character traits are authentically formed. These include, for example, the capacity to reflect upon and endorse one's desires, emotions and values.

The following paragraphs depart from the traditional discourse on autonomy and contain a short excursion into the field of theory of action in the hope of better understanding what an autonomous action means and the role of intentions in forming voluntary actions. The fundamental problem of action-theory is to explicate the contrast between what an agent genuinely does and what merely happens to him.[204] It aims to distinguish human actions from causal events of the outside world and establish a *differentia specifica* that sufficiently separates actions from ordinary events. The core dilemma of action-theory is illustrated by

---

202 Stoljar, Natalie: "Feminist Perspectives on Autonomy". In: Zalta, Edward N. (ed.): *The Stanford Encyclopedia of Philosophy*. Spring 2014. (http://plato.stanford.edu/entries/feminism-autonomy/) (04.03.2015).

203 Christman, John: "Autonomy in Moral and Political Philosophy". In: Zalta, Edward N. (ed.) *The Stanford Encyclopedia of Philosophy*. Spring 2015. (http://plato.stanford.edu/entries/autonomy-moral/) (04.06.2015).

204 Mele, Alfred (ed.): *The Philosophy of Action*. Oxford University Press: Oxford 1997, p. 42.

this question from Wittgenstein: "What is left over if I subtract the fact that my arm went up from the fact that I raised my arm?"[205]

The word action can be used in three different senses, for unintentional, intentional and autonomous actions. Actions like coughing, sneezing, or blushing are performed unconsciously and involuntarily as natural reactions to certain events of the outside world. In philosophical terms, these physical reactions can only be called 'actions' in some fairly weak sense and it seems more appropriate to say that people do not act when they cough, sneeze or blush because they occur without the intention or the volition of the subject whenever the adequate cause is present (similarly to the laws of physics). Most philosophers agree that, in order to speak about an action, the performed act must be intentional to a certain extent.[206] There seems to be a conceptual tie between action and intention. But is intention really a necessary condition of actions? Is it possible to speak of non-intentional actions? The first problem we encounter here is that intentions are dependent on different descriptions of action. The same action can be described as intentional and unintentional at the same time. Following Davidson's example, it is possible to describe the action of turning on the light in four different ways: flipping the switch, turning on the light, illuminating the room and, in a specific hypothetical situation, unknowingly alerting a prowler to the fact that the actor has arrived home.[207] All four descriptions refer to the same action but only three of them are intentional. Unknowingly alerting the prowler is an unintentional consequence that cannot explain why the action was taken. It is neither the intention, nor the cause of switching on the light. A similar example is the example of Oedipus, who, after coming to a crossroads in his journey, got into a dispute with an unknown traveller and killed him as a revenge for his insults.[208] The traveller was his unrecognized birth-father, King Laius. It is possible to describe the action of Oedipus both as intentional and unintentional: (1) Oedipus accidentally killed his father at the crossroads or (2) Oedipus intentionally killed the unknown traveller for his insults. According to Davidson, both situations involve

---

205 Wittgenstein, Ludwig: *Philosophical Investigations*. Basil Blackwell: Oxford 1968, § 621.

206 Wilson, George / Shpall, Samuel: "Action". In: Zalta, Edward N. (ed.): *Stanford Encyclopedia of Philosophy*. Summer 2012. (http://plato.stanford.edu/entries/action) (03.12.2014).

207 Davidson, Donald: "Actions, Reasons, and Causes". *The Journal of Philosophy* 60 (23) (1963), pp. 685–700, p. 686.

208 Tengelyi, László: "A cselekvés narratív értelmezése". *Aspecto* 1 (1) (2008), pp. 149–164.

human actions, because they have *at least one* intentional description.[209] Occurrences that have no intentional descriptions are not actions; they are events. A person who accidentally stumbles on the stairway and breaks a window does not act. The breaking of the window is merely an unfortunate event for which he cannot be held liable.[210] To explain actions of negligence or factual mistakes, it is important to note that the original intention of the actor should not be necessarily realized. Actions with non-intended results still qualify as actions if there is at least one intention upon which the subject acts; consider the above-mentioned example of Oedipus and his intention to kill the unknown traveller.

The relationship between action and intention is a central dilemma in the philosophy of action. The concept of intention, as it is directed towards an aim, seems to have a teleological dimension and presuppose a means-end relation. Neo-Wittgensteinian authors, such as Anscombe or Melden, stress that the relation between intention and action cannot be reduced to a causal one.[211] Actions, unlike natural events, cannot be explained on causal terms because causality is law-like: it automatically connects cause and effect to each other. Actions are unique events, where the same intention might produce different actions in different contexts. It was Donald Davidson, who 'reversed' the direction of intention and supported a causal explanation of action. According to him, actions are rationalized by reasons and they are different from mere occurrences in as much as they are caused by reasons. Whenever someone does something for a reason, he can be characterized as (a) having some sort of pro attitude (desire, want, urge, moral preference, aesthetic principle, social convention, etc.) toward actions of a certain kind, and (b) believing that his action is of that kind.[212] These two elements constitute the primary reason (the cause) for why the agent performed the action. Intention is connected to reason but it is not equivalent with it. The notion of reason seems broader than intention. To know the intention of an action is not necessarily to know the underlying reason, but to know the primary reason is to know the intention. For example, if James goes to church with the intention of pleasing his mother, then he must have some pro attitude toward pleasing his

209 Davidson, Donald: *Essays on Actions and Events*. Oxford University Press: Oxford 1980, p. 46.

210 Of course, someone can be held responsible for acting negligently: negligence already implies a certain form of intention on behalf of the actor, even if it manifests itself in omission.

211 Tengelyi 2008.

212 Davidson 1963, p. 685.

mother, but it needs more information to tell his exact reasons (e.g. he enjoys pleasing his mother, he considers it a moral obligation, etc.).[213]

Besides the intentional and causal explanations of action, there is an approach that emphasizes the role of the actor's will in the theory of action. According to the volitional theory, actions are things that someone does either because he specifically wants to do them or because he believes that they are the means to reach other things he wants.[214] The idea that actions are initiated by a simple act of will has a 'prestigious historical pedigree'.[215] However, the problem is that this theory only duplicates the problem of action at the mental stage. If bodily actions are caused by mental actions of will, what are these mental actions caused by?

Either we choose the intentional or the causal explanation, it is possible to conclude that an 'act' only qualifies as human action if and only if it has an intention under at least one description. But this does not mean that the action is performed autonomously as well.[216] Actions based on mistaken factual beliefs or performed under coercion are intentional but can hardly be considered as autonomous. To identify the conditions of an autonomous action, it is necessary to 'dig deeper' into the subject of motives, reasons or intentions. At first sight, it seems that it is the 'genuinity' or 'authenticity' of our motives that determine the autonomous character of our actions. Of course, not all genuine motives make actions autonomous. Genuine but uncontrolled desires can 'enslave' people rather than making them autonomous. A 'popular' account of autonomy stresses the capacity to critically reflect upon and endorse one's desires and preferences as the condition of authenticity.[217] In other words, an autonomous person identifies on a 'higher level' with his first order preferences and his second-order preferences 'cohere' with his first-order ones.

---

213 Ibid. 689.

214 Smith, Peter / Jones, O.R.: *The Philosophy of Mind: An Introduction*. Cambridge University Press: Cambridge 1986, p. 122.

215 Ibid. 125.

216 The question of autonomous actions constitutes a different question than intentionality. Ágnes Heller warns us not to confuse the two concepts. Heller, Ágnes: *Általános etika*. Cserépfalvi: Budapest 1994, pp. 67, 78.

217 Consider Gerald Dworkin's definition which defines autonomy as "a second-order capacity of persons to reflect critically upon their first-order preferences, desires, wishes, and so forth and the capacity to accept or attempt to change these in the light of higher-order preferences and values". However, this definition is quite empty. Critical reflection is certainly an important element of autonomy but it remains unclear how the second-order preferences are created and which values and preferences qualify exactly as such. Dworkin 1988, p. 20.

There are different ideas as to the source of our motives. Plato writes in *The Republic* that the human soul, analogously to the *polis*, is a tripartite entity: it consists of an appetitive, a spirited and a rational part. Human motives are formed through the interaction of these parts. The appetitive part requires the fulfilment of simple bodily needs – such as hunger, thirst or sexual lust. This part lacks any form of rationality; it aims only to satisfy bodily needs. A thirsty person, for example, is characterized by a pure and unqualified urge to drink, with no particular kind of drink in mind. Actions motivated by the appetitive part of the soul are 'genuine' but can hardly be called 'autonomous'. It could be said that there is not much difference between a human completely dominated by his desires and an animal. Clearly, not all human actions are motivated by appetitive desire. A thirsty person may refuse to drink if the water is unclean or contaminated. Such decisions stem from the rational part of the soul, which is logically distinct from the appetitive part.[218] The third part of the soul is the spirited part, independent from the other two parts. Anger, for example, is neither a desire nor subject to reason: children and animals have the spirited part of the soul without possessing real reason. According to Plato, there is a certain hierarchy between the three soul-parts because the rational part is capable of controlling the other two in most cases.

But why Plato's tripartite distinction of the soul is important from the viewpoint of autonomy? It is possible to draw at least two conclusions from Plato's theory at this point. (1) The genuinity of a motive does not make an action autonomous. A genuine desire might provide the intention or the cause for an action but does not make the action autonomous. (2) The discourse on personal autonomy is a distinctly modern development in the history of philosophy. Plato is not concerned with this question. He is investigating the character of

---

218 To illustrate the distinct character of the rational and the spirited part of the soul, consider the following excerpt from section 439d of the Republic:

- "Must we not say that there is one element in their minds which bids them drink and a second which prevents them and masters the first?"
- "I suppose so."
- "And isn't the element of control, when present, due to our reason, while the urges and impulses are due to our feelings and unhealthy cravings?"
- "Clearly so."
- "Then we shan't be without justification if we recognize these two elements as distinct. We can call the reflective element in the mind the reason, and the element with which it feels hunger and thirst, and the agitations of sex and other desires, the irrational appetite – an element closely connected with pleasure and satisfaction." See Plato: *The Republic*. Penguin Books: Harmondsworth 1955, p. 191.

the just individual and correspondingly, the structure of a just society. However, the scheme he developed in relation to the human soul – the delicate balance between the three parts of the soul, with a priority given to reason – resembles to the two-level 'coherentist' approach of modern authors to personal autonomy (e.g. Harry Frankfurt, Gerald Dworkin).

3.1.2 Moral autonomy

Autonomy in moral philosophy refers to the capacity of human beings to impose moral principles on themselves.[219] This formulation of the concept needs to be clarified further. Three preliminary questions shall be addressed before examining the concept of moral autonomy in details. (1) The first question is whether moral autonomy is merely a potential capacity to accept self-imposed rules or requires that the subject actually be the author of his own moral principles. In the Kantian interpretation, moral autonomy refers to a capacity which belongs to all rational human beings. But can we call someone morally autonomous who drifts through his life unconsciously, following external moral standards without truly endorsing or ever questioning them? For this reason, it is possible to agree with Gerald Dworkin who emphasizes the concept's actual character: "a person is morally autonomous if and only if he chooses his moral principles" or "if and only if the ultimate authority and source of his moral principles is his will".[220] (2) The second question is whether moral autonomy (similarly to personal autonomy) is a matter of degree. If we take it as a capacity, then all rational beings have the same amount of it. If moral autonomy depends on the actual choices we make, it seems that a person can partially follow external moral standards and can partially be morally autonomous. (3) The last question is what does it mean that moral rules are one's 'own'? Does it imply that the individual's own moral standards only belong to him and to nobody else? Does it exclude the existence of a common morality? Obviously, this is not the case. People do not own moral principles as they own things. It is possible to share a common set of principles just as it is possible to share certain preferences. To share a taste for chocolate with others, for example, does not mean that this taste is not my own.[221] Moreover, it is not necessary to invent the moral principles we follow by ourselves. In

219 Christman, John: "Autonomy in Moral and Political Philosophy". In: Zalta, Edward N. (ed.) *The Stanford Encyclopedia of Philosophy*. Spring 2015. (http://plato.stanford.edu/entries/autonomy-moral/) (04.06.2015).

220 Dworkin 1988, p. 35.

221 Ibid.

most cases, patterns of morality are provided by the society in which we live. Choosing one's own moral principles mostly means an 'internalization' of already existing external moral standards.

Moral autonomy has a central role in Kantian ethics because Kant derives the normativity of moral claims not from external factors but from the fact that the laws of morality are laws of the agent's own will. Moral autonomy means that ethical standards are internally and independently formulated, with the only condition that they must conform to the requirements of the 'universal law of reason'. The 'invention' of moral autonomy is generally attributed to Kant although the process of detaching morality from 'external sources' (i.e. God) was a process that started earlier. In this regard, Schneewind writes that Kant's "view of morality as autonomy is something new in the history of thought".[222] Attributing autonomy to all rational agents was a significant move in moral theory, since it made possible to derive the normativity of moral claims from autonomy.[223] "It is because each person's own reason is the legislator and executor of the moral law that it is authoritative for every individual."[224]

Following from his epistemology in the *Critique of Pure Reason*, Kant separates the realm of normativity (*sollen*) from the realm of nature (*sein*). Nature, its events being connected by causal relations and its laws being subject to empirical evidence, is entirely 'non-moral'. The aim of Kant's moral philosophy is to isolate the *a priori*, unchanging elements of morality, which Kant finds in the rule of the categorical imperative.

At this point, there seems to be a tension between the universality of moral law and the moral autonomy of the subject. If moral rules are predetermined by practical reason, how is it possible that people are free to give moral rules to themselves? Does not the individual become a slave of his own reason? This would certainly be the case if people were fully rational. However, "[…] obedience is not automatic because we are not wholly rational beings but are compounded of reason and of what Kant calls sensibility, in which is included all

---

222 Schneewind, Jerome B.: *The Invention of Autonomy*. Cambridge University Press: Cambridge 1998, p. 483.

223 Korsgaard, Christine M.: *The Sources of Normativity*. Cambridge University Press: Cambridge 1996, p. 19.

224 Johnson, Robert: "Kant's Moral Philosophy". In: Zalta, Edward N. (ed.): *The Stanford Encyclopedia of Philosophy*. Summer 2014. (http://plato.stanford.edu/entries/kant-moral/) (22.02.2015).

our physiological and psychological make-up".[225] We seem to reach an interesting conclusion here. On one side, the subject is predetermined by reason; on the other side, by physiological and psychological properties; and since he is predetermined by both, he is free.

The moral subject is liberated in Kantian philosophy by becoming independent from internal inclinations and external commands. Hypothetical imperatives tell people what to do in order to achieve particular goals: "If you don't want to go to prison, don't steal cars". Such imperatives do not come under the scope of morality, even if the performed act is the same what moral duty prescribes.[226] Kant's classic example is the shopkeeper who gives the correct change, not because he considers it a duty but because honesty 'pays off' by bringing more customers. In contrast to this, morality requires us to act from duty. The real content of moral autonomy is the capacity of human beings to identify their duties prescribed by the categorical imperative through the application of practical reason.

The criticisms generally brought up against Kant are based on the fact that he detaches the notion of moral duty from 'substantive' notions of ends, purposes and needs. The categorical imperative is neutral but at the same time empty as well: MacIntyre points out that with 'sufficient ingenuity' almost every moral rule can be universalized.[227] The positive increment of Kant's theory from a liberal perspective is that it liberates the individual from external authorities in a way that "it leaves the individual free to pursue whatever it is that he does, without suggesting that he ought to do something else. [...] The typical examples of alleged categorical imperatives given by Kant tell us what *not* to do [...] But as to what activities we ought to engage in, what ends we should pursue, the categorical imperative seems to be silent."[228] Thus, moral autonomy provides people with certain rules, while leaving them free to choose their own personal goals and preferences. This idea forms the basis of the liberal separation between the 'right' and the 'good' (cf. chapter 3.4).

Moral autonomy received a new interpretation in the works of Kierkegaard and Nietzsche, generally considered as the first forerunners of postmodern philosophy. In opposition to Kant, Kierkegaard holds that there are no objective rules in morality. The morally autonomous individual does not only discover

225 MacIntyre, Alasdair C: *A Short History of Ethics – A History of Moral Philosophy from the Homeric Age to the Twentieth Century*. Routledge: London 1998, p. 124.

226 Kant, Immanuel: *Groundwork of the Metaphysics of Morals*. (= Cambridge Texts in the History of Philosophy) Cambridge University Press: Cambridge 1998, p. 25.

227 MacIntyre 1998, p. 126.

228 Ibid.

ethical rules through practical reason, but 'creates' them through an act of choice. Moral rules receive authority merely by the fact that someone has chosen to utter them.[229] Kierkegaard's subjectivism comes from his conviction that rational arguments do not work for morality; they can only present us with alternatives from which we must make our own choices. There is only one obligation, the obligation to choose and either way we decide, it is the choice that makes us morally autonomous.

> "What I have said to you so often I say once more, or rather I shout it to you: either/or; aut/aut. [...] Your whole nature is in contradiction with itself. But you can only get out of this contradiction with an either/or; [...] to win what is the main thing in life: to win yourself, to take possession of yourself. [If one forgets to take this into account], the moment eventually comes when there is no longer any question of an either/or, not because he has chosen but because he has refrained from choice, which can also be expressed in another way: because others have chosen for him, because he has lost himself."[230]

From the viewpoint of moral autonomy, what we choose seems less important compared to the fact that we *make* a choice. But if there are no rational criteria for making ethical decisions, how is it possible to speak about good and bad decisions at all?

Kierkegaard's philosophy can be regarded as the 'epitaph' of Enlightenment's attempt to discover a rational justification for morality, but it is also a direct consequence of Kantian philosophy.[231] MacIntyre describes the relation of the two theories as follows:

> "Kierkegaard and Kant agree in their conception of morality, but Kierkegaard inherits that conception together with an understanding that the project of giving a rational vindication of morality has failed. Kant's failure provided Kierkegaard with his starting-point: the act of choice had to be called in to do the work that reason could not do."[232]

Nevertheless, the question still remains that if the source of morality for Kierkegaard is an 'arbitrary' choice of the subject, how is it possible to speak of authority that these choices have over others? One is tempted to draw the conclusion that moral autonomy as Kierkegaard's 'absolute' freedom of choice is inconceivable, because it fails to account for the normativity of ethical rules.

---

229 Ibid. 138.

230 Kierkegaard, Soren: *Either/Or – A Fragment of Life*. Penguin Books: London 1992, pp. 477, 482–483.

231 MacIntyre, Alasdair C.: *After Virtue: a Study in Moral Theory*. University of Notre Dame Press: Notre Dame, Ind. 2007, p. 39.

232 Ibid. 47.

Nietzsche criticizes Kant for the ideological nature of his ethical theory. Although it seems that Kant removed God from his moral philosophy, he replaced it with the 'ideology' of reason. The categorical imperative remains to be a Christian God's command disguised by 'secular' reason.

> "A virtue must be *our* invention; it must spring out of *our* personal need and defence. [...] Nothing works a more complete and penetrating disaster than every 'impersonal' duty, every sacrifice before the Moloch of abstraction. – To think that no one has thought of Kant's categorical imperative as *dangerous to life!* [...]That is the recipe for *décadence,* and no less for idiocy. Kant became an idiot."[233]

Instead of universal rules, Nietzsche advocates an ethics based on the will of the individual. Since the rational moral subject of Kant is an illusion, he proposes to 'make ourselves into autonomous moral subjects by some gigantic and heroic act of the will'.[234]

The previous overview has shown that moral autonomy is not an uncontested notion. Its original 'Kantian' understanding seems to have significantly changed during the evolution of the concept. This implies that paternalism also becomes contingent on the interpretation of moral autonomy, provided that the two concepts are related to each other. The relation between paternalism and moral autonomy is not as obvious as the relation between paternalism and personal autonomy. The capacity to choose his own moral standards makes the individual an object of respect and this is what paternalistic interventions seem to violate. Purely instrumental forms of paternalism can violate personal autonomy but do not interfere with moral autonomy. However, when evaluative decisions concerning moral values come into play in situations of self-harm, paternalism might interfere with moral autonomy.

The distinction between personal and moral autonomy seems to make sense only in the framework of Kantian philosophy. We have to understand the

---

233 Nietzsche, Friedrich: *The Antichrist*. Noontide Press: Costa Mesa, CA 1980, p. 53–54. (section 11). Another expressive passage is coming from *The Gay Science*: "And now don't cite the categorical imperative, my friend!—this term tickles my ear and makes me laugh despite your serious presence: it makes me think of old Kant who had obtained the 'thing in itself' by *stealth*—another very ridiculous thing!—and was punished for this when the 'categorical imperative' crept stealthily into his heart and *led him astray* back to 'God,' 'soul,' 'freedom,' and 'immortality,' like a fox who loses his way and goes astray back into his cage:—yet it had been *his* strength and cleverness that had *broken open* the cage!" Nietzsche, Friedrich: *The Gay Science*. Cambridge University Press: Cambridge 2001, p. 188 (section 335).

234 MacIntyre 2007, p. 114.

importance of the distinction for modern liberal theories. As I already mentioned, it provides for the separation between the 'right' and the 'good' and facilitates the ideas of value pluralism and neutrality. Morally 'right' rules belong to the sphere of moral autonomy and have a universal character guided by human reason. In turn, they are within the boundaries of personal autonomy; everyone is free to choose his own preferences that constitute a 'good life' and provide individual happiness.[235] However, the full separation of the two concepts is undesirable. They are interrelated and often overlap with each other. Certain elements of personal autonomy are indispensable to moral autonomy and there seems to be a hierarchical relation between the two concepts, which we will fail to understand "if we erect too high a wall of separation".[236]

3.1.3 The value of autonomy

It is a general presupposition that autonomy constitutes a value for individuals. However obvious this fact seems today, the value attributed to autonomy has been significantly shaped by the historical development of the concept.[237] Examining the axiological aspects of autonomy seems essential because the normative content of the concept determines how one approaches the justification of paternalism. Some of the questions that are necessarily addressed are the following: Is autonomy valuable and if yes, what gives value to it? Is the value of autonomy unconditional or dependant on its beneficial consequences or the specific social context it is situated? Is autonomy similar to other social values or does it have a distinguished place in the system of values?

---

235 As Waldron points out, this distinction is already present in Kant's philosophy. Kant writes that "[n]o one can coerce me to be happy in his way; instead each may seek his happiness in the way that seems good to him [...]". Kant calls this principle as the "principle of freedom". It seems similar to a principle of autonomy but it is not to be confused with moral autonomy. It accounts more for a principle of personal autonomy. Thus, the separation of the "right" and the "good" corresponds to the separation of moral and personal autonomy. Jeremy Waldron, *Moral Autonomy and Personal Autonomy*, in Christman / Anderson 2005, p. 308.

236 Ibid. 325.

237 The thought that the value of freedom is historically bound appears in *On Liberty*. Mill writes that "Despotism is a legitimate mode of government in dealing with barbarians, provided the end be their improvement, and the means justified by actually effecting that end. Liberty, as a principle, has no application to any state of things anterior to the time when mankind have become capable of being improved by free and equal discussion." Mill 1975, p. 11.

Kant considered moral autonomy as an inherent capacity of rational human beings. It seems quite obvious that the *fact* of autonomy (either as a potential capacity or as an actual condition, if the capacity is exercised) does not make autonomy valuable. To draw such an inference would constitute a naturalistic fallacy and violate the idea of separating the 'ought' from the 'is'. It is needless to say that not all human characteristics are valuable – even if we allow that some of them are. Moreover, the value that people tend to attribute to autonomy will vary by the specific theory of autonomy one subscribes to. It seems more demanding to explain why a formal concept of autonomy is valuable than a substantive one that associates the content of the concept of autonomy with other values.[238]

Autonomy as an 'ideal type' (as opposed to autonomy as capacity) can be valuable in two ways: in an intrinsic and in an instrumental way.[239] In support of autonomy's intrinsic value, it is possible to assert that autonomy is the very essence of humanity and the basis for self-fulfilment that accounts for the plurality of mankind. Mill writes the following in *On Liberty*: "It is not by wearing down into uniformity all that is individual in themselves, but by cultivating it and calling it forth, within the limits imposed by the rights and interests of others, that human beings become a noble and beautiful object of contemplation".[240] Based on this passage, Kultgen argues that autonomy has an 'aesthetic character' in Mill's theory that makes the concept intrinsically valuable not only for the agent but for others as well.[241] Of course, one might rightfully ask why autonomy should have value independent of the results of exercising it. John Christman poses the question: "Why is one person's autonomy intrinsically valuable when she uses it to harm herself or make rash or morally skewed choices?"[242]

Cass Sunstein differentiates between 'thick' and 'thin' versions of autonomy and argues that autonomy under both conceptions carries an intrinsic value. The 'thin' version suggests that freedom of choice is a component of welfare.

238 Dworkin 1988, p. 30.

239 For the distinction, see Kultgen 1995, p. 105. Joel Feinberg distinguishes four senses in which personal autonomy can be used: the capacity to govern oneself, the actual condition of governing oneself, autonomy as a right (derived from the individual's sovereign authority to govern himself or herself) and autonomy as an ideal. Feinberg 1989, pp.27–52.

240 Mill 1975, p. 59.

241 Kultgen 1995, p. 104.

242 Christman, John: "Autonomy in Moral and Political Philosophy". In: Zalta, Edward N. (ed.) *The Stanford Encyclopedia of Philosophy*. Spring 2015. (http://plato.stanford.edu/entries/autonomy-moral/) (04.06.2015).

Autonomy is not valuable because it leads to good consequences but it has value in itself as an ingredient of human welfare.[243] People tend to dislike when their free choices are overridden and policy makers must take into account the loss of welfare potentially caused by coercive interventions. The 'thick' version abandons welfarism and stands on strict Kantian grounds: autonomy is valuable because it is the essence of human dignity that all rational beings possess.[244] In this sense, autonomy is a 'show-stopper' because it cannot be limited for the sake of welfare or social utility; it is practically immune to empirical considerations.[245]

Even if the idea of autonomy's intrinsic value is rejected, it is hard to deny that it can be valuable in an instrumental way. Mill argues that autonomy is beneficial because it leads to new ideas, innovations and experiments which contribute to the development of humankind.[246] He warns the reader "[...] where, not the person's own character, but the traditions and customs of other people are the rule of conduct, there is wanting one of the principal ingredients of human happiness, and quite the chief ingredient of individual and social progress".[247] This passage shows the consequentialist character of Mill's reasoning: autonomy is valuable because it is an instrument for maximizing human happiness. The adoption of such view, however, presupposes a sort of 'teleology' that requires singling out and precisely conceptualising certain substantive values that autonomy promotes (e.g. happiness). Another difficulty here is that Mill, in a rule-utilitarian fashion, argues that respect for autonomy *always* increases social utility in the long run, even if autonomous decisions sometimes result in actions that are offensive or

243 Sunstein 2014, p. 124.

244 Ibid. 127.

245 Ibid. 133.

246 This reasoning is particularly striking in Mill's defense of freedom of speech. He claims that the diversity of opinions is essential to social development. He argues in the following way: "But the peculiar evil of silencing the expression of an opinion is that it is robbing the human race; posterity as well as the existing generation; those who dissent from the opinion, still more than those who hold it. If the opinion is right, they are deprived of the opportunity of exchanging error for truth: if wrong, they lose, what is almost as great a benefit, the clearer perception and livelier impression of truth, produced by its collision with error". Mill thinks that an opinion, even if wrong, is still valuable. True opinions are only appreciated if constantly challenged on the 'marketplace of ideas' and contrasted with other, possibly false opinions: "However true a [statement] may be, if it is not fully, frequently, and fearlessly discussed, it will be held as a dead dogma, not a living truth." Mill 1975, pp. 18, 35.

247 Ibid. 54.

harmful to others. We will discuss why this argument is not particularly convincing in chapter 3.2.2.

Mill thinks that autonomy is useful in two other instrumental ways for the individual. First, people learn best from their own mistakes: only by choosing do people develop their rational faculties and learn to make better choices.[248] Second, Mill claims that the individual's best judge is himself, because he knows his own values and preferences the most: "with respect to his own feelings and circumstances, the most ordinary man or woman has means of knowledge immeasurably surpassing those that can be possessed by any one else."[249] This 'epistemic argument' is often invoked to combat paternalism; Sunstein actually claims that it provides the strongest argument to support non-intervention.[250]

Joseph Raz and Gerald Dworkin also attribute instrumental value to autonomy. Gerald Dworkin warns us that overemphasizing the importance of autonomy makes autonomy inconsistent with other values, such as loyalty, commitment, benevolence and love. What is valuable about autonomy is that it makes our commitments genuinely ours and allows us to define ourselves via these commitments. Autonomy is important but so are other values: "theories that base everything on any single aspect of human personality, on any of a number of values, always tend toward the intellectually imperialistic".[251]

Raz relativizes the value of autonomy from two aspects. First, he claims that "autonomous life is valuable only if it is spent in the pursuit of acceptable and valuable projects and relationships".[252] He argues for a contingent value of autonomy in the following way:

> "Has autonomy any value *qua* autonomy when it is abused? Is the autonomous wrongdoer a morally better person than the non-autonomous wrongdoer? Our intuitions rebel against such a view. It is surely the other way round. The wrongdoing casts a darker shadow on its perpetrator if it is autonomously done by him".[253]

This shows that autonomy does not have a value on its own but relates to other, substantive values. An autonomous premeditated murder is no more valuable than a murder committed non-autonomously; in fact, it is considered to be even

248 Kultgen 1995, p. 107.
249 Mill 1975, p. 71.
250 Sunstein 2014, p. 7.
251 Dworkin 1988, p. 32.
252 Raz 1986, p. 417.
253 Ibid. 381.

worse.[254] Autonomy is not valuable *per se;* if it has any value, it lies in its instrumental character, which helps people to realize other valuable projects and goals. This makes Raz's theory compatible with value pluralism. "A moral theory which recognizes the value of autonomy inevitably upholds a pluralistic view. It admits the value of a large number of greatly differing pursuits among which individuals are free to choose."[255] Raz neither elevates autonomy over substantive values, nor equates it with them. It has a somewhat different (i.e. more 'fundamental', yet still instrumental) character. But where does this difference come from? Raz derives it from social and historical developments of modern societies. He thinks that autonomy is not a question of choice, but a fact of life in modern societies:

> "For those who live in an autonomy-supporting environment there is no choice but to be autonomous; there is no other way to prosper in such a society. [...] Since we live in a society whose social forms are to a considerable extent based on individual choice, and since our options are limited by what is available in our society, we can prosper in it only if we can be successfully autonomous."[256]

In other words, we don't have the autonomy to be non-autonomous. Our choice is predetermined by the society in which we live; the best way to survive and flourish in modern societies is to be autonomous. This is required by the need to adapt to the fast changing circumstances. Modern life gives us a whole lot of possible options to choose from. On one hand, this provides the external conditions of personal autonomy. On the other hand, it also requires us to make decisions and *compels* us to be autonomous: development produces options and options 'require' free choices. Autonomy, thus, is a fact of modern life and goes hand in hand with value pluralism: it has a distinguished role as an instrument of self-realization. This implies a perfectionist standpoint on the side of the state but not in the classical sense, which requires the promotion of substantive values and thus is incompatible with value pluralism. Modern society requires a

---

254 Jeremy Waldron draws attention to the weakness of Raz's argument. Waldron claims that the value of autonomy cannot be equated with the overall moral praiseworthiness of an autonomous person, just as the value of courage with the moral praiseworthiness of a courageous person. An act can display the virtues of courage or autonomy, yet be completely immoral from other perspectives. Autonomy and other values are not interconnected and the fact that autonomy does not add anything to the value of an act a person chooses to do is not a conclusive argument for the instrumental and contingent character of autonomy. Waldron, Jeremy: "Autonomy and Perfectionism in Raz's Morality of Freedom". *Southern California Law Review* 62 (1989), pp. 1097–1152, p. 1127.

255 Raz 1986, p. 381.

256 Ibid. 391, 394.

perfectionist promotion of autonomy. This understanding of autonomy is the foundation of Raz's liberal perfectionism which will be discussed in more details in chapter 4.3.4.

Traditional perfectionist theories deny the distinguished character of autonomy. Thomas Hurka, for example, acknowledges its importance, but only as one value amongst many others. Similarly to Raz, he argues that a plausible value theory must "acknowledge some other goods, for example that freely chosen creativity is better than freely chosen idleness, and autonomous knowledge is better than autonomous ignorance".[257] Autonomy may sometimes be outweighed by other 'perfections'.

To sum up, let us go through the different ideas concerning the value of autonomy once again. Kant regards moral autonomy as an inherent capacity of rational human beings, which is intrinsically valuable and provides the very essence of human existence by allowing the individual to impose universal rules of morality on himself. Mill can be understood to attribute both an instrumental and an intrinsic value to autonomy. His utilitarian argument is still somewhat unconditional: he claims that autonomy *always* increases utility and contributes to the development of humankind. Joseph Raz is aware of the relative character of the concept. Autonomy's value depends on other values and also on social and historical circumstances. In Raz's theory, autonomy has a different character than other, "ordinary" values. It is an instrument that helps us realize our goals and preferences but it is also a central condition in modern society without which people are unable to flourish. Perfectionists attribute no distinguished value to autonomy but they still regard it as valuable, because – in Hurka's words – it "develops human nature by exercising sophisticated rationality". All authors seem to agree that autonomy is valuable – the disagreement seems to be about the extent of this value. Accepting that the normative character of autonomy is instrumental and contingent on external social factors seems to bring us closer to a more 'realist' perception of paternalism which implies that the justification of paternalism cannot be assessed according to one universal principle but should be considered on a case-by-case basis. It also implies that the specific motives and circumstances of a paternalistic intervention cannot be disregarded and that we need to pay more attention to the idea that the value of autonomy might also stem from developing interpersonal relations as suggested by the ethics of care (cf. chapter 4.4).

---

257 Hurka, Thomas: *Perfectionism*. Oxford University Press: New York 1993, p. 149.

3.1.4 The 'myth' of autonomy

The reader might have the impression that the concept of autonomy is a specific socio-historical construct. Indeed, it seems that the 'myth' of individual autonomy began to disperse with the emergence of philosophical trends associated with the critique of modernity. Even though "[...] the program of the Enlightenment was the disenchantment of the world; the dissolution of myths and the substitution of knowledge for fancy",[258] the Enlightenment-project has created its own 'mythology' in concepts such as reason, progress and freedom. Horkheimer argues that the dominant form of reason in the modern age is 'instrumental reason' by which he refers to the capacity of selecting means necessary to attain certain ends, irrespective of what these ends might be.[259] The disregard for 'objective reason' leads to a social structure where ends are imposed on people from the outside and the individual is precluded from leading a 'genuinely' autonomous life.

Radical social critics, such as Herbert Marcuse, argue that advanced industrial societies create false needs, which integrate people into a repressive system of ceaseless production and consumption. This results in a 'one-dimensional' universe in which the possibility of critical thinking is marginalised and freedom is 'tamed' by a "society which seems increasingly capable of satisfying the needs of the individuals through the way in which it is organized".[260] Autonomous preference formation is illusory because preferences are determined by the surrounding *simulacrum* of mass media and advertising: it might be that choices are free from coercion but people are kept incapable of being autonomous through indoctrination and manipulation. The degree of human freedom is not determined by the number of options available to the individual but rather by the *content* of his or her actual choices. Freedom in the formal sense serves purely ideological reasons and "can be made into a powerful instrument of domination."[261] Consequently, freedom in advanced industrial societies turns into a state of "comfortable, smooth, democratic and reasonable unfreedom".[262]

---

258 Horkheimer, Max / Adorno, Theodor W.: *Dialectic of Enlightenment*. Verso: London 1992, p. 3.

259 Horkheimer, Max: *Eclipse of Reason*. Continuum: London; New York 2004, p. 3.

260 Marcuse, Herbert: *One-Dimensional Man: Studies in the Ideology of Advanced Industrial Society*. Routledge: London 2002, p. 4.

261 Ibid. 9.

262 Ibid. 1.

Besides 'leftist' social critics, communitarian and feminist thinkers are also sceptical about the prioritised role of autonomy in modern societies. Most of them do not completely reject the concept but argue for its critical reinterpretation focusing on autonomy's specific social and historical character. Communitarians claim that the individual cannot be separated from the social, historical and cultural reality in which he or she is embedded; their opposition to autonomy mainly stems from the individualist *identity* it fosters.[263] Charles Taylor aims to explore how selfhood and personal identity have evolved throughout the course of history.[264] He argues that people have always had some perception of themselves as individual beings but 'selfhood' as a distinct notion is a product of modernity. The way in which modern people regard themselves is essentially individualistic. "We live in a world where people have a right to choose for themselves their own pattern of life, to decide in conscience what convictions to espouse, to determine the shape of their lives in a whole host of ways that their ancestors could not control."[265] Many consider individual autonomy as one the 'finest achievements' of modern civilization, but Taylor interprets it as one of the three *malaises* of modernity. He believes that there is a price to pay for individual freedom:

> "Modern freedom was won by our breaking loose from older moral horizons. People used to see themselves as part of a larger order. [...] But at the same time as restricting us, these orders gave meaning to the world and to the activities of social life. [...] The discrediting of these orders has been called the 'disenchantment' of the world."[266]

It is individualism and partly the process of disenchantment that leads us to the second problem of modern age, the primacy of instrumental reason. With respect to the third *malaise*, Taylor echoes the concerns of Alexis de Tocqueville and emphasizes the tendency that the "atomism of the self-absorbed individual" alienates citizens from the public sphere and weakens democratic participation.[267] This might result in the loss of political freedom and bring about a soft form of despotism.

---

263 O'Shea, Tom: *Critics of Autonomy.* (Essex Autonomy Project Green Paper Report) University of Essex: 2012. (http://autonomy.essex.ac.uk/critics-of-autonomy) (07.06.2015).

264 See especially Taylor, Charles: *Sources of the Self: The Making of the Modern Identity.* Harvard University Press: Cambridge, Mass. 1989.

265 Taylor, Charles: *The Ethics of Authenticity.* Harvard University Press: Cambridge, Mass. 1992, p. 2.

266 Ibid. 3–4.

267 Ibid. 9.

Individuality, as the main component of modern identity, can be further analysed. Components of "Western selfhood" include a radically disengaged notion of freedom, a sense of inwardness and the emphasis of authenticity.[268] Disengaged freedom is related to individuality and the first of the three *malaises*: due to the fact that the disenchanted world lacks any preordered meaning, the self is 'free' to define itself without looking for an intrinsic moral order in the cosmos. The disconnectedness from a larger cosmic order brings along a sense of inwardness: "[…] for the modern, the horizon of identity is to be found within, while for the pre-modern it is without".[269] Disengaged freedom and inwardness culminate in the emphasis of authenticity in modern identity. Since everyone has an individual mode of being, the individual is encouraged to realize this authentically rather than conform to a pre-existing model or a pattern imposed from outside.[270]

The ideal of authenticity, however, does not require the person to build his or her identity completely independent of the demands of society and nature. This is a misinterpretation of authenticity which leads to 'shallow' and 'narcissistic' cultures of identity that emphasize self-fulfilment by breaking with social expectations. It is impossible to 'bracket out' history, nature, society and the demands of solidarity in the process of self-definition. Taylor believes that a non-trivial identity can only be defined if someone "exist in a world in which history, or the demands of nature, or the needs of my fellow human beings, or the duties of citizenship, or the call of God, or something else of this order matters crucially".[271]

Probably the most puzzling characteristic of the self in the process of identity-building is its *dialogical* nature. Taylor claims that self-identity cannot be worked out in isolation, but only through dialogue with others; individuality is continuously formed through human interactions and encounters. People do not acquire the 'languages of expression' needed for self-definition on their own; they learn them through exchanges with others, most importantly through exchanges with significant others.[272] Even though the dialogical aspect of selfhood has been eclipsed by the 'myth' of individualism, they are not necessarily incompatible with each other.[273] Moreover, if we accept that individuals exist within what Taylor calls 'webs of interlocution', our whole understanding of autonomous

268 Abbey, Ruth: *Charles Taylor*. Acumen: Teddington 2000, p. 79.

269 Charles Taylor quoted by Ruth Abbey. Ibid. 85.

270 Ibid. 86.

271 Taylor 1992, p. 40.

272 Ibid. 33.

273 Abbey 2000, pp.68–70.

personhood might change. A comatose person kept alive by a life-support system or a person suffering from Alzheimer's disease might not meet the criteria of personhood. However, they still exist in a web of social dialogue and interconnectedness, for example as someone's brother, father, husband or neighbour. This is not only important to consider when discussing matters of life and death such as euthanasia, but also when exercising paternalism over non-autonomous people, whose individuality continues to exist in the form of human relations they retain and the social narratives they are part of.[274] This conclusion already bears resemblance to relational theories of autonomy articulated by feminist philosophers (cf. chapter 4.4.2).

3.2 The harm principle of John Stuart Mill

In his essay *On Liberty*, John Stuart Mill designated the limits of state intervention by the harm principle:

> "The object of this essay is to assert one very simple principle [...] That the only purpose for which power can be rightfully exercised over any member of a civilized community, against his will, is to prevent harm to others. His own good, either physical or moral, is not a sufficient warrant. He cannot rightfully be compelled to do or forbear because it will be better for him to do so, because it will make him happier, because in the opinions of others, to do so would be wise or even right."[275]

The most striking feature of Mill's principle is its exclusive character. It sets a blanket prohibition to legal paternalism and moralism, legitimizing the limitation of individual liberty only if it is necessary to prevent harm to others. The harm principle in its original form seems untenable in modern societies.[276] Despite its central status in the liberal tradition, most modern liberals regard it as exaggerated. Hart, for instance, writes that "Mill carried his protests against paternalism to lengths that may now appear to us fantastic."[277]

274 Ibid. 71.

275 Mill 1975, p. 10.

276 A modern criminal code fashioned in Mill's concept would not prohibit a large number of conducts commonly regarded as criminal acts. The lack of the harm-to-others element would remove, for example, drug use, euthanasia or moral crimes from the scope of criminal law. Louis B. Schwartz, *Morals Offenses and the Model Penal Code,* in Feinberg, Joel / Gross, Hyman (eds.): *Philosophy of Law.* Wadsworth Publishing Co: Belmont 1991, p. 258.

277 Hart 1963, p. 32.

The harm principle is not as simple as Mill asserts. It has a complex, two-sided structure. The positive side of the principle accepts harm caused to others as a legitimate reason to limit individual liberty. The requirement set by the negative side is more demanding: it prohibits any kind of coercion that is not intended to prevent harm to others. Besides being overly restrictive, there is a more fundamental problem with the harm principle and this is the tension between Mill's commitment to a categorical approach towards liberty and his defense of utilitarianism. Nigel Warburton remarks that "[…] many readers of *On Liberty* have been left with the suspicion that, in his tenacious adherence to the harm principle, Mill unintentionally comes closer to advocating an absolute right to personal freedom than his professed utilitarianism would consistently allow".[278] It seems that there is a gradual shift from the utilitarian to the deontological, autonomy-based interpretation of the harm principle during its historical development, which affects the justification of paternalism as well. The potentiality of this transformation is already implicit in *On Liberty*, certain parts of which provide good starting point for autonomy-based theories. Taking into account this interpretational change, a strange paradox appears. While the absolute character of prohibition is gradually abandoned through different methods of 'softening' of the harm principle, Mill's original utilitarian justification is replaced by a deontological background that is more suitable for justifying categorical prohibitions.

3.2.1 The absolute character of prohibition

According to the original formulation of the harm principle, any interference with liberty that does not aim to prevent harm to others is excluded from the scope of legitimate state intervention. However, even in Mill's own theory, the blanket character of this prohibition seems to weaken. I will discuss five ways Mill eases the rigorousness of the harm principle: (1) the distinction between other-regarding and self-regarding actions; (2) the distinction between soft and hard paternalism; (3) the acceptance of non-coercive forms of paternalism; (4) harm to others as not always a necessary and/or sufficient condition for regulation; (5) the acceptance of the offense principle.

278 Matravers / Pike / Warburton 2000, p. 317.

3.2.1.1 Self-regarding and other-regarding actions

Mill distinguishes two maxims that correspond to the double-sided structure of the harm principle.[279] The 'liberty maxim' covers mostly the negative side of the principle. It states "that the individual is not accountable to society for his actions in so far as these concern the interests of no person but himself".[280] The 'social authority maxim' claims that "for [other-regarding] actions [...] the individual is accountable, and may be subjected to social or to legal punishment, if society is of opinion that the one or the other is requisite for its protection".[281]

These normative statements presuppose the possibility of distinguishing between conducts that are self-regarding and those that regard others. Mill makes this distinction between conducts that only affect the agent himself and conducts that affect others.[282] The traditional critique against Mill is based on the idea that there are no purely self-regarding actions and criticise him for perceiving society as a collection of atomistic individuals. Mill's contemporary critic, James Fitzjames Stephen already pointed out that "by far the most important part of our conduct regards both ourselves and others".[283]

Obviously, the scheme is not so simple. Mill admits that "the mischief which a person does to himself may seriously affect, both through their sympathies and their interests, those nearly connected with him and, in a minor degree, society at large".[284] He rightly asks the question "how [...] can any part of the conduct of a member of a society be a matter of indifference to the other members?" and adds that "no person is an entirely isolated being".[285] But do not such statements contradict Mill's whole theory based on the distinction of self-regarding and other-regarding actions?

---

279 Riley, Jonathan: *Mill on Liberty*. Routledge: London ; New York 1998, pp.111–114.

280 Mill 1975, p. 87.

281 Ibid.

282 According to Ten, the term 'self-regarding' is Mill's own invention but he does not use the expression 'other-regarding' in his essay. The concept of self-regarding offences already appears in Bentham's works. See, e.g. Bentham, Jeremy: *An Introduction to the Principles of Morals and Legislation*. Clarendon Press: Oxford 1907. (http://www.econlib.org/library/Bentham/bnthPML.html) (chapter XVI, paragraph 8). Ten, C. L.: *Mill on Liberty*. Clarendon Press: Oxford 1980, p. 4.

283 James Fitzjames Stephen quoted by Nigel Warburton. Matravers / Pike / Warburton 2000, p. 311.

284 Mill 1975, p. 75.

285 Ibid.

It is possible to distinguish between three types of self-regarding conduct. The first category contains a few trivial, purely self-regarding actions. If I prepare myself a cup of coffee or turn on the television with moderate volume, these acts could hardly affect others. Since they have no social relevance, no limitation is likely to be imposed on them. The second category is comprised of acts that provoke anger, disgust or resentment in others but do not cause harm to them (cf. chapter 2.1.3). Under the original formulation of the harm principle, these actions cannot be legitimately restricted.[286] The disgust that someone may feel, for example, at the public display of an 'immoral' behaviour is not a sufficient reason for coercion, largely because this feeling, unlike the 'objective reality' of physical harm, seems to depend on moral values chosen by the majority of society. Acts of an individual that are hurtful to others or "wanting in due consideration for their welfare" might be "justly punished by opinion, though not by law."[287] Mill has been criticized for abandoning utilitarianism at this point on the grounds that ignoring any phenomenon that decreases utility seems incompatible with utilitarianism.[288] True enough, Mill's position seems quite radical and many modern liberals have decided to "jump off the Millian ship" at this point.[289] After all, doesn't society have the right to regulate indecent public behaviour that offends others? The most promising strategy to save the integrity of the harm principle is to admit that such cases cannot be adequately covered by the concept of harm. Hart and Feinberg use the offense principle as an auxiliary principle to handle such cases.

The third category of self-regarding acts contains primarily self-harming actions that at the same time violate a "distinct and assignable obligation" to others.[290] Self-harm and other-regarding harm are inseparable: self-harm causes harm to others due to the interdependence of individuals. Mill gives some illustrations, including the man whose extravagant personal consumption leads him to violate his creditors' rights; and the policeman whose drunkenness prevents him from performing his duties. A lot of other situations exist with indirect harm. In fact,

---

286 It seems that Mill is not entirely consequent about the regulation of offensive behaviour. In Chapter 5 of *On Liberty*, Mill allows the limitation of such behaviour.

287 Ibid. 72.

288 Consider, for example, Ten's remark: "[i]n treating as irrelevant the repugnance and abhorrence of the majority towards some self-regarding actions, Mill goes against the classical utilitarian's view that all pleasures and pains are relevant in determining the rightness or wrongness of an act." Ten 1980, p. 18.

289 Riley 1998, p. 177.

290 Ten 1980, p. 15.

it is possible to identify such harm in most self-harming actions. The obligation to wear seat belts or crash-helmets may be justified by the additional medical expenses in case of accidents. Voluntary euthanasia may be opposed on the ground that the death of a relative causes mental suffering (i.e. mental harm) to family members. Moreover, the extension of the concept of harm offers a solution when the narrow possibilities of state intervention may result in social situations that are discriminatory, unequal or oppressive.[291] The censorship of pornography under the classical form of the harm principle is unacceptable, since pornography does not seem to cause direct harm to anyone. It does, however, advocate gender inequality and indirectly harms the interests of women in leading autonomous lives free of discrimination and male dominance. This way, it becomes possible to reconcile the censorship of pornography with liberal values and the requirements of the harm principle.

Mill admits that "[w]henever there is a definite damage, or a definite risk of damage, either to an individual or to the public, the case is taken out of the province of liberty, and placed in that of morality or law."[292] However, Mill did not imply that the existence of indirect harm should automatically discredit primarily self-harming actions. Apparently, the question is what the word 'primarily' means in this context. As mentioned before, harm to others is a necessary but not sufficient condition for legal coercion. A careful balancing of interests should take place before an action is prohibited. It is possible to adopt a utilitarian method for calculating competing interests; if the expected benefits (including the benefit from preserving the liberty of the person) of the self-regarding conduct are greater than the indirect harm caused to others, the prohibition seems unjustified.

An interesting argument against the distinction of self and other-regarding actions is based on Derek Parfit's view on personal identity. The 'complex view' of personal identity he advocates implies that the future self of a person can be partly identical with the present self, depending on psychological continuities between the two. Parfit suggests that a person is connected with his future self in a similar way as he is with other people with whom he is living at the moment.[293] If it is wrong to cause harm to others, it must be wrong to inflict harm on

291 David Dyzenhaus, *John Stuart Mill and the Harm of Pornography*, in Dworkin, Gerald (ed.): *Mill's On Liberty: Critical Essays*. Rowman & Littlefield Publishers: Lanham, Md. 1997, p. 31.

292 Mill 1975, p. 76.

293 Häyry, Heta: *The Limits of Medical Paternalism*. Routledge: London, New York 1991, p. 132. See also Kleinig 1983, pp. 45–48.

one's future self. Thus, Parfit's theory seems to allow paternalistic interventions.[294] Smoking or excessive alcohol use, for example, can be classified as an abuse of the future self's right to a healthy existence.

Another way to demonstrate that self-harm leads to harm to others is to show that it sets a bad example to others. This argument is only true, according to Mill, if self-harm sets "a more salutary than hurtful example to other people". If self-harm displays "painful and degrading consequences", no one is going to follow the bad example.[295] However, this presupposition is somewhat naïve of Mill. We often see that people follow bad examples, regardless of the harmful consequences.

As another sign of interconnectedness, it can be mentioned that someone may not only cause, but also suffer harm from others as a result of his self-regarding conduct. 'Natural penalties' flow as spontaneous reactions from other's dislike.[296] Nobody wants to see the self-destruction of others; avoiding someone's company because of his self-destructive lifestyle is, for instance, a natural penalty. Natural penalties are not deliberate and therefore they do not contradict the harm principle: they are unintentional psychological responses to self-harming actions. Artificial penalties (e.g. legal sanctions) are deliberate actions and they can only be imposed legitimately on those who harm others.

Feinberg also deals with the distinction of self and other-regarding conducts. He admits that public interest is always involved, at least to a small extent, when someone harms himself. The question is where to draw the line and say that a conduct is *primarily* self-regarding or other-regarding. Feinberg suggests that this threshold changes from society to society and it is also subject to the gravity of self-harm.[297] Suicide is not legally prohibited in modern democratic societies; it is considered to be a primarily self-regarding conduct. However, if we imagine a small community, the life of which is a constant struggle for survival (e.g. a garrison of settlers under continuous attacks from Indians), anyone who does not help to defend the settlement can be considered to harm the others with his or her 'passivity'. The decision to withdraw and commit suicide in such a situation is unacceptable, because it can negatively impact the life of others. Similarly, soldiers are punished if they attempt suicide or commit self-mutilation during wartime. Also, if suicide or heroin consumption reached such an extent

294 Parfit, Derek: *Reasons and Persons*. Clarendon Press: Oxford 1984, p. 320.
295 Mill 1975, p. 78.
296 Riley 1998, p. 96.
297 Feinberg, Joel: *Harm to Self*. (= The Moral Limits of the Criminal Law) Oxford University Press: New York 1989, p. 22.

in a society that it endangers its normal functioning, paternalistic intervention would become justified under the 'indirect' harm-to-others rationale.[298] The closer any society comes to the 'garrison threshold', the more interference with personal liberty is justified.

3.2.1.2 *Soft paternalism*

Mill accepts certain forms of soft paternalism. He acknowledges that people lacking the ability to make voluntary choices (minors, drunks, the mentally ill, etc.) can be restricted in their self-harming decisions. Mill would permit the state to protect people from their own ignorance in cases where an uninformed or misinformed choice would be likely to lead to consequences that are the opposite of what they actually desired:

> "If either a public officer or anyone else saw a person attempting to cross a bridge which had been ascertained to be unsafe, and there were no time to warn him of his danger, they might seize him and turn him back, without any real infringement of his liberty; for liberty consists in doing what one desires, and he does not desire to fall into the river."[299]

The same soft paternalism applies to "a child, or someone who is delirious, or in some state of excitement or absorption incompatible with the full use of the reflecting faculty".[300] Nonetheless, there is no reason why a child, a drunkard, or a mentally ill person should not be allowed to walk home across a safe bridge if there is no direct harm present. The same paternalistic rationale applies to "[...] those backward states of society in which the race itself may be considered as in its nonage."[301] Mill does not rule out the possibility of despotism "as a legitimate mode of government in dealing with barbarians, provided the end be their improvement, and the means justified by actually effecting that end."[302]

Endorsing soft paternalism is a sign that Mill is also concerned with autonomy in *On Liberty* because a strict utilitarian approach would ignore the distinction between children and adults and take everyone's pleasure equally into account in the *felicific calculus*.

298 Ibid.
299 Mill 1975, p. 89.
300 Ibid.
301 Ibid. 11.
302 Ibid.

3.2.1.3 *The scope of the harm principle*

3.2.1.3.1 *The acceptance of non-coercive forms of paternalism*

Another means to limit the absolute character of the harm principle is to limit the scope of prohibition. It was only coercion and criminal law that Mill ruled out in absolute terms. He is convinced that "[...] benevolence can find other instruments to persuade people to their good, than whips and scourges".[303] Mill supports non-coercive methods to protect people from self-harm, to promote their benefit or to improve morals within the society. His typical example is education.

> "To bring a child into existence without a fair prospect of being able, not only to provide food for its body, but instruction and training for its mind, is a moral crime, both against the unfortunate offspring and against society; and that if the parent does not fulfill this obligation, the state ought to see it fulfilled [...]"[304]

Mill seems to adopt a perfectionist approach here. The state does not only have the right to prescribe compulsory education but has a duty to do so, if parents fail to provide adequate education for their children.

3.2.1.3.2 *The limited range of the principle*

Gertrude Himmelfarb claims that Mill was wrong to assert that 'one very simple principle' can govern absolutely the complex connections between society and individual. She characterizes the harm principle as an extreme claim for liberty that modern liberals have carried to its 'logical extreme', making the individual the 'repository of wisdom and virtue' and the freedom of the individual 'the sole aim of social policy'.[305] Ronald Dworkin argues that Himmelfarb confuses the force and the range of Mill's principle.[306] The range of the principle is limited and it has absolute force only *within* this range. Unlike Bentham, who thought that the utility principle can determine every political decision by simply calculating the aggregate pleasures and pains of the community, Mill extends his principle only to cases where harm occurs. Such decisions form a very small part of governmental decisions. The harm principle, for example, does not determine how

303 Ibid. 71.

304 Ibid. 97.

305 Dworkin, Ronald: *Taking Rights Seriously*. Harvard University Press: Cambridge, Mass. 1977, p. 260.

306 Ibid. 261.

to distribute scarce resources or how to reconcile situations in which liberty and human rights clash with consequentialist policy considerations.

3.2.1.4 Harm as a necessary and sufficient condition for coercion?

A somewhat similar question is whether the existence of harm is a necessary and/or sufficient condition for coercion. According to the literal interpretation of the harm principle, harm to others is a necessary but not sufficient condition for coercion (cf. "the only purpose for which power *can* be rightfully exercised [...] is to prevent harm to others"). Sufficiency in Mill's theory would probably be determined by a utilitarian calculation (cf. the previously mentioned 'social authority maxim'; "for other-regarding actions [...] the individual is accountable, and *may* be subjected to social or to legal punishment, if society is of opinion that the one or the other is requisite for its protection").

If we take into account other passages and examples from *On Liberty*, the picture changes a bit. In most cases, the prevention of harm to others seems to be a sufficient reason for legal coercion – sufficient in the 'weak sense', meaning that harm is a weighty but not conclusive reason for regulation.[307] The necessity condition is not so obvious, because Mill seems to believe that besides harm, the promotion of benefits can also be a good reason for coercion. "There are also many positive acts for the benefit of others, which he may rightfully be compelled to perform; such as to give evidence in a court of justice; [...] and to perform certain acts of individual beneficence, such as saving a fellow-creature's life."[308] Of course, if one decides to include the loss of benefit in the concept of harm and accept that omissions are sometimes just as harmful as actions, the tension between the previous and the present paragraph is resolved. Moreover, non-coercive benefit promoting paternalism (e.g. compulsory education) is unconditionally allowed in Mill's theory.

3.2.1.5 Offense principle

The original formulation of the harm principle does not include the offense principle. Other parts of *On Liberty* imply that Mill was nevertheless sympathetic towards the idea of restricting offensive behaviour. He writes in the last chapter

307 A regulation is unacceptable, for example, if the regulation causes more harm than the behaviour in question. Brink, David: "Mill's Moral and Political Philosophy". In: Zalta, Edward N. (ed.): *The Stanford Encyclopedia of Philosophy*. Fall 2014. (http://plato.stanford.edu/entries/mill-moral-political/) (10.05.2015).

308 Mill 1975, p. 12.

that "there are many acts, [...] which, if done publicly, are a violation of good manners, and coming thus within the category of offences against others, may rightfully be prohibited."[309]

3.2.2 The utilitarian justification of the harm principle

Opinions are divided whether Mill based his defence of the harm principle on utilitarian or deontological grounds. Himmelfarb claims that the notion of liberty in *On Liberty* is a 'deviation' from the notion in Mill's earlier works. She attributes this change to the influence of Mill's wife, Harriet Taylor.[310] Mill basically defends his principle on utilitarian grounds but it is true that respect for an absolute right to liberty permeates the whole essay, even if Mill explicitly denies this in the first chapter. He states that his case for liberty is not based on "the idea of abstract right, as a thing independent of utility" and he regards "[...] utility as the ultimate appeal on all ethical questions; but it must be utility in the largest sense grounded on the permanent interests of man as a progressive being".[311] While not denying Mill's utilitarian intentions, I think that one can make a convincing case for the deontological approach if he or she manages to show that (1) utilitarianism is less capable of prescribing an absolute respect for self-regarding conducts; (2) Mill himself is not consistently utilitarian in his reasoning; (3) the utilitarian justification of the harm principle has to face the same criticisms that all consequentialist ethical theories are subject to.

Mill's utilitarian reasoning starts from the presumption that abiding by the harm principle always maximizes social utility. Putting aside the question of paternalism for the moment, the principle of utility seems to violate some basic intuitions concerning fundamental rights when regulating other-regarding behaviour. Supposing that the quality of life of a thousand people can be substantially improved by sacrificing the life of just one, utilitarianism seems to demand this sacrifice.[312] In other words, classical utilitarianism seems to relativize the value of human rights and allows deviation from categorical prohibitions when the principle of utility so dictates. A blanket prohibition of self-harming

309 Ibid. 91.

310 See Himmelfarb's editorial introduction to *On Liberty.* Mill, John Stuart: *On Liberty*. Penguin Books: London 1985, p. 27. See also Dworkin 1977a, p. 260.

311 Mill 1975, p. 12.

312 A well-known example of 'Jim and the Indians' comes from Bernard Williams. Smart, J.J.C. / Williams, Bernard: *Utilitarianism: For and Against.* Cambridge University Press: Cambridge 1973, p. 98.

conducts seems even more difficult to be defended on utilitarian grounds. It is hard to prove, for instance, that preventing people from voluntarily selling themselves to slavery always constitutes a lesser evil than allowing them to do so; there will be situations when the calculus of 'pleasure and pain' demands the opposite. The blanket prohibition comes from the presupposition that individuals know their interests best, therefore utility is maximized if people are allowed to act on their own preferences. Even if self-harm causes pain and pain is considered to decrease utility, someone can plausibly assert that the self-harming conduct will increase his happiness in the long run. From today's point of view, the claim that humans are infallible in self-regarding matters and can always determine their 'real' preferences seems an 'exaggeration' of the age of Enlightenment.[313] Moreover, if paternalism is too risky because an external observer is incapable of knowing someone's preferences, then other legal actions, including the prevention of harm to others, are too risky as well.[314]

An additional non-utilitarian element in Mill's theory is that Mill thinks that the dislike and disgust of others caused by self-harming conduct is not a good reason for coercion (at least in the original formulation of the harm principle, cf. chapter 3.2.1 on self-regarding and other-regarding actions). By treating the disgust of the majority towards some self-harming actions as irrelevant, Mill goes against the classical utilitarian view that *all* pleasures and pains are relevant in determining the rightness or wrongness of an act.[315] But why is Mill ignorant of such indirect offenses? He argues that a person's liberty in self-regarding matters is more valuable than the satisfaction others might feel at suppression of his conduct. Personal liberty is prized higher than any form of disgust or dislike, a value choice that has no utilitarian justification.

---

313 The same point is made by Hart in *Law, Liberty and Morality:* "No doubt if we no longer sympathize with this criticism this is due, in part, to a general decline in the belief that individuals know their own interest best. […] [Mill endows the average individual with] too much of the psychology of a middle-aged man whose desires are relatively fixed, not liable to be artificially stimulated by external influences; who knows what he wants and what gives him satisfaction of happiness; and who pursues these things when he can." Hart 1963, p. 32.

314 Lyons, David: *Ethics and the Rule of Law.* Cambridge University Press: Cambridge 1984, pp. 173–174.

315 Ten 1980, p. 18.

3.2.3 Reconciling Mill's utilitarianism with the harm principle

Rule utilitarianism provides a plausible alternative to argue for the categorical character of the harm principle. Rule utilitarians understand utility as dictating not particular actions but general rules or policies. They say that public good in the long run is best served by complying with an optimal set of rules and not by endorsing acts that maximize utility in specific situations. The problem with traditional act utilitarianism is that it justifies too much and, when circumstances dictate, it allows for the violation of absolute rights. Consider the example that "[…] if some kind of very cruel crime becomes common, and none of the criminals can be caught, it might be highly expedient […] to hang an innocent man, if a charge against him could be so framed that he were universally thought guilty".[316] As Rawls argues, the utility provided by the stability and foreseeability of rules outweighs the *ad hoc* negative consequences of blanket regulations.

Whether Mill was a rule utilitarian is a matter of controversy.[317] In Chapter 5 of *Utilitarianism*, Mill defends the concept of rights in terms of utility: the principle of utility can support a notion of rights if rights are defined by rules that maximize the 'general' utility of the community. "To have a right, then, is, I conceive, to have something which society ought to defend me in the possession of. If the objector goes on to ask, why it ought? I can give him no other reason than general utility."[318] Mill believes that an ethical theory that is independent of utility cannot explain the diversity and multifaceted character of rights: "[…] if justice be totally independent of utility, and be a standard *per se* […]; it is hard to understand why that internal oracle is so ambiguous, and why so many things appear either just or unjust".[319]

Elements of rule utilitarianism are also traceable in *On Liberty*. Mill regards "[…] utility as the ultimate appeal on all ethical questions, but it must be utility in the largest sense, grounded on the permanent interests of man as a progressive

316 This example originally comes from Carritt and it is mentioned by John Rawls. Rawls, John: "Two Concepts of Rules". *The Philosophical Review* 64 (1) (1955), p. 10. For the Hungarian translation, see John Rawls, *Kétfajta szabályfogalom,* in Lónyai, Mária (ed.): *Tények és értékek – A modern angolszász etika irodalmából.* Gondolat: Budapest 1981, p. 364.

317 Urmson defends a rule utilitarian reading of Mill. J.O. Urmson, *The Interpretation of the Philosophy of J.S. Mill,* in Lyons, David (ed.): *Mill's Utilitarianism.* Rowman & Littlefield Publishers: Lanham, Md. 1997, p. 3.

318 Mill, John Stuart: *Utilitarianism.* Collins: London 1962, p. 308.

319 Ibid. 310.

being".[320] Even if utility is not served by an act prescribed by the harm principle in a specific case, Mill implies that following the dictates of the principle will maximize 'utility in the largest sense'. His reasoning is similar to the reasoning he follows in the case of freedom of speech. The same reasons that justify a policy of free speech without exception (i.e. freedom of speech always leads to maximal social utility even if the articulated opinion is false or morally wrong) can also justify an absolute anti-paternalist policy.[321]

The main objection against rule utilitarianism is that it collapses into act utilitarianism. Consequent rule utilitarians have to make exceptions to general rules whenever doing so will maximize utility, otherwise they would just be 'rule worshipers' who only care about rules but forget about total utility.[322] For example, it seems that there are certain situations when telling lies produces more good than telling the truth. To overcome this, rule utilitarians would formulate exceptions as sub-rules to the general rule 'thou shall not lie'. However, in the end, there will be as many sub-rules as exceptional cases, so rule utilitarianism ultimately prescribes the very same acts that act utilitarianism requires.[323]

The relation of liberty and utility seems largely to turn on the kind of preferences that are considered to be relevant when calculating the balance of pleasure and pain. Ronald Dworkin argues that utilitarianism can be reconciled with the ideals of freedom and equality by excluding 'external preferences' from calculating the utility of political decisions.[324] External preferences are those that are assigned to other people's enjoyment of goods, while personal preferences are connected to a person's own enjoyment of certain goods or opportunities. The dilemma raised by Dworkin seems to go back to the issue how preferences are formed. He argues that realizing a *prejudicial* external preference held by the majority might increase the overall utility of society but it can lead to the unequal treatment of those with different preferences. The problem with counting external preferences is that it can override personal preferences and violate people's right to 'equal concern and respect' which is a basic assumption of utilitarian theories (i.e. everyone's utility counts equally in the *felicific calculus*). Consider, for example, that people hold racist views and their external preference is such that

---

320 Mill 1975, p. 12.

321 Arneson, Richard: "Mill versus Paternalism". *Ethics* 90 (4) (1980), pp. 470–489, p. 480.

322 Hampton, Jean: *Political Philosophy*. Westview Press: Boulder, Co. 1997, p. 132.

323 Hooker, Brad: "Rule Consequentialism". In: Zalta, Edward N. (ed.): *The Stanford Encyclopedia of Philosophy*. Spring 2011 (http://plato.stanford.edu/archives/spr2011/entries/consequentialism-rule/) (03.04.2015).

324 Dworkin 1977a, p. 236.

a black person's vote should count less than that of a white. Taking into account this preference can lead to the implementation of oppressive social policies.[325]

Utilitarian arguments can be used not only to defend but also to criticize liberal anti-paternalism.[326] James Fitzjames Stephen argues that legal and moral coercion is a necessary element of social life. Contrary to Mill, he believes in the superiority of a moral 'elite' and claims that "the wise minority are the rightful masters of the foolish majority".[327] Morally right actions are those that contribute to the greatest happiness of greatest numbers. Compulsion, if it fulfils this criterion, can legitimately be exercised. Since individual happiness, contrary to the liberal conviction, does not always contribute to the general happiness of mankind, coercion is an effective instrument to motivate people to advance the good of society instead of their own interests. "My motive for doing what is right and avoiding what is wrong is that unless I do so I will be punished by other people, either through legal procedures, or by the use of social and moral sanctions".[328] As for paternalism, Stephen abandons the harm principle's categorical prohibition. If utility requires, it is possible to allow coercive forms of paternalism and moralism.[329] According to Ten, Stephen's less tolerant approach can be explained by his changes in the method of utilitarian calculation. Following Bentham's classical view, he attaches value to the pleasures of 'malevolence'.[330] Punishing or prohibiting immoral or self-harming acts that offend or cause distress to others yields 'malevolent' pleasures to the majority and this can modify the outcome of the *felicific calculus*. As discussed earlier, Mill was reluctant to take into account the negative utility of offensive behaviour that triggers disgust or distress in others. Consequently, it seems that Mill also rejected pleasures that could be derived from punishing such forms of behaviour.

---

325 C. L. Ten argues that excluding external preferences is wrong when it means excluding altruistic external preferences. Suppose that parents who do not swim have a strong external preference to build a new swimming pool for their children, which is stronger than any personal preference they might have. Dworkin would not allow the swimming pool to be built in this example, which seems unfair to the parents. Of course, it is possible to argue that altruistic preferences are actually not external preferences, but personal ones. Ten 1980, pp. 32–33.

326 Häyry 1991, p. 79.

327 Stephen, James Fitzjames: *Law, Equality, Fraternity*. Liberty Fund: Indianapolis, Ind. 1993, p. 172.

328 Ibid.

329 The legal moralism of Stephen is discussed in chapter 5.2.1.

330 Ten 1980, p. 35.

3.2.4 The shift to deontology

Gerald Dworkin claims that there is a non-contingent argument (i.e. independent of utilitarian calculation) that runs through *On Liberty*.[331] People shall be treated as ends in themselves and not as means to an end – this requirement is guaranteed by providing and safeguarding a sphere of personal liberty with respect to each human being. The boundaries of this sphere are designated by the harm principle which seems to resist utilitarian considerations. The priority of liberty is demonstrated by Mill's approach to slavery contracts; he rejects the validity of voluntary slavery contracts which can be interpreted as a form of 'autonomy-maximizing' hard paternalism. The justification cannot be utilitarian here because it is possible that slavery contracts yield greater utility than blank prohibition in some circumstances. Instead, Mill argues that:

> "[…] by selling himself for a slave, [the individual] abdicates his liberty; he foregoes any future use of it beyond that single act. He therefore defeats, in his own case, the very purpose which is the justification of allowing him to dispose of himself […] The principle of freedom cannot require that he should be free not to be free. It is not freedom to be allowed to alienate his freedom."[332]

Mill is concerned here with the value of individual liberty *per se* with no regard to consequences. However, critics argue that by allowing hard paternalism in this case, Mill deviates from the requirements of the harm principle and his theory becomes inconsistent. Consequently, one must either disregard the harm principle or the passage concerning perpetual slavery contracts.[333] Those who defend the harm principle might try to transform the problem into soft paternalism and claim that a person who enters into such a contract necessarily shows that his choice is not fully voluntary.[334] Another possibility, somewhat similar to Parfit's argument on personal identity, is to claim that voluntary enslavement causes harm to 'others', that is, to the future self of the subject. It seems probable that after some time spent in slavery, a person would regret having made the contract.

331 Dworkin, Gerald: "Paternalism". *The Monist* 56 (1) (1972), pp. 64–84, p. 72. Dworkin quotes Mill to support his claim: "there is a part of the life of every person who has come to years of discretion, within which the individuality of that person ought to rein uncontrolled either by any other person or by the public collectively".

332 Mill 1975, p. 95.

333 Arneson 1980, p. 473.

334 Feinberg 1989, p. 79. See also Robert Young, *John Stuart Mill, Ronald Dworkin and Paternalism*, in Ten, C. L.: *Mill's On Liberty – A Critical Guide*. Cambridge University Press: Cambridge 2009.

Thus, his or her actual will would 'trump' any previous orders and continued external coercion to keep him enslaved would be unacceptable under the harm-to-others principle.[335]

Overall, what seems to be behind Mill's utilitarian argument is an unconditional respect for autonomy. According to Isaiah Berlin:

> "[Mill's] propositions are very like those defended on metaphysical grounds by the traditional upholders of the doctrine of natural rights. [...] At the centre of Mill's thought and feeling lies, not his utilitarianism, nor the concern about enlightenment, nor about dividing the public from the private domain, [...] but his passionate belief that men are made human by their capacity for choice – choice of evil and good equally."[336]

Some recent liberal authors, such as Feinberg, try to reconcile Mill's radical prohibition of paternalism with the obvious need for certain paternalistic interventions. Feinberg writes that "the problem is to reconcile somehow our general repugnance for paternalism with the apparent necessity, or at least reasonableness, of some paternalistic regulations".[337] From another point of view, Feinberg also needs to break with the apparent utilitarianism of Mill and emphasize the role of autonomy in the interpretation of the harm principle in order to save it from the 'Millian' inconsistencies and preserve it as a central tenet of his theory.[338] Thus, "Feinberg explicitly distinguishes his brand of anti-paternalism from that of J. S. Mill, on the ground that, in On Liberty, Mill does not oppose paternalism on principle but only contingently".[339] The challenge of resolving these two tasks simultaneously – i.e. to design a theory that leaves adequate space for paternalism while it places the harm principle on a deontological ground – seems to remain unmet in Feinberg's theory.

3.3 Hard cases for the 'soft' paternalist

The previous chapter discussed some of the theoretical problems that emerge in relation to the consequentialist and autonomy-based interpretations of Mill's harm principle. The aim of this chapter is to present some hard cases that

---

335 Ten 1980, p. 117.

336 Isaiah Berlin, *John Stuart Mill and the Ends of Life,* in Matravers / Pike / Warburton 2000, p. 340.

337 Feinberg 1989, p. 111.

338 Feinberg believes that liberalism is "the view that the harm and offense principles, and only these, state good and relevant reasons for state coercion by means of the criminal law". Ibid. 3.

339 Arneson 2005, p. 273.

illustrate the practical difficulties with respect to the principle's strict deontological reading. I consider these cases 'hard' because there seems to be an apparent tension between one's moral intuitions and the way the harm principle instructs us to resolve these examples of paternalism.[340] Most of the following cases present self-harming actions that cannot be prohibited by the harm principle because (subject to one's understanding of harm) they do not seem to cause harm to others. Neither can they be prohibited on soft paternalistic grounds since the decisions are based on perfectly voluntary choices. Still, one's moral intuition might tell that some of these self-harming actions are just 'not right' and should be restricted (or at least, there is nothing wrong with restricting them). The cases suggest that following the harm principle, based either on consequentialist grounds or derived from a substantive conception of autonomy, does not always lead to a 'morally adequate' solution.

Joel Feinberg tries to defend the moderate liberal position that "[...] the harm and offense principles, duly clarified and qualified, between them exhaust the class of good reasons for criminal prohibitions".[341] Despite all his efforts, some 'stubborn counterexamples' prevent him from reaching this goal. As a difficult case for liberal opponents of legal paternalism and moralism, Feinberg cites Irving Kristol's hypothetical example of a "gladiatorial contest in Yankee Stadium before a consenting adult audience [...] between well-paid gladiators who are willing to risk life or limb for huge stakes".[342] This case involves a 'free-floating evil', which neither harms nor offends other individuals except for the consenting gladiators, who are 'exempted' from harm due to the *volenti non fit iniuria* principle. These evils are independent of anyone's interests but Feinberg still thinks that such an evil (i.e. several thousand adults deriving great pleasure from bloodshed and suffering) should not be allowed. Although he tries to justify legal prohibition on the ground that the gladiatorial contest will brutalize the audience and indirectly lead to an increase in violent crimes, it is very difficult to actually

340 It is possible to draw an analogy with Ronald Dworkin's theory of hard legal cases. According to Dworkin, a legal case is 'hard' if the judgment does not follow from a legal rule and a description of the facts. Such a situation is the result of various legal gaps that Peczenik categorises as insufficiency, inconsistency, indeterminacy and axiological gaps. The hard cases discussed here seem to be related to axiological legal gaps: although there is a valid rule (i.e. a moral rule and its legal equivalent), it contradicts one's values and moral convictions. Dworkin 1977a, p. 81. Peczenik, Aleksander: *On Law and Reason*. Springer: New York 2008, pp. 18–19.

341 Feinberg 1990, p. 12.

342 Ibid. 128.

establish any solid connection between the event and its supposed harmful effect. Applying the argument of indirect harm may also open the door to extreme and unreasonable restrictions. Following the slippery slope, it is to be feared that the indirect harm argument could, for example, lead to the prohibition of violent computer games, then violent television programs, and finally toy soldiers and plastic revolvers. The harm principle seems unable to handle 'free-floating' evils the way many people would expect. It seems necessary to include some form of a perfectionist argument to justify coercion in cases connected to 'free-floating' evils. Feinberg accepts that "it can be morally legitimate for the state to prohibit certain types of action that cause neither harm nor offense to anyone, on the grounds that such actions constitute evils of other (free-floating) kinds".[343]

Commentators of Feinberg generally agree that he fails to provide a consequent defence of liberalism in *The Moral Limits of the Criminal Law*, because he cannot handle these 'stubborn counterexamples'. Actual judicial decisions also demonstrate the shortcomings of 'traditional' anti-paternalism based on the harm principle. Four controversial issues of paternalism will be analysed in the following chapters: physical protection, health regulations, euthanasia and the protection of human dignity. The related cases are all instances of hard paternalism in that they restrict fully voluntary self-harming actions. Although these 'hard cases' do not provide a *conclusive* argument against the harm principle, they raise some doubts about its traditional deontological interpretation.

3.3.1 Physical protection

Paternalism that aims to protect bodily integrity can take various forms. Consider, for example, regulations requiring the use of safety-belts or crash helmets; prescribing safety equipment for construction workers; establishing restrictive rules for dangerous sports such as boxing or motor racing; or simply prohibiting the

343 Ibid. xx. Another group of free-floating evils distinguished by Feinberg is the category of 'harmless wrongdoings'. These acts do not constitute harm or offense to others, but one might still consider them as 'wrongs'. Consider Ripstein's example of a harmless trespass. Suppose that a burglar breaks into someone's house, while the owner is away. He does not damage the house or steal anything but decides to take a nap in the owner's bed. Although the burglar does no harm in the traditional sense of the word and the harm principle cannot be invoked for protection, such act still seems to violate the privacy rights of the owner. Arthur Ripstein, *Beyond the Harm Principle,* in Feinberg, Joel / Coleman, Jules (eds.): *Philosophy of Law*. Cengage Learning: Belmont, CA 2008, p. 265.

exercise of dangerous activities (e.g. base-jumping).[344] The traditional objection against these restrictions makes an appeal to the autonomy of the individual, but the 'liberal conscience' seems to be divided on the subject[345]: today only radical libertarians would question the appropriateness of helmet or seat belt regulations. From a utilitarian viewpoint, statistical evidence seems to verify compulsory helmet legislations and makes a strong case for hard paternalism.[346] Liberals focusing on the value of autonomy have three possibilities if they want to avoid hard paternalistic reasoning.[347]

First, they can argue that riding a motorcycle without a helmet is presumably a non-voluntary choice because it is irrational and unreasonable. This line of reasoning is an effort to transform the problem into soft paternalism: if a choice is non-voluntary, it can be legitimately restricted even by 'strict' liberal standards. Besides the obvious problem of equating autonomy with voluntariness, there is also the issue of introducing substantive values to the concept of autonomy through the requirements of reasonableness and rationality. It is possible to presume, as Gerald Dworkin does, that the choice of not wearing a helmet is the result of erroneous calculation of preferences in most cases. However, there is a small minority of motorcyclists that still prefer to ride a motorbike without a helmet purely out of 'romantic' sentiments (for example, commitment to speed, freedom and adventurous lifestyle).[348] These people are fully competent and

---

344 Kleinig 1983, p. 81.

345 Raz 1986, p. 422.

346 While seat belts do seem to save many people from serious injuries, some argue that they can have negative consequences as well. Wearing a seat belt can pose a threat to the life of passengers because, in case of an accident, it can prevent them from leaving the burning car. Allegedly, it can also interfere with the working of pacemakers. These arguments were made before the Hungarian Constitutional Court in a petition that questioned the constitutionality of compulsory seat belt regulations. 60/1993 (XI. 29) AB. For an analysis of the case, see Takács, Péter: *Nehéz jogi esetek*. Napvilág Kiadó: Budapest 2002, p. 156.

347 Feinberg 1989, p. 135.

348 The commitment to speed or adventurous lifestyle may not be a convincing argument against compulsory helmet legislation. On the other hand, if we consider a conviction regarded as more significant, the case becomes totally different. Take the case of the Sikh man who denied wearing the crash-helmet because of his religious convictions. His right to wear the turban can hardly be questioned. But should society decide on the relative importance of personal convictions? *R v Crown Court at Aylesbury, ex parte Chahal* [1976]; *X v. United Kingdom*, 7992/77. Decision of the European Commission of Human Rights.

aware of the risks they take. It is only that they endorse different values than the majority. Their choices might be unreasonable by majority standards but they are not necessarily irrational or non-voluntary.

The second argument that can be invoked in support of mandatory helmet laws is based on the need to protect third parties under the harm-to-others principle. Some claim, for example, that motorcyclists can be struck in the face by stones propelled upward by their own or other vehicles' tires.[349] This may cause the cyclist to lose control of his vehicle and harm others in the accident. This argument seems somewhat strained: if the true purpose of crash helmet regulations were to protect from flying objects, a requirement to install windshields on motorcycles would be suitable to reach this objective. A more serious argument makes reference to the costs of accidents that indirectly harm the interests of third parties and, in general, the whole society.[350] These costs include the salaries of policemen, doctors, nurses and paramedics; material expenses, such as medicines; indirect costs, like lost productivity and lost tax payments. However, if the legislator is worried about such expenses, it is theoretically possible to require motorcyclists to purchase extra medical insurance that covers expenses in case of an accident. A more problematic point is the psychic harm caused to others by the accident. Adopting a wholly anti-paternalistic approach which contends that bikers should 'pay the price' for their own foolhardiness, seems insensitive, cruel and inhuman. It is one thing to reject paternalism in theory and it is another to actually let someone die on the side of the road on the principled basis that he did not wear a crash helmet and refused to contribute extra money to the social security system. Any person with a 'sound emotional life' will face a moral dilemma in such cases. Consequentially, "we might seek protection *for ourselves* from such moral extortion" by restricting helmetless motorcycle riding.[351] Mental harm takes other forms as well – e.g. the trauma of witnesses and other motorists involved in the accident or the suffering caused to the victim's family members. I tend to agree with Feinberg that the appeal to psychic costs is probably the strongest non-paternalistic argument for helmet regulations.[352]

---

349 Feinberg 1989, p. 138; Kleinig 1983, p. 91. Kleinig calls this argument the 'argument from danger to others'. A similar line of reasoning can be used to justify the prohibition of smoking or the use of cell phones during driving.

350 Kleinig divides the indirect harm-to-others argument in three parts: the argument from loss of productivity, the public charge argument and the public disaster argument. Kleinig 1983, p. 92.

351 Feinberg 1989, p. 140.

352 Ibid. 141.

The third alternative is to follow the deontological interpretation of the harm principle and accept that the restrictive statutes are morally unjustified because they infringe personal autonomy. However, since autonomy is a matter of degree, non-coercive measures adopted to increase safety will be received with less hostility. Such alternative measures include improved licensing procedures and education of motorcyclists to raise awareness to the dangers of helmetless biking.

3.3.2 Health regulation and dangerous substances

Until the early part of the twentieth century, contagious diseases were a common cause of death.[353] Today, in developed countries, death from contagious diseases is relatively rare and more people die from illnesses such as cancer or heart disease, often caused by an unhealthy lifestyle (e.g. smoking, alcohol consumption, unhealthy diet, etc.). In the case of contagious diseases, public health measures can be justified by appeal to the harm principle. The regulation of smoking, unhealthy diets or alcohol use is a question of paternalism, since these 'lifestyle choices' are primarily self-regarding.

The soft paternalistic strategy against smoking refers to circumstances that make someone's choice to smoke non-voluntary.[354] Feinberg argues that the greater the risk or the gravity of harm, the higher the level of voluntariness that is required (cf. chapter 2.2.1). Though the gravity of potential harm is significant in the case of smoking, harm is not as imminent as in the case of heroin use, for example. It seems difficult to argue that those who decide to light up make a nonvoluntary choice in the traditional sense of the word, because smoking is not *manifestly* unreasonable. Consequently, coercive interventions seem excessive and paternalism is mostly restricted to non-coercive methods, e.g. financial disincentivising, provision of information and other 'nudges'. Nonetheless, the addictive character of smoking might complicate the question by weakening the subject's will and undermining his or her long-term preferences.

Goodin also seems to follow a soft-paternalistic strategy when distinguishing between 'surface' and 'deeper' preferences.[355] Surface preferences are not always autonomously formed and public officials should only refrain from paternalism if they are convinced that someone is acting on his own 'deeper' (i.e. 'relevant'

353 Kleinig 1983, p. 106.

354 Pope 2000, p. 482.

355 Robert E. Goodin, *Permissible Paternalism: Saving Smokers from Themselves*, in LaFollette, Hugh (ed.): *Ethics in Practice: an Anthology*. Blackwell: Malden, Mass. 2002, p. 308.

and 'settled') preferences. Similarly to soft paternalism, such approach legitimizes methods such as warnings and increased taxes that are aimed to help to prevent smoking by shaping surface preferences while still showing respect for the value judgments of the individual. The separation of higher and lower-order preferences seems to solve the problem of *akrasia* as well.

The ban on smoking in public places is usually justified by reference to harm caused to others. Today, it is well known that environmental tobacco smoke causes physical harm to non-smokers 'varying from minor irritations to demonstrable respiratory, cardiovascular, and carcinogenic effects'.[356] Besides its negative effects on health, restrictions often refer to the indirect social harm (e.g. increased medical costs) and to the nuisance caused to others by smoking.[357] The harm and offense principles, taken together, seem to provide sufficient basis for limiting smoking in public – a statement that is being increasingly confirmed by recent policy developments throughout Europe.[358]

In 1998 the European Commission of Human Rights considered a complaint that claimed that German laws did not provide effective protection for non-smokers because of the extent to which they were exposed to smoking in public places and buildings.[359] The case raised the question whether the German State, under the positive obligation to protect the life and privacy of the people residing in its territory, should have enacted legislation completely prohibiting smoking in public. The Commission observed that the means calculated to secure compliance with the State's positive obligations prescribed by the Convention is a matter that falls within the States' margin of appreciation. The Commission noted that German law contained provisions limiting the advertising of tobacco products and prohibiting smoking in certain public areas, and that the German authorities also started a public information campaign on the injurious effects of smoking. It concluded that "the absence of a general prohibition on advertising

---

356 Pope 2000, p. 441.

357 Although smoking imposes serious costs on society (in the form of health care costs and lost future earnings), its net economic impact seems to be positive due to increased tax income. Ibid. 444.

358 To date, 17 EU countries have introduced comprehensive smoke-free regulations: Ireland (2004); Italy (2005); Sweden (2005); United Kingdom (2007); Finland (2007); Estonia (2007); Slovenia (2007); Lithuania (2007); The Netherlands (2008); France (2008); Latvia (2010); Spain (2011); Greece (2010); Malta (2011); Hungary (2012); Bulgaria (2012). See, e.g. www.smokefreepartnership.eu (04.05.2015).

359 *Wöckel v Germany*, Decision of the European Commission of Human Rights, 16 April 1998.

of tobacco products and on smoking does not amount to a failure on the part of the German State to ensure the applicant's rights under Articles 2 and 8 of the Convention."[360] So there is no obligation under the European Convention for a complete ban of smoking in public places.

The flipside of the previous issue, i.e. the question whether limitations on smoking are compatible with the fundamental rights of smokers, is also worthy of examination. A widespread smoking ban was introduced in England in 2006, making it illegal to smoke in all enclosed public places from 1 July 2007.[361] Certain exemptions were nevertheless granted, including the possibility to smoke in psychiatric institutions until 1 July 2008.[362] A recent case before the High Court involved the claim of mental health patients that the ban on smoking in the psychiatric institution where they were detained violated their right to privacy as enshrined in Article 8 of the ECHR.[363] But does the right to privacy provide protection from non-smoking policies? In other words, is there a 'right to smoke'?

The Counsel of the petitioners argued that "respect for private life involves permitting someone to do what they want to do, however foolish others might consider the activity".[364] Lord Justice Pill, however, refused to attribute the same scope to the right to privacy as to the harm principle:

> "We do not accept that the respect required by Article 8 is coextensive with the right of absolute independence contemplated by John Stuart Mill. The law may place restrictions on a person's freedom of action without necessarily interfering with the right to respect required by Article 8. The expression 'personal autonomy', used by the ECtHR in *Pretty*, undoubtedly resonates with Mill's philosophy but [...] the protection 'falls some way short of protecting everything a person might want to do even in that private space.'"[365]

---

360 Ibid.

361 The prohibition came into force earlier in Wales (2 April 2007). Smoking was banned separately in Northern Ireland and Scotland by the Smoking (Northern Ireland) Order 2006 and by the Smoking, Health and Social Care (Scotland) Act 2005. They took effect 30 April 2007 and 26 March 2006, respectively.

362 The prohibition was introduced by the Health Act 2006 and the exemptions by the Smoke-free (Exemption & Vehicles) Regulations 2007.

363 *R (G) v Nottinghamshire Healthcare NHS Trust* [2008] EWHC 1096.

364 Ibid. para. 50. The Counsel explicitly cited John Stuart Mill's harm principle: 'The only part of the conduct of anyone, for which he is amenable to society, is that which concerns others. In the part that merely concerns himself, his independence is, of right, absolute. Over himself, over his own body and mind, the individual is sovereign'.

365 *R (G) v Nottinghamshire Healthcare NHS Trust* [2008] EWHC 1096, para. 100.

In other words, the Court was convinced that to prevent someone from smoking does not affect that individual's 'physical or moral integrity' and it rejected the idea that the right to privacy could involve an 'absolute right to smoke' wherever one is living. The Court of Appeal, upholding the decision of the High Court, argued that both the nature of the activity and the nature of the place where the activity is exercised must be taken into account when determining the scope of privacy.[366] Although not denying that the mental health institution can be considered as 'home' to the patients, the Court established that "[t]here is no basis for distinguishing the loss of freedom to choose what one eats or drinks in such an institution and the ban on smoking".[367]

Prohibiting or coercively restricting smoking in cases where no other regarding harm is present qualifies as hard paternalism. Thus, legislators often resort to non-coercive means to discourage people from smoking, like raising the prices of cigarettes or imposing restrictions on trade and advertising. There are three legislative trends aimed at reducing tobacco consumption in the European Union: the regulation of tobacco advertising,[368] the increasing of excise duties[369] and the labelling regulations raising awareness to the risks of smoking on the packaging of tobacco products.[370]

---

366 *R (E) v Nottinghamshire Healthcare NHS Trust* [2009] EWCA Civ 795.

367 Ibid. para. 46.

368 The Television Without Frontiers Directive (Directive 89/552/EEC amended by Directive 2007/65/EC) banned all tobacco advertising and sponsorship on television in the European Community. This ban was extended by the Tobacco Advertising Directive (2003/33/EC) to cover other forms of media such as the internet, print media, radio and sports event. However, the directive does not prohibit indirect advertising on merchandising products, billboards or in local cultural and sporting events. An attempt (Directive 98/43/EC) to prohibit these was struck down by the European Court of Justice in its judgment *Germany v. Parliament and Council,* C-376/98 [2000] ECR I-8419. The ban of such advertisements was considered to be unnecessary for the free movement of goods and free provision of services within the EC since these products and services do not have cross-border effects.

369 Directive 92/79/EEC on the approximation of taxes on cigarettes; Directive 92/80/EEC on the approximation of taxes on manufactured tobacco other than cigarettes; Directive 95/59/EC on taxes other than turnover taxes which affect the consumption of manufactured tobacco.

370 The provisions of the first and second Labelling Directives (Directives 89/622/EEC and 92/41/EEC) were deemed to be insufficient due to the warnings' small size and lack of visibility. The currently valid European regulations are based on the Directive on Packaging and Labelling of Tobacco Products (2001/37/EC). See, for example:

Restrictions on the trade of alcoholic drinks are also often justified by reference to the health of consumers. In the famous 'Cassis de Dijon' case, the public health argument was invoked to restrict the importation of a French liqueur to Germany.[371] Interestingly, the problem of the German authorities was not the too high, but the too low alcohol content of the liqueur: "[...] fixing of the minimum alcohol contents by national legislation is to avoid the proliferation of alcoholic beverages on the national market, in particular alcoholic beverages with a low alcohol content, since [...] such products may more easily induce a tolerance towards alcohol than more highly alcoholic beverages."[372] The European Court of Justice rejected this argument because a high variety of weakly alcoholic beverages had already been accessible for German consumers without any restriction on their trade. This also shows that the primary aim of the restriction was not paternalism but the protection of Germany's domestic market. The ECJ came to a somewhat different conclusion in relation to the Portuguese restriction on internet gambling sites. The Court ruled that Portugal's domestic regulation of internet gambling sites was not contrary to EC law and the freedom to provide services.[373] Although not a direct question of paternalism, the Portuguese government stated that the aim of the regulation is "the protection of consumers of games of chance against fraud on the part of operators".[374] The regulation can be interpreted as protection from harm to others (i.e. protection from fraud), but also as indirect paternalism, because people enter into gambling contracts voluntarily. The limitation imposed on the service provider has a paternalistic effect on the consumers. The question is whether the motive behind the restriction was really consumer protection or rather the protection of state gambling monopoly.

Recreational drugs are also commonly considered as dangerous substances. There are numerous arguments both for and against the decriminalization of drugs; it is not my aim here to explore these in detail. From an autonomy-based perspective, prohibition of drugs is hard paternalism.[375] Of course, if someone

---

www.who.int/tobacco/training/success_stories/en/european_community_labelling.pdf (10.05.2011).

371 C-120/78, *Rewe-Zentral AG v. Bundesmonopolverwaltung für Branntwein* [1979] ECR 649.

372 Ibid. para.10.

373 C-42/07, *Liga Portuguesa de Futebol Profissional v Departamento de Jogos da Santa Casa da Misericórdia de Lisboa* [2009] ECR I-07633.

374 Ibid. para. 62.

375 Presupposing that the choice of using the drug is made voluntarily (e.g. knowing the possible harmful effects, being aware of one's own preferences, not being addicted to the drug).

shows that the choice of drug use is the result of erroneous calculation of preferences, it is possible to transform the problem into soft paternalism (cf. Feinberg's example in chapter 2.2.1). It is also possible to argue along consequentialist lines and claim that (1) drugs cause overall more harm than good to society and (2) prohibition decreases the harms associated with them. It seems plausible to accept the first premise, although it is worth mentioning that there are many non-criminalized self-harming practices that can lead to negative social utility – smoking is probably one of the most prominent examples here. Following a consequentialist reasoning, the state should criminalize smoking in the first place as, according to statistical evidence, it kills many more people than drug use.[376] The second premise is more often criticized than the first one: many experts seem to agree that prohibition does not work and it is not an effective method to discourage drug consumption and reduce harm associated with it. Those who still want to defend prohibition might invoke the harm-to-others (e.g. harm to family and to society by additional social security expenses, violent behaviour, increased crime rate, etc.) and the offense-to-others (e.g. being intoxicated in public) principles. Appealing to perfectionist ideals might be another strategy for prohibition. Perfectionists claim that law can prohibit drugs because (1) drug use is degrading and it is detrimental to individual character, and (2) the state has a duty to improve the character of its citizens.[377] Note that this strategy is also applicable to the excessive use of alcohol.

3.3.3 Euthanasia

The European Court of Human Rights discussed the problem of voluntary active euthanasia in the Pretty v United Kingdom case.[378] The applicant, Mrs. Diane Pretty, suffered from motor neurone disease, which causes severe weakness in the arms and legs, acute breathing difficulties and later paralyzes the patient.[379] Death inevitably occurs as the sufferer becomes increasingly unable to breath. The patient's intellect and capacity to make decisions remains unimpaired during the illness. Diane Pretty made an application to the Director of Public

---

376 For an overview of possible arguments and statistical data, see Smith, Paul: *Moral and Political Philosophy: Key Issues, Concepts and Theories*. Palgrave Macmillan: Basingstoke 2008, pp. 1–19.

377 Ibid. 10.

378 *Pretty v United Kingdom*, Judgment of 29 April 2002.

379 Ibid. para. 7.

Prosecutions to give an undertaking not to prosecute her husband should he assist her to commit suicide in accordance with her wishes. The UK authorities refused to give this undertaking. The applicant brought the case before the European Court, claiming that the refusal violated her right to life (which, according to the applicant, also includes her right to terminate her own life), human dignity, right to privacy, freedom of conscience and the principle of non-discrimination (as opposed to those ill persons, who are able to end their life without assistance).[380] The Court held that there has been no violation of any of these rights and rejected the petition: "[...] the Court cannot but be sympathetic to the applicant's apprehension that without the possibility of ending her life she faces the prospect of a distressing death".[381]

The core of Mrs. Pretty's complaint involves Article 3 of the Convention. She submitted that the suffering she faced qualifies as degrading treatment and violates human dignity. She suffered from a terrible, irreversible disease and she would die in an exceedingly distressing and undignified manner. Two of the Convention's most fundamental provisions seem to clash here: Article 2 protecting the right to life and Article 3 prohibiting torture and inhuman or degrading treatment. The Court gives preference to the right to life because it observes that human dignity does not demand positive action from the state in this case. Member States have an obligation to refrain from inhuman and degrading treatment but should not actively assist in suicides. Such claim would place a new and extended construction on the concept of inhuman and degrading treatment, which goes beyond the ordinary meaning of the word 'treatment'.[382]

An individual's approach towards euthanasia seems to be largely determined by the type of ethical theory he or she adopts. The deontological view, focusing on the autonomy of the patients, claims that it is unjustified hard paternalism to restrict voluntary self-harming decisions. The central question here is how to ascertain the voluntariness of the patient's decision. Since suicide is irrevocable, a very high degree of voluntariness is needed to validly accept it. Although a certain level of depression is 'understandable' on the part of seriously ill patients, severe clinical depression interferes with voluntary decision-making capacity and must be cured before a request for euthanasia can be accepted.[383] The alternating moods of the patient should also be taken into consideration. Full voluntariness is generally sought to be verified by expert committees and guaranteed by

380 Articles 2, 3, 8, 9 and 14 of the European Convention on Human Rights, respectively.
381 *Pretty v United Kingdom*, para. 55.
382 Ibid. para. 54.
383 Feinberg 1989, p. 354.

prescribing a compulsory 'cooling off' period after the decision.[384] Living wills and health-care proxies (i.e. documents stipulating the refusal of certain medical treatments or appointing someone else to make the decision on euthanasia) also aim to protect the autonomy of the patient.[385] Living wills and proxies raise similar questions as the issue of 'prior consent' to paternalism discussed earlier (cf. chapter 2.2.1).

Proponents of euthanasia must confront a deeply embedded social 'prejudice' of the sanctity of human life. But is it desirable to keep people alive under all circumstances? Philippa Foot suggests that it is only 'ordinary' human life that is intrinsically valuable:

> "It seems, therefore, that merely being alive even without suffering is not a good. The idea we need seems to be that of life which is ordinary in human life in the following respect – that it contains a minimum of basic human goods. What is ordinary in human life [...] is that a man is not driven to work far beyond his capacity; that he has the support of a family or community; that he can more or less satisfy his hunger; that he has hopes for the future; that he can lie down to rest at night. [...] Disease too can so take over a man's life that the normal human goods disappear."[386]

This passage implies that the minimum of 'basic human goods' is subject to certain external circumstances which are partly social in nature. Proponents of euthanasia face the following problem here. Someone may decide to choose euthanasia because he or she suffers from an extremely painful disease. Yet, it is possible that the disease is only painful because the patient cannot have access to good medical care in his or her country. Under these circumstances, the choice of euthanasia is dependant on the reigning economic regime and on moral luck.[387] What is more, having additional options does not necessarily increase autonomy. Offering the possibility of euthanasia, as an additional choice, may encourage patients to question the justifiability of their continued existence.[388] Many, who suffer from painful but not necessarily terminal illnesses, would only think about euthanasia because it is accessible. There is an additional cultural element here, namely that our modern culture does not tolerate very well sick, idle, or dependent individuals. "Establishing a right to die in our culture may

---

384 Dworkin 1972, p. 81. Dworkin refers to these expert committees as 'suicide boards'.

385 Dworkin, Ronald: *Life's Dominion*. HarperCollins: London 1993, p. 180.

386 Foot, Philippa: "Euthanasia". *Philosophy & Public Affairs* 6 (2) (1977), pp. 85–112.

387 LaFollette, Hugh (ed.): *Ethics in Practice: an Anthology*. Blackwell: Malden, Mass. 2002, p. 20.

388 Dworkin 1993, p. 192.

thus be like establishing a right to duel in a culture obsessed with honor."[389] This also shows that autonomous choices are often influenced by external social and cultural factors (cf. chapter 3.1.1).

Euthanasia is not entirely self-regarding. Depending on one's understanding of harm, it is possible to apply the harm-to-others principle to prohibit euthanasia. Indirect harm takes various forms, including psychical and emotional harm inflicted on those who maintain a close relation with the ill person. Moreover, it is possible to argue that euthanasia and suicide in general can threaten the preservation of society, if too many people choose to die in a specific situation. The idea here is similar to Feinberg's 'garrison threshold' concept (cf. chapter 3.2.1). True enough, a soldier's decision to withdraw and commit suicide in the middle of the battlefield can harm fellow soldiers. However, in normal circumstances, it's hard to see how euthanasia could bring society close to the 'garrison threshold'. Also, terminally ill patients are mostly unable to contribute to the survival of society, so their death would not affect negatively the survival of society.

From a utilitarian perspective, the benefit of permitting active euthanasia is that it can prevent unnecessary suffering. Even though modern medical science provides effective painkilling methods, some kinds of pain cannot be eliminated with drugs and only a small minority of patients has access to such treatments. Euthanasia also allows a better resource allocation: the money and expertise that is devoted to keeping alive terminally ill patients – often in agonizing pain – could be better spent to cure other people.[390] The possibility of a mistaken diagnosis and the possible appearance of future cures, on the other hand, are good reasons against legalisation.[391] A practical argument against euthanasia is the 'slippery slope' argument: the fear is that the legalization of voluntary euthanasia, if not controlled sufficiently, may lead to non-voluntary or involuntary euthanasia.[392]

---

389 J. David Velleman, *Against the Right to Die*, in LaFollette 2002, p. 36.

390 Brad Hooker, *Rule Utilitarianism and Euthanasia*, in LaFollette 2002, p. 26.

391 The risk of mistaken diagnosis can be decreased by prescribing compulsory consultation for the therapist with other doctors. However, we have to acknowledge that the legalization of voluntary euthanasia would inevitably mean the deaths of some people who would have otherwise recovered. Nevertheless, on a utilitarian basis, this is counterbalanced by the large amount of suffering eliminated by euthanasia. Singer, Peter: *Practical Ethics*. Cambridge University Press: Cambridge 1993, p. 197.

392 Conceptual confusion often surrounds the meaning of the term euthanasia. Distinction can be made between voluntary, nonvoluntary and involuntary euthanasia. Involuntary euthanasia is imposed on the subject against his will or without his consent. It qualifies as murder and it is rarely discussed, let alone defended by anyone. In the case of nonvoluntary euthanasia, the patient is not mentally competent to make an

While active euthanasia is mostly forbidden, passive euthanasia (i.e. the rejection of treatment) is legalised in plenty jurisdictions. Physician assisted suicide is also becoming more and more accepted.[393] These facts demonstrate that the distinction between killing and letting someone die has moral significance in most people's eyes: "[…] most people think that while killing Bengali children would be morally heinous, refusing to provide these same children with food, medical, and economic assistance is not immoral".[394] Such view can be associated with deontological ethics, which requires the agent to refrain from violating certain categorical moral duties, for example the duty not to kill other people. Utilitarianism does not place specific moral weight on this distinction since the consequences of an act and an omission are often indistinguishable.[395] There is not much difference between stopping feeding a comatose patient and actually giving him a lethal injection. Still, Bernard Williams claims that there is a fundamental difference between killing someone, and someone else killing someone as a result of something I have done.[396] Williams' point is that moral decisions help to preserve our psychological integrity while 'impersonal' utilitarianism loses this distinction. It requires the agent to abandon his own projects and his

informed choice (e.g. infants or people in coma). Voluntary active euthanasia involves someone's direct contribution to the patient's death, while in cases of physician assisted suicide (PAS), the patient is the 'final link' in the causal chain and the doctor 'only' assists in the process (e.g. by providing the necessary drug). This distinction is recognized by many jurisdictions by criminalizing assistance in suicide separately from active euthanasia which qualifies as homicide in most cases. Feinberg 1989, p. 345; Singer 1993, pp. 176–181.

393 Physician assisted suicide is legal in five states of the USA (Oregon, Montana, Washington, Vermont, New Mexico). It means the possibility of acquiring prescriptions for lethal doses of medications. See, e.g. http://time.com/3551560/brittany-maynard-right-to-die-laws/ (04.03.2015).

394 LaFollette 2002, p. 21.

395 Singer 1993, p. 207.

396 Smart / Williams 1973, p. 117. A well-known argument of Williams against utilitarianism centers on Jim, a botanist doing research in a South American country led by a brutal dictator. One day, Jim meets a captain of the dictator's army, who has arrested twenty Indian rebels. He makes an offer to Jim – if he kills one of the Indians, the others will be released; if he does not, they will all be killed. Utilitarianism demands from Jim to kill one person in order to save the others. However, Williams claims that from the viewpoint of personal integrity, it does matter if someone actively kills another human being or lets him die under the compulsion of external circumstances. Utilitarianism is indifferent to this distinction. Ibid. 98.

own personal integrity for the 'impartial point of view' of maximizing general welfare.[397]

3.3.4 Human dignity and paternalism

The following cases demonstrate the potentially paternalistic implications of the constitutional concept of human dignity. Harm is not imminent in these cases. They seem to involve evils of a 'free-floating' kind, meaning that the harm principle cannot be directly invoked to impose limitations on the contested practices. The analysed judgments resort to a broad interpretation of human dignity and argue that it is incompatible with the activities in question. It is important to note that not all legal systems make the same use of the concept of dignity; the German constitutional jurisprudence is probably the most prominent example of a 'dignitarian' approach.[398]

The following two judgments are examples that show how far the protection of human dignity can go in restricting individual freedom. This concern was articulated in other cases as well. The dissenting opinion of Judges Spielmann and Jebens in *Vereinigung Bildender Künstler v Austria* emphasizes that the abstract concept of human dignity can be "dangerous since it may be used as justification for hastily placing unacceptable limitations on fundamental rights".[399] The judges refer, inter alia, to David Feldman who argues that "[t]he notion of dignity can easily become a screen behind which paternalism or moralism are elevated above freedom in legal decision-making."

3.3.4.1 Wackenheim v France

Manuel Wackenheim, a French citizen suffering from dwarfism, began to appear in 'dwarf tossing' events organized by a company called *Société Fun Productions*.[400] Wearing suitable protective gear, he would allow himself to be thrown

397 Chappell, Sophie Grace: "Bernard Williams". In: Zalta, Edward N. (ed.): *The Stanford Encyclopedia of Philosophy*. 2015 Spring (http://plato.stanford.edu/entries/williams-bernard/).

398 Kommers, Donald P.: *The Constitutional Jurisprudence of the Federal Republic of Germany*. Second edition. Duke University Press: Durham, NC 1997, p. 298.

399 *Vereinigung Bildender Künstler v Austria*, Judgment of 25 January 2007, joint dissenting opinion of Judges Spielmann and Jebens, para. 9.

400 *Wackenheim v France* CCPR/C/75/D/854/1999; *Conseil d'Etat*, 27 Octobre 1995, N° 136727, *Commune de Morsang-sur-Orge*. For an overview of the whole legal process, see Husson, Céline: ""Lancer de nain" ou "lancer de nains"? Variations sur un thème".

short distances onto an air bed by clients of local discotheques. French authorities prohibited the practice of 'dwarf tossing' on the ground that it violated human dignity; the prohibition was upheld by the *Conseil d'Etat* in the subsequent proceedings. The case was finally brought before the UN Human Rights Committee, which found that the French prohibition neither violated human dignity, nor was discriminatory against dwarf people.[401]

The applicant's petition emphasizes that banning him from working had an adverse effect on his life and represents an affront to his dignity. He claims that France violated his rights to freedom, employment, respect for private life and an adequate standard of living and Mr. Wackenheim also claims to be a victim of discrimination and further states that there is no work for dwarves in France and that his job does not violate his dignity since dignity consists in having a job.

Even if there is a general consensus that such form of entertainment is degrading for human beings, perfectionist reasoning may open a large door to unjustified 'moral paternalism' in similar cases. One should constantly pay attention to this possibility. The applicant's counsel criticized the French policy:

> "To the tripartite structure of public order in France as normally portrayed – order (tranquility), safety (security) and public health – a fourth component – public morals, embracing respect for human dignity – has been added. Case law of this kind at the dawn of the twenty-first century revives the notion of moral order [...] directed against an activity that is both marginal and inoffensive when compared with the many forms of truly violent, aggressive behavior that are tolerated in modem French society. The effect [...] is to enshrine a new policing authority that threatens to open the door to all kinds of abuse: are mayors to become censors of public morality and defenders of human dignity? Are the courts to rule on citizens' happiness?"[402]

Without implying that the case was not decided correctly, it is possible to point out that the applicant has a strong argument as well. It definitely goes against the ideals of Kantian morality to use another human being for such bizarre entertainment. However, it is hard paternalism to force someone to quit his voluntarily

---

Revue l'Europe des Libertés 4 (11) (2003). (http://leuropedeslibertes.u-strasbg.fr/) (03.04.2015).

401 Differentiation constitutes discrimination when it is not based on objective and reasonable grounds. The ban on dwarf-throwing applies only to dwarves, because they are the only persons capable of being thrown. Thus, the differentiation between dwarfs and 'ordinary' people is based on an objective reason and is not discriminatory in its purpose. *Wackenheim v France*, para. 7.4.

402 *Wackenheim v France*, para. 5.2.

chosen job, just because the majority finds his activity degrading or humiliating. Moreover, hard paternalism brings up the questions of perfectionism and state neutrality. A better way to approach this case might be to refer more explicitly to the public offense caused by dwarf-tossing.

3.3.4.2 The Omega case

The Omega case is an important improvement in the field of human dignity in the jurisprudence of the European Court of Justice.[403] Omega GmbH, a German company started running a laser game facility called 'Laserdrome' in 1994. The objective of the game was to 'shoot and kill' the enemy players by tagging them with gun-like infrared targeting devices. The German authorities soon prohibited the operation of Laserdrome, claiming that simulated homicide and the trivialization of violence were contrary to the ideal of human dignity.[404] The case was referred to the European Court of Justice: the company stated that the prohibition violated its freedom to provide services, since the equipment worn by the players was lawfully produced in the United Kingdom and franchised to Omega in Germany.

The major part of the Advocate General's opinion deals with the possible justification of the restriction imposed on the freedom to provide services on the ground that they infringe human dignity.[405] Advocate General Stix-Hackl recalls the Schmidberger case and gives a general review on the status of human rights in the Community legal order. She states that "[fundamental rights] are to be considered part of the [EU] primary legislation and therefore rank in hierarchy at the same level as other primary legislation, particularly fundamental freedoms".[406] In the second step, the role and function of human dignity must be assessed whether it can be used as an independent human right to limit fundamental freedoms or it can only be used as a principle of interpretation. The Advocate General argues for the first alternative based on the jurisprudence of the ECJ (Netherlands v Parliament and Council) and on Article 1 of the Charter of Fundamental Rights, which seems to reflect a comparatively wide understanding

403 C-36/02 *Omega Spielhallen und Automatenaufstellungs GmbH v Oberbürgermeisterin der Bundesstadt Bonn*, 2004.

404 Jean-Yves Gilg, *ECJ ruling in laser game ban re-opens moral exception*. http://lawzone.thelawyer.com (10.04.2008.).

405 Ackermann, Thomas: "Case Law Review – C-36/02 Omega Spielhallen und Automatenaufstellungs GmbH v Oberbürgermeisterin der Bundesstadt Bonn". *Common Market Law Review* 42 (4) (2005), pp. 1107–1120.

406 C-36/02 *Omega Spielhallen,* para. 49.

of human dignity.[407] By accepting human dignity as an independent right, it becomes possible to confirm the decision of the German authorities. Sticking to the concept of dignity as an interpretational or subsidiary principle would have precluded the Advocate General to deliver her opinion because the shooting game did not violate other fundamental rights. The judgment of the Court follows the opinion, but it is less elaborate and makes no reference to the Charter.

The Omega decision was the subject of extensive criticisms. The Court was criticized for giving the Member States 'green light' to restrict fundamental freedoms in the name of human dignity.[408] The slippery-slope argument also applies. Based on Omega, Member States may decide to prohibit any other products (movie films, computer games, even sports like wrestling or boxing) that entertain people by presenting violence.

The Omega and Wackenheim cases demonstrate that human dignity can be used to impose paternalistic measures on individuals. Human dignity, interpreted as having 'objective' moral content may become a means to moral paternalism. Dignity is a complex notion which is capable of raising controversies due to its complexity: it can, for example, come into conflict with the two basic principles behind paternalism, autonomy and beneficence. In the discussed cases, dignity trumps the principle of autonomy but also goes against the principle of beneficence in a certain sense, as the imposition of external moral standards might have a benevolent motivation, but it does not necessarily serve the actual best interests of the subject (i.e. Mr. Wackenheim lost his job as a result of the ban on dwarf-tossing).

3.4 Liberal neutrality and paternalism

According to Wojciech Sadurski, conventional contemporary liberalism has two fundamental precepts: (1) the liberal neutrality of the state, i.e. that the state should be neutral between competing conceptions of the 'good life' and (2) the harm principle, understood as a non-perfectionist principle, designating the limits of permissible state coercion.[409] These precepts seem to go hand in hand, the harm principle being an 'element' of the more comprehensive ideal of state neutrality. At this point, the discussion of paternalism elevates to a 'higher' level, that

---

407 C-377/98 *The Netherlands v European Parliament and the Council*, 2001.

408 Jean-Yves Gilg, *ECJ ruling in laser game ban re-opens moral exception*. http://lawzone.thelawyer.com (10.04.2008.).

409 Sadurski, Wojciech: "Joseph Raz on Liberal Neutrality and the Harm Principle". *Oxford Journal of Legal Studies* 10 (1990), p. 122.

of political philosophy, and centres on the liberalism versus communitarianism debate. This chapter discusses how liberal neutrality relates to the autonomy-based interpretation of the harm principle and on what grounds the idea of state neutrality has been criticized.

Implications of the ideal of autonomy go beyond the harm principle aimed at safeguarding personal integrity. Citizens in modern pluralistic societies hold different views of what constitutes a 'good life' to them; neutrality does not only demand that the state refrains from coercive paternalism but also from non-coercive interventions that promote a specific conception of the 'good'. State neutrality has become a central concept among contemporary liberal theorists.[410] However, the neutrality principle often requires liberals to go against their own convictions.[411] The problem for them is how they can 'take pride in defending what they oppose': for instance, how can a liberal defend the right to free speech while deeply disagreeing with the speech's content or support recreational drug use even if he or she is convinced that drugs are harmful to the consumer.[412] The solution is to draw a distinction between 'the right' and 'the good' and claim the priority of the right over the good. The sphere of the right seems to be designated by the harm principle which remains neutral towards personal preferences of what constitutes a good life – it might be that someone is convinced that drugs are bad but still disagree with their criminal prohibition because it is primarily self-regarding and fits the requirements of the harm principle. 'Kantian' liberals emphasize that someone's actions should comply with rationally constructed rules that do not presuppose any particular conception of the good.

Observing the rules of the right is necessary for social co-existence. Reason dictates, for instance, a more or less absolute prohibition on harm to others. Self-harming decisions, on the other hand, seem to belong to the sphere of the good: liberals argue that autonomous choices (even if self-harming) are means of self-fulfilment and integrity. In contrast, paternalism is morally wrong, because it forces a certain idea of the good on people. Instrumental forms of paternalism (e.g. safety-belts, crash helmets, etc.) are the exception as they do not normally involve the enforcement of substantive values. So what is at stake here from the

410 Although the historical ideal of an ideologically and religiously neutral state goes back to the time of reformation and religious wars, neutrality as a central topic of political philosophy emerged in the 1970s with the publication of John Rawls' *A Theory of Justice*.

411 Sadurski, Wojciech: *Moral Pluralism and Legal Neutrality.* (= Law and Philosophy Library) Springer Netherlands: Dordrecht 1990b, p. 90.

412 Michael Sandel quoted by Sadurski. Sadurski 1990b, p. 90.

viewpoint of paternalism is its moral justification: if the ideal of neutrality is 'compromised', paternalism becomes theoretically unobjectionable. This is how *some* communitarian authors argue. They claim that the idea of neutrality is built on false metaphysical presuppositions and on a false value attributed to individual autonomy (cf. chapter 3.1.4) and, therefore, it should be abandoned for a perfectionist ideal of the state.

Not all forms of liberalism regard state neutrality as a centrally important concept. The most well-known versions of 'neutrality liberalism' are the theories of John Rawls and Ronald Dworkin.[413] Even though one would expect that these theories are radically hostile towards paternalism, a closer look at them reveals a certain amount of tolerance to paternalistic interventions.

Rawls built his theory of justice on Kantian grounds. He emphasizes the absolute priority of justice over other values: "[...] justice is the first virtue of social institutions, as truth is of systems of thought".[414] Justice as fairness stands both against utilitarianism and perfectionism and rejects teleological theories that impose a certain conception of good on individuals:

> "One of the deepest distinctions between political conceptions of justice is between those that allow for a plurality of opposing and even incommensurable conceptions of the good and those that hold that there is but one conception of the good which is to be recognized by all persons, so far as they are fully rational. [...] Plato and Aristotle and the Christian tradition, as represented by Augustine and Aquinas, fall on the side of the one rational good. Such views tend to be teleological and to hold that institutions are just to the extent that they effectively promote this good."[415]

The Kantian inspiration of Rawls is reflected in the construction of his two principles of justice. The first principle, aimed at safeguarding basic rights and personal autonomy, states that "[...] each person is to have an equal right to the most extensive scheme of equal basic liberties, which is compatible with a similar scheme of liberties for others".[416] The second principle contains the rule

413 The neutrality principle has been articulated by other authors as well. Bruce Ackerman imposes neutrality as a dialogic constraint ('neutral dialogue') on public debate: "No reason is a good reason if it requires the power holder to assert [...] that his conception of the good is better than that asserted by any of his fellow citizens." Ackerman, Bruce: *Social Justice in the Liberal State*. Yale University Press: New Haven 1980, p. 11.

414 Rawls 1999, p. 3.

415 Rawls, John: "Justice as Fairness: Political not Metaphysical". *Philosophy & Public Affairs* 14 (3) (1985), pp. 223–251, p. 248.

416 Rawls 1999, p. 53.

of distribution of goods: "[...] social and economic inequalities [...] [must be ordered] to the greatest benefit of the least advantaged members of society".[417] Although not utilitarian in the strict sense, the second principle seems to have teleological characteristics. It prescribes an egalitarian model of distribution in order to serve the 'greatest benefit' of the least advantaged. However, the first principle has priority over the second one. If, for example, just distribution required the violation of fundamental liberties, respect for fundamental rights would override this. In other words, consequences cannot trump autonomy in Rawls' theory.[418]

The two principles together form the sphere of 'right', which sets limits, but also creates the framework for different conceptions of the 'good':

> "The concept of justice is independent from and prior to the concept of goodness in the sense that its principles limit the conceptions of the good which are permissible. A just basic structure and its background institutions establish a framework within which permissible conceptions can be advanced. Elsewhere I have called this relation between a conception of justice and conceptions of the good the priority of right (since the just falls under the right)."[419]

Thus, Rawls' two principles of justice that together constitute the sphere of the 'right' seem to prescribe 'more' than Mill's harm principle because for Rawls, the sphere of the 'right' also includes rules of just social distribution. Still, the function of the principles of the 'right', just as the function of the positive side of the harm principle, is to regulate other regarding actions (i.e. 'conflicting claims that persons make upon one another') in order to maintain peaceful social coexistence.[420] The negative side of the harm principle, which excludes interference related to self-regarding matters, provides space for realizing different conceptions of the 'good'.

Rawls justifies the two principles of justice by a hypothetical contractarian reasoning. He argues that rational individuals in the 'original position' (where the 'veil of ignorance' prevents them from knowing their future position in society,

417 This is the so-called 'difference principle'.

418 The theory of Rawls can be considered as a mixed conception of justice where priority is given to deontology over consequentialism. It forms a middle way between the liberal traditions of Locke and Rousseau, between 'liberty' and 'equality'. His first principle gives greater weight, with Constant's terminology, to the 'liberties of the moderns', while his second principle to the 'liberties of the ancients'. Riley 1998, p. 152. Rawls 1985, p. 227.

419 Rawls 1985, p. 249.

420 Sadurski 1990b, p. 93.

their race and sex, their abilities or their conception of good life) would choose his principles to build a just social order. This reasoning rules out perfectionist approaches to justice because people do not know their conception of the good in the 'original position'. Although Rawls does *not* explicitly articulate the principle of state neutrality, excluding the knowledge of the 'good' from the original position seems to carry a commitment to neutrality.[421]

It seems that one of the main questions in this theoretical framework is how to determine which acts belong to the sphere of the right and which to the sphere of the good. The common answer is that claims about the good are essentially controversial while the "principles of justice [i.e. the sphere of the right] are objective and interpersonally recognizable in a way that conceptions of the good are not".[422] Furthermore, the sphere of the right extends only to constitutional essentials and to principles that regulate the basic structure of society. The state may legitimately regulate these basic and 'interpersonally recognizable' issues but must remain neutral to controversial social questions that fall outside this sphere. Rawls, as opposed to Kant, bases the separation of right and good on *political* and not on metaphysical grounds in his later works: "[…] the idea is that in a constitutional democracy the public conception of justice should be, so far as possible, independent of controversial philosophical and religious doctrines."[423] The idea of overlapping consensus expresses Rawls' belief that people with conflicting metaphysical and/or religious views could still agree on the questions of governance and on the regulation of the basic structure of society (i.e. on the sphere of justice). In an overlapping consensus, citizens support the same basic laws for different reasons: each citizen affirms the same political conception of justice (a liberal conception) for reasons internal to his own comprehensive doctrine (i.e. religious beliefs, moral convictions).[424] For example, Catholics, Muslims and atheists all have their own good reason to accept the liberal right to religious freedom. Thus, neutrality does not require a specific world view to be accepted: it comes around as an overlapping consensus between groups that have very different moral and religious convictions.

---

421 Klosko, George / Wall, Steven (eds.): *Perfectionism and Neutrality: Essays in Liberal Theory*. Rowman & Littlefield Publishers: Lanham, Md. 2003, p. 3.

422 Arneson, Richard: "Liberal Neutrality on the Good: An Autopsy". In: Wall, Steven / Klosko, George (eds.): *Perfectionism and Neutrality: Essays in Liberal Theory*. Rowman & Littlefield Publishers: Lanham, Md. 2003, pp. 191–218, p. 195.

423 Rawls 1985, p. 223.

424 Wenar, Leif: "John Rawls". In: Zalta, Edward N. (ed.): *The Stanford Encyclopedia of Philosophy*. Winter 2013. (http://plato.stanford.edu/entries/rawls/) (05.03.2015).

Rawls' neutrality is not as radical as his critics generally claim.[425] He does not require that governmental interventions always have neutral consequences. Government actions may help some ways of life more than others; neutrality is 'only' required in the justification of state policies. He writes that even if "[...] even if political liberalism can be seen as neutral in procedure and in aim, it is important to emphasize that it may still affirm the superiority of certain forms of moral character and encourage certain moral virtues."[426] The requirement to distinguish between an action's justification and its actual consequences seems to be present in the case of paternalism as well.[427] As we have seen in chapter 2.1.2, not paternalistically motivated interventions with *unintended* paternalistic consequences do not seem to qualify as paternalism.

As a consequence of his commitment to neutrality, one would presume that Rawls rejects perfectionist public policies, including hard paternalism. However, Robert P. George, a contemporary perfectionist argues that "Rawls himself has neither argued for the harm principle as such nor criticized specific forms of morals legislation in the light of his theory of justice."[428] Still, Rawls' aversion to paternalism is perceptible in two of his arguments. (1) He disagrees that public institutions such as universities or theatres should be subsidized on the grounds that they are intrinsically valuable.[429] Although such perfectionist policies can promote the benefit of some individuals, there is no proof that it is for the good of the least advantaged in society. (2) Rawls is more permissive in the case of soft paternalism towards children or the mentally ill. He uses the hypothetical consent scheme (cf. chapter 2.2.1) to decide on the justifiability of paternalistic interventions. His argument for soft paternalism is based on the idea that rational individuals would want to insure themselves in the original position in case it turns out, after lifting the veil of ignorance, that they are incapable of leading an autonomous life. Rawls instructs us how to design soft paternalistic

425 Raz, for example, argues that Rawls endorses consequential neutrality. Kymlicka defends Rawls by showing that two basic tenets of Rawls' theory (the respect for civil liberties and equality of resources) necessarily have non-neutral consequences. Raz 1986, p. 117. Kymlicka, Will: "Liberal Individualism and Liberal Neutrality". *Ethics* 99 (4) (1989), pp. 883–905, p. 884.

426 Rawls, John: "The Priority of Right and Ideas of the Good". *Philosophy & Public Affairs* 17 (4) (1988), pp. 251–276, p. 263.

427 Although an action's public justification and the motivation behind the same action seem to be related, they cannot be equated with each other.

428 George 1995, p. 140.

429 Rawls 1999, p. 291.

interventions: "Paternalistic interference is to be guided by an appeal to the individual's own settled preferences and interests, in so far as these are not irrational or, failing a knowledge of these, by the theory of primary goods".[430] It is easy to see that such formulation leaves space for perfectionism from two perspectives. First, the requirement that the individual's settled preferences should not be 'irrational' is subject to how the concept of irrationality is constructed. Second, Rawls believes that primary goods are goods that everyone wants to possess but critics point out that there could be certain sorts of people to whom the theory of primary goods does not apply.[431] Rawls, perhaps to avoid these problems, immediately suggests that individuals, after their rational powers have been restored or developed, should approve what the paternalistic actor did for them in the past. As pointed out in chapter 2.2.1, the problem with such subsequent consent is that it is not autonomously formed; in the case of children, for example, the subject will probably approve of those values that he was conditioned to internalize during his upbringing.

It is possible to build a theory of liberal neutrality on other grounds than Kantian philosophy. Kant and Rawls derives equal moral agency from the *rational capacity* of humans to make moral choices. Another form of liberalism, however, sees human beings as sharing similar *passions,* which can also provide a uniform conception of the 'right' or the 'just'.[432] Thomas Hobbes argued that good and bad opinions do not have an 'objective' natural basis and, as a consequence, people disagree about what is good and bad, but they can all agree on the need for peace and security (i.e. the sphere of just).[433] Sadurski seems to connect the Hobbesian 'equal passion' tradition to Ronald Dworkin's theory of equal moral agency.[434] Ronald Dworkin argues that state neutrality is necessary in order to respect individuals' right to moral independence and to treat all persons with 'equal concern and respect'.

In Sovereign Virtue, Dworkin sets up a conceptual framework for paternalism that is somewhat different from the one in the 'dominant' discourse. He makes

430 Rawls 1999, p. 219.
431 Haksar, Vinit: *Equality, Liberty and Perfectionism*. Oxford University Press: Oxford 1979, p. 184.
432 Sadurski, Wojciech: "The Right, the Good and the Jurisprude". *Law and Philosophy* 7 (1) (1988), pp. 35–66, p. 42.
433 Sadurski 1990b, p. 92.
434 Sadurski 1988, p. 44.

a distinction between 'volitional' and 'critical' interests.[435] Volitional well-being is improved whenever the person achieves something he wants (e.g. good food, fewer visits to the dentist, etc.). Volitional interests are not particularly valuable: it is good to have these things, but the lack of them does not make one's life substantially poorer. Critical interests, on the other hand, are things that people think that they *should* want because they feel that their life would be poorer without them (e.g. close relationship with their children, professional success). These interests are valuable not because people want them but because people think that their life would be poorer without them. Following this distinction, Dworkin introduces the notions of volitional and critical paternalism. "Volitional paternalism supposes that coercion can sometimes help people achieve what they already want to achieve and, for that reason, it can be in their volitional interest. Critical paternalism supposes that coercion can sometimes provide people with lives that are better than the lives they currently think of as good and so it can be in their critical interest."[436] It seems that Dworkin accepts volitional paternalism (because it does not interfere with 'substantive' preferences and values) but he is more hostile towards critical paternalism. Critical paternalism is only justifiable if the subject *endorses* those 'life-components' that are paternalistically imposed on him. If a homosexual does not lead a homosexual life out of fear of punishment but neither endorses heterosexuality, his life cannot be said to have improved as a result of the paternalistic intervention. A set of questions need to be clarified at this point, e.g. what exactly counts as endorsement; what are the conditions and circumstances of 'genuine' endorsement and if critical paternalism can manipulate people to actually endorse an imposed restriction. If a 'small amount' of endorsement suffices or if the endorsement can take place a long time after the paternalistic intervention, then the endorsement constraint can be seen as a fairly weak condition of paternalism.[437]

Besides distinguishing between volitional and critical paternalism, Dworkin also identifies 'crude', 'endorsed', 'substitute' and 'conceptual' forms of paternalism.[438] Conceptual paternalism is a subtle form of critical paternalism that exercises paternalism through controlling people's access to knowledge about

435 Ronald Dworkin, *Liberal Community*, in Dworkin, Ronald: *Sovereign Virtue: The Theory and Practice of Equality*. Harvard University Press: Cambridge, Mass. 2000, p. 216.

436 Ibid.

437 Arneson 2003, p. 201.

438 For a summary of Dworkin's categorization, see Wolfe, Christopher: "Liberalism and Paternalism: A Critique of Ronald Dworkin". *The Review of Politics* 56 (4) (1994),

different options (i.e. it manipulates choice architecture similarly to libertarian paternalism). For example, laws prohibiting homosexual acts could be aimed at eliminating homosexuality as part of 'the conceptual menu' so that future generations will not be able to imagine such a life.[439]

Probably the most extensive critique of liberal neutrality is provided by communitarian authors. They believe that the idea of neutrality should be abandoned for a 'politics of the common good'.[440] In a communitarian society, the common good is conceived of as a *substantive* conception of the good life that is prior to what individuals believe to be in their best interests. Communitarians argue that some ways of life are objectively better than others. This claim seems plausible at first glance: theatre-going, for example, is probably more valuable than watching reality shows on television because it is more stimulating, intellectually challenging and aesthetically satisfying. But how can someone know this for sure? Who specifies the domain of valuable and invaluable activities? Is it the majority, the ruling elite or the whole community? If it is the community, who belongs to the community? These are questions that liberals may rightfully ask.

A common liberal counterargument, following Mill, claims that the individual always knows best what is good for him. Whether this statement is right seems to be an empirical question. As Sunstein points out, behavioural sciences have shown that people do not always act in ways that are in their best interests: they are, for example, often 'myopic', preferring short-term gains over long-term ones.[441] A similar counterargument against a substantive understanding of the 'common good' can be based on the Dworkinian endorsement-constraint. If a value is not internally endorsed, it is useless to impose it externally on the subject. It does not make much sense to oblige people to go to the theatre, if they refuse to do so voluntarily. Of course, communitarians would reply that a value will become endorsed as soon as people realize its worth and a 'little' hard paternalism does not 'hurt' to drive people in the right direction. Putting aside these perfectionist implications until the next chapter, the following paragraphs will deal with the communitarian critique of liberal neutrality.

(1) Communitarians question the value that liberals attribute to individual autonomy. They criticize the so-called 'unencumbered' view of the self and claim

---

pp. 615–640, p. 620. See also Robert Young, *John Stuart Mill, Ronald Dworkin and Paternalism*, in Ten 2009, pp. 209–228.

439 Wolfe 1994, p. 622.

440 Kymlicka, Will: *Contemporary Political Philosophy*. Oxford University Press: Oxford 1992, p. 206.

441 Sunstein 2014, pp. 8–9.

that we cannot make autonomous decisions without the knowledge of our particular social identity. Freedom makes sense only if it is situated in a framework of constraints; it loses its meaning if it cannot be contrasted with an opposite notion. Charles Taylor writes that 'complete freedom would be a void in which nothing would be worth doing, nothing would deserve to count for anything. The self which has arrived at freedom by setting aside all external obstacles and impingements is characterless [...]'.[442] Isaiah Berlin expresses a similar view in the *Two Concepts of Liberty*:

> "For am I not what I am, to some degree, in virtue of what others think and feel me to be? When I ask myself what I am, and answer: an Englishman, a Chinese, a merchant, a man of no importance, a millionaire, a convict – I find upon analysis that to possess these attributes entails being recognized as belonging to a particular group or class by other persons in my society. [...] I am not disembodied reason."[443]

Sandel's critique of Rawls is also based on the idea that the self in the 'original position' is unable to create the principles of justice (i.e. the rules of the 'right') merely by following the dictates of reason. He proposes to replace liberalism's unencumbered view of the self with the 'embedded self', in which the self is not prior, but rather it is constituted by its ends.[444] We are, at least partly, constituted by ends that stem from external social factors and which are not freely chosen; we "merely" discover them by being embedded in a shared social context. This does not entail full predetermination as the subject can make choices about which of the possible purposes he will pursue and which he will not. In other words, the self, constituted by its ends, can be reconstituted by choice.[445] The question is whether we can reject these constitutive attachments entirely or we are always determined by them to a certain degree.

(2) Another common argument against state neutrality is that it is self-defeating. Liberals believe that a state which intervenes in the 'marketplace of ideas' to encourage or discourage any particular way of life restricts people's self-determination. However, it seems that non-intervention in the cultural marketplace eventually fails to prevent the spread of ideas that undermine pluralistic cultural structures.[446] For example, in the case of freedom of speech, unregulated populist

442 Charles Taylor quoted by Will Kymlicka. Kymlicka, Will: *Contemporary Political Philosophy: an Introduction*. 2nd ed. Oxford University Press: Oxford 2002, pp. 221–222.
443 Berlin 1969, p. 155.
444 Sandel, Michael J.: *Liberalism and the Limits of Justice*. Cambridge University Press: Cambridge 1982, pp. 15–24, 47–59, 120.
445 Kymlicka 1992, p. 210.
446 Kymlicka 1989, p. 894.

or intolerant ideas have a tendency to suppress other ideas. One possible way out for liberals is to deny that autonomy depends on pluralism. The other possibility is to "insist that good ways of life will sustain themselves without state assistance".[447]

(3) Finally, it is possible to argue that individual preference formation and the development of a specific conception of 'good' always take place in a social setting. This argument seems to be the reformulation of the classical *zoon politicon* argument. Communitarians claim that the individual can only create his personal identity and reach self-fulfilment *within* the context of the political community, through a process of collective deliberation and exchange of experiences.

It is important to mention that there are non-communitarian arguments against liberal neutrality as well. At least two such arguments can be distinguished: the argument from incoherence and the argument of impossibility.[448]

The argument from incoherence is probably the most evident and straightforward argument against liberal neutrality. It is based on the observation that the choice of neutrality already reflects moral presuppositions. The essence of the argument is that liberals are not acting neutrally when they endorse neutrality because neutrality is part of a specific ideology and a distinct world-view. Thus, the principle of neutrality is inherently incoherent.

Raz argues that political neutrality is impossible. It is not that the state should not be neutral; it simply cannot be so.[449] Raz describes two scenarios when action and non-action both represent a non-neutral commitment,[450] in connection to a hypothetical state of war between Somalia and Ethiopia. In the first one, an external third country, Uruguay starts supplying militarily useful materials to one of the parties (e.g. Somalia). In the second scenario, Uruguay does not do so, though it has the materials. It is clear that the first scenario is non-neutral, because Uruguay provides help to only one of the parties. However, Raz argues that the second scenario is also non-neutral because Uruguay hinders Somalia by not helping it. It seems that there is no possibility for neutral behaviour in this situation.[451] Although it is clear that the example of Raz

447 Ibid.

448 Kis, János: *Az állam semlegessége*. Atlantisz: Budapest 1997, pp.76–77.

449 Sadurski 1990a, p. 122.

450 Raz 1986, p. 120.

451 Sadurski claims that Raz's argument is not entirely correct. Both Ethiopia and Somalia engage in the conflict with a set of expectations about their military resources, including information about their foreign allies and suppliers. Uruguay's non-intervention

does not necessarily mean that the state can *never* act neutrally, it is true that in many cases governmental non-action tacitly represents a commitment or value choice. The state, when legalizes or prohibits abortion, tacitly endorses a particular view on the human character of foetuses. There is no neutral, 'third' option in this case.[452]

is only non-neutral if Somalia indeed had some strong grounds for believing that Uruguay would start supplying it with military materials after the outbreak of the conflict with Ethiopia. Sadurski 1990a, p. 126.

452 Kis 1997, p. 76.

4. Alternative approaches

4.1 The emergence of virtue ethics

The previous chapters demonstrated some of the problems that deontology and consequentialism have to face when it comes to the justification of paternalism. These ethical theories have been criticized on a more general level as well. MacIntyre asserts that disagreements over central moral issues cannot be settled in the present social and cultural order.[453] Modern ethical theories, rooted in what MacIntyre calls the 'Enlightenment project', sought to replace the religious foundations of morality with secular principles that any rational person could accept, irrespective of his or her personal beliefs.[454] However, these theories are often unable to resolve moral dilemmas because their allegedly rational action-guiding principles are "mutually antagonistic" and 'protagonists' of rival theories tend to "invoke incommensurable forms of moral assertions against each other".[455] These ethical systems seem to hide an 'emotivist' approach to morality, meaning that people's approach to central moral debates (such as the value of human life, e.g. abortion or euthanasia) is only seemingly rational and moral choices, in fact, are personal, non-rational choices that are merely "expressions of attitude and feeling".[456]

The inability of deontology and consequentialism to resolve moral dilemmas triggered two responses.[457] Some 'anti-theorists', like Bernard Williams, criticized the idea that an impersonal 'morality system' grounded in universally applicable principles can prescribe moral obligations that are always consistent with each other. Williams argues that conflicts of moral obligations are not merely apparent and they cannot simply be eliminated by rejecting one of the conflicting 'oughts' the way the dominant morality system dictates. The fact that an otherwise valid moral obligation was not applied in a given situation

453 Veitch, Scott: *Moral Conflict and Legal Reasoning*. Hart Publishing: Oxford 1999, p. 5.

454 Alasdair MacIntyre, The Claims of After Virtue, in Knight, Kelvin (ed.): *The Macintyre Reader*. University of Notre Dame Press: Notre Dame, Ind. 1998, p. 70.

455 Ibid. 69.

456 Ibid.

457 Baron, Marcia / Pettit, Philip / Slote, Michael: *Three Methods of Ethics: A Debate*. Wiley-Blackwell: Cambridge, Mass. 1997, p. 179. See also Beauchamp / Childress 2009, p. 51.

"is registered by all sorts of facts in our moral experience", including agent-regret, i.e. the feeling that we experience toward an action's bad consequences for which we are causally but not morally responsible.[458] Another sign that our moral understanding is too complex to be reduced to principles is the inability of moral systems to accommodate the phenomenon of moral luck. Modern moral theories, especially those of Kantian origin, emphasize that an action's moral character depends entirely on the actor's voluntary choices. In reality, we tend to blame people not only for what they have done voluntarily but luck also plays a role here. Consider, for example, the case of a driver who accidentally swerves into the oncoming traffic lane: the action is judged differently if he or she causes an accident or if, out of pure luck, there is no oncoming traffic and hence no accident.[459] Consequently, Williams advocates a particularistic and anti-theoretical approach to morality that places more emphasis on emotions such as shame and takes into account a person's connections with friends, family and with other members of society in general.[460]

The other response to the problems of modern moral philosophy was provided by the revival of virtue ethics. In her seminal paper,[461] Elizabeth Anscombe criticized modern moral philosophy, including Mill's utilitarianism and Kant's deontology, for adopting a 'law conception of ethics' that emphasizes the notion of obligation and relies heavily on the application of universal principles.[462] Inspired by Aristotle, Anscombe urged moral philosophers to return to concepts such as character, virtue and flourishing.

Philosophers, following Anscombe, developed different approaches to virtue ethics. The best way to demonstrate the common characteristics of these is to contrast them with deontology and consequentialism.[463] (1) Virtue ethics is essentially agent focused, meaning that it focuses on the character of the moral agent, while deontology and consequentialism concentrates on the morality of discrete actions. From the viewpoint of paternalism, this means that emphasis

---

458 Sussman, David: *Is Agent-Regret Rational?* (Working paper, 47th Chapel Hill Colloquium in Philosophy, University of Illinois at Urbana-Champaign).

459 The example comes from Thomas Nagel. Cf. Baron / Pettit / Slote 1997, p. 181.

460 Crisp, Roger / Slote, Michael (eds.): *Virtue Ethics*. Oxford University Press: Oxford 1997, p. 7.

461 Anscombe, Elizabeth: "Modern Moral Philosophy". *Philosophy* 33 (124) (1958), pp. 1–19 See also Lónyai 1981, pp.615–652.

462 Athanassoulis, Nafsika: "Virtue Ethics". In: *Internet Encyclopedia of Philosophy* (http://www.iep.utm.edu/ virtue/) (06.04.2015).

463 Baron / Pettit / Slote 1997, p. 182.

shifts from the autonomy-violating character of paternalistic interventions to the character of paternalistic agents. (2) Virtue ethics uses *aretaic* ethical terms like 'morally good', 'admirable' or 'virtuous' to describe moral character. *Deontic* terms such as right, wrong, duty or obligation all refer to compliance with certain rules and this limits the scope of ethics to a narrow range of concerns.[464] An act, for example a paternalistic white lie, can be empathic, yet dishonest at the same time. Instead of viewing it merely in a rule-based dimension, it is possible to evaluate such acts by reference to broader concepts. Paternalism may exhibit virtues (i.e. caring) and vices (i.e. disrespect for autonomy) at the same time – the question is how virtue ethics can resolve such tensions. (3) The last difference that virtue ethicists usually emphasize in contrast to deontology is that the agent does not act from duty – he is motivated because he has desires that virtuous people have. Thus, if the motivation of the paternalistic actor corresponds to virtuous desires (i.e. improving his character, caring for others, preserving valuable social relations, etc.), the absolute character of the harm principle is pushed into the background. The subject's autonomy and the hard-soft distinction become less important because he is no longer bound by a categorical rule that defines the scope of paternalism.

To demonstrate that virtue ethics provides a different rationale to regulate paternalism than deontology or consequentialism, consider Michael Sandel's example on price gouging (i.e. the seller setting a much higher price than which is considered to be reasonable or fair). In 2004, Hurricane Charley swept across Florida causing numerous fatalities, injuries and serious damages to property.[465] Shopkeepers, exploiting the vulnerable situation of people, raised the price of certain essential products (e.g. bottled water, ice, etc.) to an unreasonably high level. One can rightfully ask whether it is morally wrong for shopkeepers to take advantage of natural disasters, and if it is permissible for the legislator to interfere with the prices of the free market.[466] Price gouging is very similar

464 Ibid.

465 Sandel, Michael J.: *Justice: What's the Right Thing to Do?*. Allen Lane: London 2009, p. 3.

466 Thirty-four US states had regulations against price gouging in 2008. Zwolinski distinguishes three definitional elements of price gouging: (1) period of emergency (e.g. natural disasters); (2) necessary items (i.e. restrictions only apply to items that are essential to survival); (3) price ceilings (prescribed either by exact percentage or with words such as 'excessive' or 'unconscionable'). For more details, including an analysis of the relation between price gouging and moral character, see Zwolinski, Matt: "The Ethics of Price Gouging". *Business Ethics Quarterly* 18 (03) (2008), pp. 347–378.

to usurious lending. A limitation on these practices can be considered indirect paternalism to protect vulnerable parties from entering into disadvantageous contracts. Consequentialists could defend anti-gouging laws by arguing that the free market does not always lead to 'optimal' results and society's overall welfare is not served by introducing astronomical prices in situations of emergency. Representatives of deontological ethics would probably refer to the coercive and exploitative character of usury and price gouging and transform the problem to soft paternalism (i.e. that the person entered into the contract under duress). The virtue argument, by contrast, would trace back the wrongness of price gauging and usury to the vice of *greed*. "Greed is a vice, a bad way of being, especially when it makes people oblivious to the suffering of others. [...] A society in which people exploit their neighbors for financial gain in times of crisis is not a good society. Excessive greed is therefore a vice that a good society should discourage if it can."[467]

The central question of virtue ethics is how to identify the virtues of a given society. To build a normative ethical theory on virtues, one must clearly see which character traits qualify as virtues and which as vices. Aristotle starts from a teleological viewpoint: "[...] every craft and every line of inquiry, and likewise every action and decision, seems to seek some good; that is why some people were right to describe the good as what everything seeks".[468] Good ends differ in each case: health is the end of medicine, victory of generalship, and wealth of economics (i.e. 'household management'). However, these good ends may only be means to further ends, so there must be an ultimate *telos* that all human beings strive for and which is 'complete without qualification'.[469] Aristotle calls this *eudaimonia*, which can be translated as well-being, happiness, flourishing or prosperity. *Eudaimonia* is the activity of the soul in accordance with virtue. It is achieved by

467 Sandel 2009, p. 7.

468 Aristotle: *Nicomachean Ethics*. Hackett Publishing: Indianapolis, Ind. 1999, p. 1. (Book 1, Chapter 1).

469 Aristotle gives an account of the good which is particular and universal at the same time. Many modern virtue ethicists believe that it is impossible to rationally devise a single universal rule of flourishing; virtues are relative and they are formed by the traditions and practices of local societies. However, Martha Nussbaum argues that Aristotle also defended the idea of a single objective account of human flourishing. MacIntyre 2007, p. 148. See also Martha Nussbaum, *Non-Relative Virtues: An Aristotelian Approach*, in Shafer-Landau, Russ (ed.): *Ethical Theory: an Anthology*. 2nd ed. Wiley-Blackwell: Chichester, West Sussex ; Malden, MA 2013, pp.630–631. Ross, David: *Aristotle*. Routledge: London, New York 1995, pp.120–121.

exercising virtues and by developing a virtuous character.[470] Virtues are human capacities that help us to realize the internal goods of practices (health, victory, wealth, etc.) and also *eudaimonia*. Aristotle differentiates between moral and intellectual virtues. While intellectual virtues can be directly taught and learned, virtues of character develop through practice and experience. The virtue of courage, for example, cannot be learned from books, but only through practice and experience. Virtues of character are always located between extremes of vices. Courage is a virtuous trait that is midway between the vice of rashness and the vice of cowardice.[471] But isn't it a *petitio principii* to claim that becoming virtuous requires the exercise of virtue? Without knowing the virtue, one would hardly ever start to exercise a practice, which is the only way to know the virtue. The answer lies in external 'compulsion': someone may start to practice a virtue because of upbringing or education.

Virtues and practice are deeply intertwined in Aristotle's philosophy. When he speaks of excellence, he generally refers to some type of human practice: flute-playing, farming, physics, politics and so on. By exercising a practice, there are two kinds of good somebody can achieve. Consider the example of a child whom I wish to teach to play chess even though the child has no desire to learn the game.[472] Therefore I offer him candies each time he plays chess with me. It is clear that he will play chess only because of the candies and not because he wants to improve or obtain human capacities that are connected to the game (e.g. strategic thinking). There are internal goods and there are goods externally and contingently attached to chess playing (in the case of the child, candy; in the case of adults, prestige and money that can be earned by playing professional chess). Thus, MacIntyre defines virtue as an "acquired human quality, the possession and exercise of which enables us to achieve those goods which are internal to its practices".[473] Virtues are embedded in practices and they develop by exercising

470 Virtues and *eudaimonia* are not in a simple means-end relation. Virtues seem to be necessary but not sufficient conditions of flourishing. An ill or poor person, even though virtuous, cannot reach *eudaimonia*. Virtues are unlike simple means that someone chooses in order to reach certain ends – virtues are chosen for themselves and also to attain *eudaimonia* at the same time. "For what constitutes the good for man is a complete human life lived at its best, and the exercise of the virtues is a necessary and central part of such a life, not a mere preparatory exercise to secure such a life." MacIntyre 2007, p. 149.

471 Shafer-Landau 2013, p. 611.

472 MacIntyre 2007, p. 188.

473 Ibid. 191.

practices. The process how virtues lead to *eudaimonia*, besides realising the internal goods of certain practices, is not entirely clear. Making reference to the works of the main representative of positive psychology, Mihaly Csikszentmihalyi, Julia Annas relates *eudaimonia* to the flow experience, a mental condition associated with a state of absorption and an active exercise of one's practical capacities.[474]

MacIntyre provides a historical analysis of the development of virtues, from heroic societies, through classical Greece and Christian Europe, up to the modern age. The diversity of virtues raises the question whether it is possible to identify certain 'core virtues' that are the same in every society or virtues are specific to a given historical period. Ethical relativism is tempting, especially if we take into account that most forms of virtue ethics reject the possibility of an all-encompassing, universal principle of morality. However, it might be the case that moral virtues are founded on a universally shared aspect of human life, independent of time and culture.[475] Perfectionism relates to virtue ethics at this point. Perfectionist writers advance an objective account of the human good and develop an account of politics that is informed by this account. Objectivity can offer a strong basis for perfectionism, including hard paternalism and moralism.

4.2 Paternalism and virtues

So how does virtue ethics relate to paternalism? Critics of virtue ethics claim that it is unable to guide actions in the same way as deontology or consequentialism: a moral theory built on *aretaic* concepts is too vague to be capable of telling people what they should do in a specific situation. Rejecting these criticisms, Hursthouse argues that virtue ethics does provide a general rule of right action, namely "[a]n action is right if and only if it is what a virtuous person would characteristically do in the circumstances".[476] As a consequence, each virtue generates a prescription (and each vice a prohibition) in the form of a *v-rule*, such as 'do what is honest, charitable, generous' and 'do not do what is dishonest, uncharitable, mean'.[477] Obviously, a well-developed virtue theory must address some further questions, for example, who qualifies as a virtuous person, what is the exact content of a virtue and how to resolve situations when virtues seem to collide.

474 Annas, Julia: *Intelligent Virtue*. Oxford University Press: Oxford 2011, p. 70.

475 Cf. Martha Nussbaum, *Non-Relative Virtues: An Aristotelian Approach*, in Shafer-Landau 2013, pp.630–644.

476 Hursthouse, Rosalind: *On Virtue Ethics*. Oxford University Press: Oxford 1999, p. 28.

477 Ibid. 33.

If we approach paternalism from the perspective of virtue ethics, it seems plausible to abandon the 'rigor' of the harm principle and adopt a casuistic approach which examines what a virtuous person would do in a specific paternalistic situation. Instead of paternalistic interventions (i.e. finding the 'right action'), it focuses on the character of paternalistic actors. If paternalism promotes virtues, it seems to become morally less objectionable because it develops individual character. There are two questions that shall be addressed at this point: (1) Is paternalism (i.e. paternalistic character) a virtue in itself? (2) Do paternalistic practices promote the development of other virtues?

(1) It does not seem likely that paternalism (i.e. paternalistic character) qualifies as a virtue. Firstly, it seems difficult to directly relate paternalism to one specific type of practice. Paternalism appears in various forms, in a multitude of human practices and relations (e.g. medical practice, pedagogy, parent-child relations, politics, legislation, etc.) and, as a consequence, it can exhibit other virtues (i.e. other than paternalism) depending on the specific situation (e.g. care, love, family values, devotion, professional commitment, etc.). In other words, paternalism is hardly a fundamental character trait: there are other virtues that lie behind it. Furthermore, paternalism with non-benevolent motivation does not seem to promote character at all.

(2) The other question to be examined is whether paternalism, even if it is not a virtue in itself, promotes other virtues or values. Such virtue-promoting paternalism can be affiliated with the idea of moral paternalism, which emphasizes the role of paternalism in shaping character and desires.[478] In contrast to pure legal moralism, which attaches moral values to acts, moral paternalism seeks to promote good character. This type of perfectionist paternalism is vulnerable to the 'virtue cannot be coerced' objection. However, this argument is not necessarily fatal. It is true that coercion, in the short run, may cause 'immoral' people to comply with moral rules for surface reasons (cf. MacIntyre's example of internal and external goods). Virtues, on the other hand, develop by practice: it might be reasonable to expect that people – in the long run, as a psychological effect – will endorse previously rejected moral principles. Writing thank-you letters seems to be out of fashion nowadays.[479] A lot of people assume that as long as they feel grateful, they do not need to write thank-you letters. Moral perfectionists argue

478 Scoccia, Danny: "Moral Paternalism, Virtue and Autonomy". *Australasian Journal of Philosophy* 78 (2000), pp. 53–71, p. 56.

479 Sandel 2009, p. 198.

the other way around: it is the writing of thank-you letters that will eventually cause the feeling of gratitude to emerge and build up in people's psyche.[480]

4.3 Perfectionism

4.3.1 Perfectionist ethics

The transition from virtue ethics to perfectionist politics seems a natural one to make. Even though it is tempting to build perfectionism on the foundations of virtue ethics, not all perfectionist authors follow this option.[481] The 'temptation' might be explained with the close relationship between Aristotle's ethics and politics and with the perfectionist ethical function Aristotle attributes to the political community:

> "Any *polis* which is truly so called, and is not merely one in name, must devote itself to the end of encouraging goodness. [...] What constitutes a *polis* is an association of households and clans in a good life, for the sake of attaining a perfect and self-sufficing existence. [...] It is therefore for the sake of good actions, and not for the sake of social life, that political associations must be considered to exist."[482]

If we accept that the *telos* of human beings is *eudaimonia* and that this is attained by developing a virtuous character through practice, it is easy to see why the *polis* must care for the moral character of its citizens. According to Aristotle, most people are unable to reach moral perfection by themselves and they do not listen to rational or moral arguments. They "do not by nature obey the sense of shame, but only fear, and do not abstain from bad acts because of their baseness but through fear of punishment".[483] It is the task of the state to improve the character of citizens through coercion: 'statecraft' inevitably becomes 'soulcraft' in the Aristotelian framework.[484]

Although both virtue ethics and perfectionism have foundations in Aristotle's philosophy, not all perfectionist theories are built on virtue ethics and not all

480 Ibid.

481 Hursthouse writes that "[w]hether virtue ethics can be expected to grow into 'virtue politics' – i.e. to extend from moral philosophy into political philosophy – is not so clear." Hursthouse, Rosalind: "Virtue Ethics". In: Zalta, Edward N. (ed.): *The Stanford Encyclopedia of Philosophy*. Fall 2013 (http://plato.stanford.edu/entries/ethics-virtue/) (06.05.2015).

482 Aristotle 1998 See also George 1995, pp.21–22.

483 Aristotle / Ross, W. D. / Brown, Lesley: *The Nicomachean Ethics*. Oxford University Press: Oxford 2009, p. 199. Book 10, Chapter 9. See also George 1995, p. 22.

484 Feinberg 1989, p. 278.

forms of virtue ethics have neo-Aristotelian foundations. It is possible to distinguish between two strands of perfectionism.[485] 'Human nature perfectionism' emphasizes the development of human character and defines perfectionist goods as those goods that contribute to the development of human nature. Thomas Hurka writes that the most important feature of perfections (i.e. virtues) is that they "develop human nature by exercising sophisticated rationality".[486] Virtue ethics seems to be related to this strand of perfectionism. By contrast, 'objective goods perfectionism' does not make reference to human character and identifies perfectionism with the realization of a list of objective goods irrespective of their effect on human nature (cf. chapter 2.2.2).

4.3.2 Perfectionist politics

Perfectionist politics is based on the idea that the state should promote particular moral or political ideals and it should not strive to be neutral between competing conceptions of the good. Perfectionism seems to challenge the harm principle and state neutrality at the same time. A plausible argument in support of perfectionist politics is that the doctrine of state neutrality is 'self-defeating': in order to preserve freedom and value-pluralism, the state cannot tolerate intolerant views that aim to undermine pluralism. As Raz puts it, strict adherence to the doctrine of state neutrality "would undermine the chances of survival of many cherished aspects of our culture".[487] The German constitutional concept of militant democracy (*streitbare Demokratie*) seems to draw inspiration from this approach. In response to those who fear that perfectionism might be the first step towards authoritarian governance, perfectionist authors stress that state neutrality is not the only way to establish social cooperation and to prevent the abuse of state power. Perfectionist politics can leave the protective arrangements of the rule of law unaffected. Sher writes that "[...] a non-neutral state can retain most, if not all, of the classical liberal protections. Such a state is obviously compatible with a fixed constitutional framework, a settled procedure of amending the constitution, and the separation of different branches of governments."[488]

---

485 Wall, Steven: "Perfectionism in Moral and Political Philosophy". In: Zalta, Edward N. (ed.): *The Stanford Encyclopedia of Philosophy*. Winter 2012 (http://plato.stanford.edu/entries/perfectionism-moral/).

486 Hurka 1993, p. 150.

487 Raz 1986, p. 162.

488 Sher, George: *Beyond Neutrality: Perfectionism and Politics*. Cambridge University Press: Cambridge 1997, p. 6.

4.3.3 Perfectionism and paternalism

This chapter examines paternalism in the framework of 'human nature perfectionism'. It seems that the 'objective goods' strand of perfectionism gives a wide access to both coercive and non-coercive forms of paternalism, thus, it is neither that interesting nor very attractive for further investigation. Representatives of this approach do not require that the objective value be endorsed by the subject of paternalism: "A slave might be forced to do theoretical physics, and do it surpassingly well; the conditions under which the achievement is made do not extinguish the value of the achievement."[489]

Paternalism that promotes human nature is justifiable in the case of 'human nature perfectionism'. The relevant harm to be avoided is the harm to the individual's future perfection or capacity to future perfection. As opposed to 'objective' perfectionism, endorsement *can* have a role in this framework. Legal paternalism without endorsement might cause more harm than good because people in a paternalistic state will not be compelled to exercise and develop their capacity for future perfection on their own.[490]

Instrumental forms of paternalism that do not affect fundamental life plans do not have perfectionist implications. Clarke mentions 'neutral paternalism' as a legitimate liberty-limiting principle.[491] Such intervention is guided by neutral considerations that are compatible with a lot of different conceptions of the good life. In other words, the goods that neutral paternalism aims to protect seem to be part of (almost) everyone's life plan.[492] Compulsory hygiene regulations for food manufacturers are paternalistic because they take away options from consumers but avoiding contaminated food seems to be compatible with all, even radically different conceptions of the good life. The same goes for traffic regulations, vehicle safety regulations and laws against misleading advertising.

Generally speaking, perfectionism is not as hostile towards hard paternalism as autonomy-based liberal theories, especially when it contributes to the

---

489 Arneson, Richard J.: "Perfectionism and Politics". *Ethics* 111 (1) (2000), pp. 37–63, p. 44.

490 Hurka 1993, p. 153.

491 Clarke, Simon: "Debate: State Paternalism, Neutrality and Perfectionism". *Journal of Political Philosophy* 14 (2006), pp. 111–121, p. 119.

492 I have previously touched upon the issue how seemingly instrumental limitations of liberty may actually have an 'evaluative' character. The question of wearing a crash helmet can sometimes constitute a part of the good life, for example in the case of the Sikh motorcyclist. Regulations against junk food and risky sports can also be non-neutral; they imply a particular ranking of neutral goods.

development of human nature. This does not mean that paternalism is unconditionally allowed and most perfectionist theories set limits to the state intervening in citizens' self-regarding actions.[493] The harm principle and its prohibition concerning paternalism are not entirely suppressed by perfectionism. It is 'only' the absolute character of the principle that is pushed into the background. The deontological harm principle is based on the presupposition that autonomy is the most essential value (to use Dworkin's expression, a moral 'trump card'), because it guarantees the self-fulfilment of the individual. Hurka admits that autonomy is important, because it is a 'perfection' itself, but it does not have a prioritized role among other values. There must be other intrinsic goods besides autonomy which explains why "freely chosen creativity is better than freely chosen idleness, and autonomous knowledge is better than autonomous ignorance".[494] Some of the previously discussed cases have also shown that just because a self-harming action is voluntary, it does not mean that it is not objectionable on other grounds. Voluntary self-mutilation or other forms of 'free-floating' evils seem 'inherently' wrong even if they are performed fully voluntarily (cf. chapter 3.3).

A plausible theory of perfectionism treats autonomy only as one good among others, which can be outweighed sometimes by other 'perfections'. Imagine that Mozart, as a young boy, was 'forced' to practice playing the piano all the time, so his life lacked autonomy in the substantive sense of the word.[495] However, we cannot claim that Mozart's whole life, with its great musical achievements, contained less perfection than if he had been given freedom in his youth not to practice and develop his musical skills. The loss of autonomy seems to be counterbalanced by other values and autonomy cannot outweigh the goods associated with Mozart's music. Thus, paternalism seems legitimate in this case.[496]

The harm principle in the perfectionist framework becomes an auxiliary principle. On the one hand, it allows for certain forms of paternalism, typically benefit-promoting 'moralistic' paternalism that develops human capacities and virtues. On the other hand, it protects and promotes autonomy and ensures that paternalism is not unconditionally allowed. In this respect, it is necessary to mention Feinberg who argues that *coercive* legal perfectionism (i.e. perfectionism through the means of criminal law) has significant limits because it seems

493 Klosko / Wall 2003, p. 125.

494 Hurka 1993, p. 149.

495 Ibid.

496 Hurka's example is unfortunate because the coercion of young Mozart, being not yet a fully competent person, can be considered soft paternalism. Such interference can also be justified under the deontological framework.

"absurd to threaten people with punishment in order to give them wisdom, style, integrity, or a better sense of humor".[497] According to Feinberg, legal coercion can, at best, promote 'negative virtues' (i.e. prevent vices) by suppressing character defects but cannot develop positive character traits. Someone who is not cruel to others might still have a poor character and nobody would call him a virtuous person. Consequently, coercive legal perfectionism must be confined to the category of 'negative virtues'. However, the harm and offense principles could also warrant the criminalization of acts that stem from harmful or offensive character deficits. Does it make a difference which argument we use? Feinberg suggests that the applicability of harm and offense principles makes the principle of legal perfectionism superfluous.[498]

4.3.4 The liberal perfectionism of Joseph Raz

The political theory of Joseph Raz can be described as a form of liberal perfectionism.[499] Although the expression seems to contain a contradiction, the paradox might be resolved by showing how perfectionist politics can contribute to increasing personal autonomy. On Raz's view, the harm principle is "superseded by a so-called autonomy principle that captures the truth in it while avoiding its exaggerations".[500] Raz seems to abandon the idea of liberal neutrality; the harm principle is no longer supported by the requirement of neutrality but rather by the principle of autonomy which he interprets in a perfectionist manner.[501]

If it is the duty of the state to promote the welfare of citizens and if autonomy is an essential component of welfare in modern industrial societies, it seems plausible to assert that the government needs to create an environment that is conducive to personal autonomy. The harm principle, backed up by 'perfectionist

---

497 Feinberg 1989, p. 281.

498 Ibid. 285.

499 Liberal perfectionism has other representatives besides Raz. Arneson mentions Martha Nussbaum's and Amartya Sen's attempts to develop a liberal perfectionist egalitarian approach to politics. Arneson 2000, p. 39. Nussbaum defines perfectionist liberalism as a type of 'comprehensive liberalism' that bases political principles on some comprehensive doctrine about human life. Cf. Nussbaum, Martha C.: "Perfectionist Liberalism and Political Liberalism". *Philosophy & Public Affairs* 39 (1) (2011), pp. 3–45.

500 Wall, Steven: "Perfectionism in Moral and Political Philosophy". In: Zalta, Edward N. (ed.): *The Stanford Encyclopedia of Philosophy*. Winter 2012. (http://plato.stanford.edu/entries/perfectionism-moral/) (06.04.2014).

501 Sadurski 1990a, p. 131.

autonomy' is reinterpreted by Raz as a principle that permits the coercive enforcement of at least *some* self-regarding duties. Thus, his theory is tolerant towards *some* forms of paternalism. Sadurski claims that there are two presuppositions that stand behind this idea.[502] The first is the perfectionist interpretation of autonomy. The second presupposition is the connection between the perfectionist account of autonomy and the harm principle. I discuss these presuppositions in more details, dealing with the first presupposition in my first point and with the second presupposition in points 2 to 4.

[1] Perfectionist principle of autonomy

The perfectionist character of autonomy stems from the 'contextual', or, as I have called it, the 'contingent' value attributed to autonomy (cf. chapter 3.1.3).[503] "Since autonomy is morally valuable, there is reason for everyone to make himself and everyone else autonomous. But it is the special character of autonomy that one cannot make another person autonomous."[504] Thus, the normative implications of the value of autonomy are twofold. Firstly, there is a *negative* duty to respect the autonomy of others. However, "[...] there is more one can do to help another person have an autonomous life than stand off and refrain from coercing or manipulating him".[505] There are also *positive* duties to promote and sustain social conditions that contribute to the realization of autonomy, for example the duty to help in creating the inner mental capacities required for the conduct of an autonomous life (e.g. cognitive abilities such as the ability to absorb, remember or use information and essential character traits such as loyalty or stability).[506]

[2] Positive side of the harm principle – harm to others

Raz does not deny that it is possible to justify state coercion in case of harm to others. Harm diminishes autonomy, just as coercion, but if coercion is less

502 Ibid.

503 Raz attributes a contextual value to autonomy. He seems to endorse the communitarian view that the individual is a social being and values are dependent on social context. David McCabe criticizes this approach and claims that individuals can envision and pursue goals that are different from those made available by the social forms of their community. McCabe, David: "Joseph Raz and the Contextual Argument for Liberal Perfectionism". *Ethics* 111 (2001), pp. 493–522, p. 495, 512.

504 Raz, Joseph: *The Morality of Freedom*. Clarendon Press: Oxford 1986, p. 407.

505 Ibid. 408.

506 Ibid.

restrictive than harm, coercion can be legitimately exercised.[507] Raz writes that "[...] a moral theory which values autonomy highly can justify restricting the autonomy of one person for the sake of the greater autonomy of others or *even of that person himself in the future.* That is why it can justify coercion to prevent harm, for harm interferes with autonomy."[508]

[3] Negative side of the harm principle – exclusion of coercion if no harm is present

The negative side of the harm principle prohibits state coercion if there is no other-regarding harm. As a consequence, immoral, bad or unwise decisions that do not have impact on others cannot be restricted. However, according to perfectionist ideals, autonomy is only valuable if geared to morally good actions. The prohibition of coercion can still be justified, if we argue that morally bad choices does not diminish autonomy, while coercion imposed out of perfectionist considerations does. Raz claims that "[...] the availability of repugnant options, and even their free pursuit by individuals, does not detract from their autonomy", while coercive interference violates the autonomy of its victims.[509] Coercion violates independence and expresses a relation of domination and disrespect for the coerced. Coercion by criminal penalties is also a global and indiscriminate invasion of autonomy. Imprisoning a person prevents him from almost all autonomous pursuits. Other forms of coercion may be less severe, but they all invade autonomy in a similar manner.[510]

[4] Paternalism

The main difference between the deontological and the perfectionist interpretation of the harm principle is that the latter seems to be more tolerant of paternalism. Raz reformulates the harm principle as a rule "that regards the prevention of harm to anyone *(himself included)* as the only justifiable ground for coercive interference with a person".[511] His idea is that most forms of harm and offence, including *voluntarily* inflicted self-harm, diminishes autonomy by limiting the number of available options open to the individual. Consequently, coercive

507 Waldron 1989, p. 1140.

508 Raz 1986, p. 419. Emphasis added.

509 Ibid.

510 Sadurski criticizes Raz for his arguments that coercion violates the condition of independence and that criminal penalties are an indiscriminate invasion of autonomy. Sadurski 1990a, p. 132. Cf. Waldron 1989, p. 1141.

511 Raz 1986, pp.412–413. Emphasis added.

paternalism is justifiable when it prevents self-harm and, by doing so, increases the autonomy of the subject.

Raz suggests that liberals are mistaken when they emphasize the harm principle's absolute prohibition of coercion and fight 'major last ditch battles' against compulsory (i.e. coercive) seat-belt or crash helmet legislations, while tolerating or encouraging indirect, non-coercive forms of paternalism. Liberals "clamour for laws improving safety controls and quality controls of manufactured goods".[512] These laws are non-coercive, and thus fall outside the scope of the harm principle, but their effect can be to reduce people's options and consequently their autonomy (cf. different forms of libertarian paternalism that work by manipulating preferences and choices). Different forms of paternalism have different effects on personal autonomy that can be assessed on a case-by-case basis; thus it seems better not to take an *a priori* position towards paternalism.

Raz seems to accept non-coercive forms of benefit-promoting paternalism more easily than coercive paternalism. For example, he thinks that the state may tax activities that are morally 'depraved' (e.g. fox hunting) in order to discourage them and subsidize 'valuable' activities instead. As Waldron shows, the problem with these methods is that they can be reduced to coercion (which is rejected by Raz as well when it comes to benefit-promoting paternalism).[513] Waldron argues that altering the costs and payoffs of an activity looks like coercion, because the threat of coercion actually does the same (i.e. it adds an artificial cost to a certain activity). Furthermore, taxes and fines are backed up by the state's coercive force: any fox hunter who goes hunting without paying the 'fox-hunting' tax will be forcefully prevented in his hunting activity.[514] Waldron thinks that "even if governmental activity is not overtly coercive, still, in the last resort, the government's ability to undertake any activity at all rests on its coercive power".[515] Raz, on the other hand, is not convinced that the use of force is a distinctive characteristic of states.[516]

---

512 Ibid. 422.

513 Waldron 1989, p. 1141.

514 Ibid. Waldron's example is outdated because fox-hunting is banned in the UK nowadays.

515 Ibid. 1140.

516 Raz, Joseph: "Facing up: A Reply". *Southern California Law Review* 62 (1989), pp. 1153–1235, p. 1232.

[5] Summary

Raz believes that Mill's harm principle is not a comprehensive doctrine of freedom, but merely a part of the wider autonomy principle.[517] Personal autonomy can be limited by other means than coercion and it is a mistake to simply equate political freedom with freedom from coercion. The significance of the harm principle is rather that it indicates the right way in which the state can promote the well-being of people. This seems to involve mainly the use of non-coercive methods to promote autonomy, because coercion always invades autonomy, unless it is done to promote autonomy by preventing harm.

It is possible to summarize the practical consequences of Raz's perfectionist harm principle in the following way. (1) Coercion is permissible to protect individuals from harm caused by others. (2) The harm principle prohibits coercive interference with a person's liberty in order to promote morals or other values. Therefore, perfectionist liberalism is not perfectionist in the 'traditional' sense of the word: moral education (i.e. moralistic paternalism) is not a good reason for legal coercion. (3) As long as it is confined to the creation of conditions of autonomy, non-coercive promotion of certain values (e.g. by taxation or subsidies) is allowed.[518] (3) Most importantly, coercion might be permissible to protect individuals from self-harm. Raz seems to accept paternalism as a potential liberty-limiting principle, the justification of which does not depend on the voluntariness of the subject's self-harming choice but rather on the question whether the state's coercive interference increases personal autonomy in the long run. Put differently, one should weigh the loss of autonomy caused by paternalistic coercion against the loss of autonomy that would have been caused by the self-harming conduct. Since each case of self-harm is different, it does not make sense to take a stand against paternalism in general. As a rule of thumb, paternalism that affects instrumental values (e.g. the use of unsafe consumer goods) is more easily justified, than the limitation of activities which are considered to carry intrinsic values (e.g. doing risky sports where risk is considered to be an unavoidable part of a self-defining activity).

517 Raz 1986, p. 420.
518 Ibid. 423.

4.4 Paternalism as caring

4.4.1 Care and virtues

In light of the problems associated with the consequentialist and autonomy-based approaches of paternalism and the problems of modern moral philosophy in general, it seems plausible to explore whether a theory of paternalism drawing inspiration from virtue ethics and the ethics of care is better at handling some of the mentioned shortcomings. Being aware of that a 'paradigm shift' can bring along the loss of old questions and make previously long-standing solutions redundant, a virtue-based approach might significantly change one's approach to paternalism.[519] The aim of this chapter is to briefly present the basic precepts of the ethics of care and examine its potential implications for a virtue-based approach to paternalism.

Care ethics was developed from feminist ethics as a response to traditional ethical theories that, according to feminist writers, follow a predominantly male rationale.[520] They claim that women tend to reason in a 'different voice' than men. Carol Gilligan demonstrates this difference through describing the approaches of an 11-year-old boy and girl to the moral dilemma of whether a man should steal a drug he cannot afford in order to save the life of his ill wife.[521] The boy's reasoning reflects rationality, logic and abstraction and he concludes a firm moral judgment (i.e. that the man should steal the drug to save his wife). The approach of Amy, the small girl is less black and white. She does not see the dilemma as a mathematical problem independent of human relations. When arguing against stealing the drug, she does not focus on property rights but on the possible effects stealing can have on the relationship of husband and wife. For example, if the husband is arrested, he has to leave his sick wife, which is even worse than having no medications. Similarly, when arguing for stealing the drug, she concentrates on the effects that the wife's death would have on her family. She is disturbed by the lack of information concerning human relations in the particular case. From a 'male' viewpoint, her position seems insecure and immature: she admits that the man should not steal but neither should he let his

519 Kuhn, Thomas S.: *A tudományos forradalmak szerkezete*. Osiris: Budapest 2000, p. 35.

520 The claim that women tend to treat moral problems differently than men was first articulated by Carol Gilligan. Gilligan, Carol: *In a Different Voice: Psychological Theory and Women's Development*. Harvard University Press: Cambridge, Mass. 1982 See also Slote, Michael: *The Ethics of Care and Empathy*. Routledge: London, New York 2007, p. 3; Kymlicka 1992, p. 263; Kultgen 1995, p. 26.

521 Gilligan 1982, p. 24.

wife die. Her solution lies in improving interpersonal relations. She is confident that "if Heinz [i.e. the husband], and the druggist had talked it out long enough, they could reach something besides stealing."[522] Thus, Amy understands morality in a framework of relationships and tries to resolve moral dilemmas through communication.

Although it is contested whether there is an actual division between genders when it comes to applying 'male' and 'female' versions of moral reasoning, the example of Gilligan is particularly useful for understanding the basic characteristics of care ethics. (1) In opposition to Kantian ethics and consequentialism (i.e. the 'ethics of justice'), the ethics of care rejects universal moral principles and focuses on particular human relations and situations.[523] Instead of learning universally applicable, 'rational' moral principles, it emphasizes the need for developing correct moral dispositions (e.g. sensitivity that allows someone to accurately perceive others' needs in specific situations).[524] (2) Opposition to universal rationality brings along opposition to impartiality. Impartiality, a general requirement of the ethics of justice, is based on the presupposition of detached individuals and neglects the moral relevance of 'subjective' emotional ties that exist in human relations.[525] We have limited resources for caring and we preserve these resources to those with whom we are bound in a positive emotional tie. Far from being a sentimental theory, the 'toughness' of care ethics compels us to make priorities in caring and dictates actions that are sometimes opposite to the principles of deontological ethics (e.g. killing a husband who has been brutally abusing his wife and children for years).[526] (3) The traditional notion of autonomy, conceived as individuality and separateness is also challenged in the framework of care ethics. If people are mutually interdependent, autonomy can only be realized through positive human relations fostered by caring for each other. Somewhat paradoxically, care ethicists claim that human relations and interdependence increase autonomy because autonomy is not simply equivalent with the lack of obligations or with the number of available options. (4) Finally, an important difference between the two ethical approaches is that the ethics of justice emphasizes respecting individual rights-claims, while care focuses on

---

522 Ibid. 28.

523 The following characterisation of care ethics relies mainly on Kymlicka's *Contemporary Political Philosophy*.

524 Kymlicka 2002, p. 400.

525 Kymlicka 1992, p. 268.

526 Nel Noddings, *Caring*, in Held, Virginia (ed.): *Justice and Care: Essential Readings in Feminist Ethics*. Westview Press: Boulder, Co. 1995, p. 25.

accepting responsibilities.[527] Justice seems to emphasize the negative aspect of liberty (i.e. non-interference with the rights of others), while caring requires positive concern for the welfare of others. However, as Kymlicka notes, most theories of rights (with the exception of radical libertarian ones) also recognize the existence of positive obligations.

The rejection of universal moral principles seems to be a central element in both virtue ethics and the ethics of care. There are other points where the two approaches come close to each other, such as the emphasis of character and the role of subjectivity, emotions and social interconnectedness in the ethical decision-making process. Thus, it is not surprising that some authors categorize care ethics as a form of virtue ethics that attributes a prominent function to the virtue of care.[528] Two *caveats* shall be made before applying these conclusions to paternalism. Firstly, the distinction between ethics of justice and ethics of care is not necessarily a gender distinction. Though it might be true that men tend to argue along the rationale of justice and women along the rationale of care, it is not an exclusive categorization. Secondly, the two approaches seem to compliment, rather than exclude each other.[529] Care ethics is not necessarily incompatible with Kantian deontology which can serve as a 'supplementary' theory providing an additional check to care ethics and guaranteeing that the recipient of care is not used as means to an end in caring relations.[530] As Kultgen remarks, "the tenderness of caring and the rigor of rules go hand in hand in a 'well-ordered' society".[531]

4.4.2 Outlining a care-based approach to paternalism

If we collect the problems that puzzle us in the 'traditional approach' (cf. chapter 3), it will become clear how a 'combination' of virtue and care ethics can respond

527 Kymlicka 1992, p. 275.

528 Sander-Staudt, Maureen: "Care Ethics". *Internet Encyclopedia of Philosophy.* (http://www.iep.utm.edu/ care-eth/) (05.03.2015).

529 Pieper, Annemarie: *Van -e feminista etika?.* Áron Kiadó: Budapest 2004, p. 102.

530 Sander-Staudt, Maureen: "Care Ethics". *Internet Encyclopedia of Philosophy.* (http://www.iep.utm.edu/ care-eth/) (05.03.2015).

531 "Real societies are not composed of fully developed and completely caring people. People who do care must deal with many who do not. [...] Rules prohibiting wrongful behavior with a certain rigor and strictness are particularly in place in this context." Kultgen 1995, p. 33.

to these questions.[532] Far from providing clear-cut rules for paternalism, this chapter aims to outline some basic characteristics and normative implications of this approach. By applying care ethics' reinterpreted notion of autonomy, it seems possible to reconcile 'our general repugnance' towards hard paternalism with its 'apparent necessity' without resorting to a perfectionist rationale. Instead of looking for a comprehensive justificatory theory, the aim here is to specify when there is a 'need' for paternalism, whereby 'need' implies a need for caring. It seems important to take into account the following elements when examining the justification of paternalistic interventions:

1. The relational concept of autonomy
2. The virtue of care
3. Contextuality and case-based approach
4. The lack of a comprehensive theory
5. The responsibility for paternalistic care
6. The possibility of care in public relations

4.4.2.1 A reinterpreted notion of autonomy

It can be argued that if care is placed in the centre of a moral theory, it implies giving up the concept of autonomy. This seems unnecessary and even undesirable if one reinterprets autonomy in a way that it focuses on the importance of human relations instead of individuality and disengaged rationality. At first sight, 'relational autonomy' seems an oxymoron, at least if one understands autonomy as complete independence from external influences. If we consider autonomy as social in nature, self-authorship depends on how someone interacts with others,[533] and it develops through the development of human relations. This approach emphasizes the external conditions of autonomy; roughly speaking, the more (positive) relations we have, the more choices open to us and the more autonomous we become. Such process of development can be observed in the case of children, where caring is central to establish future autonomy. However, it also applies in the case of competent adults. Realization of personal preferences and life plans require cooperation with others. Caring social interactions can provide people with additional options by increasing positive liberty but they also have a role in the creation of self-identity and in the formation of preferences, which

532 Connecting the concepts of paternalism and care is not particularly common. The works of John Kultgen (1995) and Tom Beauchamp – James Childress (2009) must be mentioned in this respect.

533 Slote 2007, p. 67.

constantly change in response to input from the outside world. Thus, autonomy's internal conditions are also affected by human interactions (cf. communitarian ideas about the embedded self and externalist theories of personal autonomy in chapters 3.1.1 and 3.4).

The conceptual starting point is somewhat 'reversed' in the relational framework. Personal autonomy is not seen here as a 'metaphysically' given condition that is limited by external circumstances. Instead, social relations seem to have a constitutive or, at least, an important contributory role in the formation and the exercise of autonomy and autonomy affects social relations in exchange.[534] Relational autonomy has many different versions that can be categorized following the procedural – weakly substantive – strongly substantive classification. Those that belong to the procedural category are praised for their alleged content-neutrality. They are comparable to 'historical' conceptions of autonomy as they emphasize the role of critical reflection in the historical process of preference formation and claim that autonomy is the result of a developmental process independent of the substantive content of preferences.[535] Representatives of 'relationally' procedural theories, like Diana Meyers, add that autonomy-skills (i.e. skills necessary for the realization of autonomy, e.g. introspection, imagination, self-definition, self-discovery) are formed by human relations and can also be damaged by oppressive gender socialization.[536]

Strongly substantive approaches to autonomy set normative constraints with respect to the content of preferences and values. Representatives of this approach claim that not everything can be wanted autonomously; there are objectively 'wrong' (e.g. self-harming or autonomy-diminishing) preferences that are incompatible with a substantive understanding of autonomy. But does it matter what kind of 'external' relations constitute autonomy? Irrespective of personal preferences, caring social relations seem to improve, while repressive and debilitating ones seem to undermine autonomy. Marina Oshana's 'externalist' account sets objective requirements for the quality of social relations instead of the content of internal preferences and values. People living under severe social constraint are not autonomous, even if they accept the oppressive relation and endorse the values

---

534 Ashley, Viv: Philosophical Models of Autonomy. (=Essex Autonomy Project Green Paper Report) 2012. (http://autonomy.essex.ac.uk/philosophical-models-of-autonomy) (03.04.2014).

535 Stoljar, Natalie: "Feminist Perspectives on Autonomy". In: Zalta, Edward N. (ed.): *The Stanford Encyclopedia of Philosophy*. Spring 2014. (http://plato.stanford.edu/entries/feminism-autonomy/) (04.03.2015).

536 Ibid.

associated with it. An oft-cited example is the case of Muslim women in fundamentalist societies who seem to 'willingly' accept their subordinated role but their acceptance is most likely the result of continuing repression and conditioning.[537] It is possible to argue that a "woman who willingly embraced the strictures imposed on her by the Taliban in Afghanistan should not be considered autonomous, whatever her attitude toward her social role may be".[538] As critics point out, such a substantive view of relational autonomy has built-in moral (egalitarian) presuppositions, consequently it is suspect for 'undue' perfectionism.[539]

Under the strongly substantive theories, exercising care that establishes positive social relations increases autonomy, even if the subject's actual preferences are not taken into account. In the procedural model, paternalistic interventions seem to be legitimate if they are limited to the development of autonomy skills that contribute to the formation of autonomy. There is an additional guarantee in care ethics that protects from 'undue' perfectionism, especially if care is linked to emotions such as empathy.[540] For Michael Slote, the question is how respect (a notion quite distant from emotions in its traditional sense) can be conceptualized in a sentimentalist framework of ethics. His answer is that someone respects another person's autonomy if he or she "exhibits appropriate emphatic concern" for the person when dealing with him.[541] For example, if someone feels emphatically towards the subject of compulsion (even if compulsion seems to violate autonomy in the traditional sense), he shows respect to the subject's autonomy. A mother, who takes her unwilling child to the hospital, can be fully emphatic with the child's fear of the doctor and, consequently, show respect for the child's autonomy.[542] Lack of respect for autonomy would be the lack of help; not caring about someone means not taking him as a human being, not recognizing his individuality, not recognizing his 'otherness'. This is how empathy can bring along respect for autonomy. Empathetic caring means that the actor can place himself

---

537 Oshana, Marina: *Personal Autonomy in Society*. Ashgate: Aldershot 2006, p. 101.

538 Westlund, Andrea C.: "Rethinking Relational Autonomy". *Hypatia* 24 (4) (2009), pp. 26–49, p. 30.

539 Ibid. See also Holroyd, Jules: "Relational Autonomy and Paternalistic Interventions". *Res Publica* 15 (4) (2009), pp. 321–336, p. 324–325.

540 Slote advocates such a sentimentalist approach in his recent book. He does not consider autonomy as a 'noumenal' feature of human beings which establishes respect for others, but in the other way around. He bases autonomy in respect, which is grounded in empathy. Slote 2007, p. 55.

541 Ibid. 57.

542 Ibid.

in the 'shoes' of the subject, which ensures that the subject of paternalism will not be handled as an instrument or as a means to an end. Emphatic caring does not only require focusing on a particular individual but also requires *engrossment* in the other person.[543] Someone who cares deeply and genuinely about someone else is open and receptive to the thoughts, desires, fears, etc. of the other human being. This seems to ensure that the paternalistic actor does not simply impose his own ideas about the good on the subject.

It is possible to conclude that relational autonomy seems generally less harsh on paternalism than the 'traditional' autonomy-based approach. There are disagreements about this statement. Slote, for example, writes that "it is less clear that care ethics will or should want to disagree with liberalism about paternalistic examples".[544] Obliging motorcyclists to wear crash helmets against their wishes is not only a violation of personal autonomy in the traditional sense. Such intervention can be regarded as being inconsistent with 'good relationships', even if the paternalistic actor is fully emphatic of the preferences of motorcyclists, which was Slote's previously articulated condition of respect for autonomy. The difference between this case and the parent-child example is that grown-up motorcyclists will (probably) not acknowledge the use of coercion later, thus paternalism seems to have a negative effect on relationships and seems to be inconsistent with relational autonomy. Coercion can surely ruin relations sometimes. Nevertheless, a certain degree of paternalistic coercion might be compatible with relational autonomy when the element of care 'shines through' the coercive character of a situation and builds a 'relational bridge' between the actor and the subject which strengthens mutual trust in the long run.

4.4.2.2 The virtue of care

It is an interesting question whether care and virtue ethics can be connected by classifying care as a fundamental moral virtue.[545] Care seems to develop human nature through developing the capacities of empathy in individuals, thus it

---

543 Ibid. 12.

544 Ibid. 84.

545 It is disputed whether the ethics of care is part of virtue ethics or it is separate from it. Some care-ethicists deny that care is a virtue in itself. Noddings understands care as a framework that gives rise to the development of virtues (e.g. patience). Virginia Held suggests that care is a virtue from which all other virtues flow. Some claim that conceptualizing care as a virtue leads to an overly restrictive theory because it limits care only to the sphere of personal relations (i.e. only to those people with whom someone happens to be in a caring relation). Cf. Noddings in Held 1995, p. 23; Slote

corresponds well to an 'Aristotelian' definition of virtues. Caring about others is an important element of human life, even in individualistic and alienated modern societies.[546] John Kultgen argues that care is an essential element of humanity:

> "Care is not only an essential structure of the way we exist, it is at the core of the way we should exist. We should care for and take care of ourselves. We should take care of certain others as we do ourselves. [...] To be human, is to be able to care, to want to care, and to care deeply and widely. The companions of care are commitment, obligation, anxiety, and inevitably failure and guilt. [...] When we endure a lifetime of care, we become careworn. But we also become human. The crow's-feet of care are marks of humanity."[547]

In a relational framework, care does not only increase the autonomy of the recipient of care, but also the autonomy of the care-giver by fostering a positive relation between the two. Care can make people autonomous, provided that it is given in moderation. Moreover, it seems to improve human character in general. Care has a source in universal human feelings (i.e. empathy) but it develops only by exercising it. In other words, everyone has an innate capacity to care and it can be developed by practice (or suppressed if not practiced). Thus, the intrinsic good of *caritas* seems to be that it establishes and strengthens positive social relations while fostering human character as well. Care, however, must stay in the 'golden middle' to qualify as virtue: both an exaggerated form of care (i.e. overcaring that involves excessive violation of autonomy) and the lack of care (i.e. that culminates in egoism and negligence towards others) transform to vice. Just as in the case of other virtues, the determination how to exercise care in the 'right' way is determined by *phronesis*, an intellectual virtue that is generally translated as 'practical wisdom' or 'prudence'. Caring can be wrong in many different ways: for example, one can care for the wrong person or for the wrong reasons; one can

---

2007, p. 9; Herring, Jonathan: *Caring and the Law*. Hart Publishing: Oxford 2013, p. 76.

546 In the Christian tradition, 'charity' or *caritas* (in the sense of *agape* or love) is one of the three fundamental theological virtues. "Though I speak with the tongues of men and of angels, and have not charity, I am become *as* sounding brass, or a tinkling cymbal. And though I have *the gift of* prophecy, and understand all mysteries, and all knowledge; and though I have all faith, so that I could remove mountains, and have not charity, I am nothing. And though I bestow all my goods to feed *the poor*, and though I give my body to be burned, and have not charity, it profiteth me nothing. [...] And now abideth faith, hope, charity, these three; but the greatest of these *is* charity." Paul's First Letter to the Corinthians, 13.

547 Kultgen 1995, p. 7.

exhibit care at the wrong time or for the wrong thing.[548] The appropriate exercise of care seems to be situation-specific and subject to the exercise of practical wisdom.

An additional question is whether care is a virtue distinct from other virtues or it can be subsumed under seemingly similar practices or character traits. Love might be considered a similar phenomenon to care, insofar as loving relations imply caring for the loved ones. However, love is reserved for a 'closed set' of people while care does not seem to exclude formal relations in which care is exercised toward indefinite subjects. Moreover, love is not a character trait such as e.g. bravery; it is an emotion and emotions cannot be virtues in the Aristotelian framework. Friendship is another possible candidate to equate care with; Aristotle mentions friendship (friendliness) as a moral virtue that stands between the vices of 'obsequiousness' and 'sulkiness'.[549] The word has a wider meaning in the Nicomachean Ethics than in ordinary English: it can stand for any mutual attraction between two human beings.[550]

It can be argued that paternalistic practices, if genuinely motivated by benevolence, exhibit – as a common denominator – the virtue of care. Overall, care seems to be an important element of justifiable paternalism. If paternalistic practices exhibit care and care is a virtue, then paternalism contributes to the development of a virtuous character and to the self-fulfillment of individuality: it helps people to reach 'completeness' (*eudaimonia*). At this point, the bad connotations attached to paternalism in the deontological framework are removed: paternalism becomes not only non-objectionable but in some cases morally valuable.

4.4.2.3 Contextuality and case-based approach

The term 'contextuality' might refer to a general ontological feature of human existence, i.e. the phenomenon of being 'thrown into the world' at a particular place and time in a particular network of relationships.[551] Some ethicists aim to establish a notion of care on Heidegger's central ontological concept, *Sorge*.[552]

548 Halwani, Raja: "Care Ethics and Virtue Ethics". *Hypatia* 18 (3) (2003), pp. 161–192, p. 182. See also Bennett, Frederick Joseph: The Virtuoso Human: A Virtue Ethics Model Based on Care. MA thesis, University of South Florida: 2011, p. 76.

549 Ross 1995, p. 195.

550 Ibid. 143.

551 Kultgen 1995, p. 34.

552 For a critique of these approaches, see Paley, John: "Heidegger and the Ethics of Care". *Nursing Philosophy* 1 (1) (2000), pp. 64–75.

The following is a short excursion to Heidegger's phenomenology in order to examine its possible implications for paternalistic care. For Heidegger, *Geworfenheit* is a basic existential characteristic of *Dasein* (the 'human self'). Being thrown into existence, the *Dasein* is characterized by *Angst* and *Sorge*, a constant worried 'concern' or 'care' about itself and its future.[553] *Dasein's* mode of being is basically Being-in-the-world but it also implies Being-with-others in the world. "The world of Dasein is a with-world [*Mitwelt*]. Being-in is *Being-with* Others."[554] In this Being-with Others, *Sorge* transforms from concern to a different form of care called solicitude (*Fürsorge*). "But those entities towards which Dasein as Being-with comports itself, do not have the kind of Being which belongs to equipment ready-to-hand, they are themselves Dasein. These entities are not objects of concern, but rather of *solicitude*."[555] Solicitude is an essential ontological characteristic of the *Dasein*.

Regarding its positive modes, solicitude has two extreme forms, resembling somewhat to the soft-hard distinction of paternalism. Solicitude can take away 'care' from the Other and put itself in his position in concern: it can *leap in* for him. "In such solicitude the Other can become one who is dominated and dependent, even if this domination is a tacit one and remains hidden from him [i.e. hard paternalism]."[556] Solicitude can also *leap ahead* of the Other, not to take away his 'care' but rather to give it back to him [i.e. soft paternalism that protects and respects the authenticity and the autonomy of the subject]. Though *Sorge* is a central concept of Heidegger's philosophy, a lot of commentators are reluctant to directly connect this concept to paternalistic care, because this would attribute direct ethical implications to Heidegger's ontology.[557] Solicitude is a fact of life, a mode of being but Heidegger does not say which way of solicitude should be followed (i.e. the one which dominates or the one which liberates).

From this short phenomenological excursion, it is possible to draw the conclusions that individuals are ontologically related to each other and that contextuality (*Geworfenheit)* and care (*Sorge*) are basic ontological features of human

---

553 The translation of the word *Sorge* as care is misleading because it lacks the connotation of 'worries' that the German word has. Mahlmann, Matthias: "Heidegger's Political Philosophy and the Theory of the Liberal State". *Law and Critique* 14 (3) (2003), pp. 229–252, p. 235.

554 Heidegger, Martin: *Being and Time*. Blackwell: Oxford 1962, p. 155. Emphasis as in the original.

555 Ibid. 157. Emphasis as in the original.

556 Ibid.

557 See Paley's critique of deriving a normative ethical theory from Heidegger's ontology.

life. Besides its ontological aspects, contextuality might be an attribute of certain decision-making procedures as well. Arguably, if life has a 'contextual' character, decision-making should be also sensitive to the specificities of life. The importance of a theory that leaves adequate space for the consideration of the details of cases has been stressed in bioethics by authors who criticize 'principlism', i.e. the approach that derives action-guiding rules from a closed set of abstract normative principles.[558] A potential alternative to principlism is 'casuistry', an inductive form of reasoning which decides cases on the basis of 'paradigmatic' decisions that show similarities to the case in question.

With virtue ethics in the centre of our attention, the question is not how to derive right action from previous paradigmatic decisions, but how to derive right action from virtuous character. Thus, a care-based approach to paternalism seems to call for a context-based decision-making process that answers the question what would a virtuous (caring) person do in the specific situation. This can be called '*ad hoc* paternalism' as opposed to paternalism that rests on comprehensive ethical principles. "To be an *ad hoc* paternalist is to admit that one has no powerful, overarching test that will allow anything more than intuitive confidence (either before or after one acts) that one is on the right side of this line."[559] Kennedy's understanding of *ad hoc* paternalism is, however, different from a virtue-based account because it emphasizes 'intuitive confidence' as the only guidance that someone can have about paternalistic interventions. For him, the basis of paternalism is 'lived intersubjectivity'.[560] When facing a paternalistic choice in most cases, we cannot start 'hypothesizing' how the other feels, which ethical rules are 'for' or 'against' the paternalistic intervention, etc. We simply have to act, and we act to protect the other, because if he or she is harmed, we are harmed as well. This is due to the 'intersubjective unity' that exists between the paternalistic actor and the subject in the given situation. Thus, paternalism comes from the instinct of self-preservation and from the paternalistic actor's wish to avoid the pain of the other. On the other hand, care is something we need, enjoy and something that provides fulfillment.[561] The feeling of 'intersubjective unity' seems to develop on the basis of certain special relations or emotional ties that exist between the subject and the paternalistic actor. This unity probably exists between strangers as well but it is a matter of degrees. If unity is a matter

558 Gert, Bernard / Culver, Charles M. / Clouser, K. Danner: *Bioethics: a Return to Fundamentals*. Oxford University Press: New York 1997, pp.71–93.

559 Kennedy 1982, p. 638.

560 Ibid. 639.

561 Ibid. 640.

of degrees, we make priorities in caring and also in paternalism; it is natural that we care more for those whom we love, and this may justify a higher degree of paternalism towards them. To sum up, if 'intersubjective unity' develops through relations and emotional ties, it is necessary to thoroughly assess the context of paternalism to decide about paternalism's necessity.

4.4.2.4 *The lack of a comprehensive theory*

Closely related to the *ad hoc* character of paternalism, it seems necessary to acknowledge the impossibility of a comprehensive or universal theory that could always specify the 'right' thing to do in a situation of paternalism. As I tried to demonstrate in the previous chapters, various efforts have been made to interpret the harm principle in ways to save its comprehensive character; Mill's original intention was to create a principle that can "govern absolutely the dealings of society with the individual". Some would probably argue that the harm principle reflects the expectations of 'masculine justice' to provide objective, impartial and logical answers to all questions that comes within its scope. However, such an expectation seems exaggerated in relation to paternalism. It is probably better to work out 'guidelines' for evaluating paternalistic interventions:

> "Guidelines help us take into account what must be taken into account in the pursuit of a good life; they in no way relieve us of the burden of careful judgment that sometimes forces us to transcend the whole fabric of general truths to fulfill special demands of care in the flux of concrete relations with particular things and people."[562]

Kennedy also criticizes *principled* anti-paternalism for not being capable of explaining the actor's decision to intervene with the subject's autonomy. His argument is very similar to what I have asserted in relation to 'hard cases', i.e. that the autonomy-based approach to paternalism is unable to handle autonomous evaluative decisions. Kennedy's basic argument is that "when one collects the cases of paternalist intervention that can't be plausibly explained by a notion like capacity, it becomes clear that we can't be any more than ad hoc in our opposition to intervention".[563]

4.4.2.5 *The responsibility for paternalistic care*

In certain cases, paternalism is not only justified, but the actor seems morally responsible to act paternalistically. Under the traditional autonomy-based

562 Kultgen 1995, p. 34.
563 Kennedy 1982, p. 643.

framework, non-intervention seems to be the general rule. A duty to act paternalistically is exceptional and it is mostly related to cases when the subject is incompetent (e.g. mentally ill, minor, etc.). Caring paternalism, on the other hand, accepts the responsibility for caring and it is by this acceptance that the paternalistic actor shows adequate concern for the other. Overall, it is possible to say that the ethics of care does not only justify but sometimes necessitates 'hard' paternalistic interventions. Moreover, if care is a moral virtue, it is fostered through practice, an additional reason to practice caring paternalism in certain situations.

4.4.2.6 The possibility of care in public relations

Some moral philosophers assert that the public and private spheres operate according to different moral codes.[564] The public sphere is typically governed by abstract principles, i.e. by the ethics of justice, which is better suited to handle the public domain determined by the values of self-interest, competition and autonomy. The private sphere, on the other hand, is the domain of care ethics, which is sensitive to the issues of altruism and dependence. This separation seems plausible. However, it seems necessary to extend the ethics of care to the public sphere if someone wants to apply a care-based approach to paternalism in the sphere of legal institutions. Some writers have indeed challenged the public-private dichotomy. Slote argues that the ethics of care does not only complement classical ethical theories but offers an alternative to them.[565] It is unnecessary to restrict the notion of caring to people with whom we have an actual relationship; "one can have a caring attitude towards (groups of) people one is never going to be acquainted with".[566] Others claim that there is no need to apply different ethical theories for the public and private spheres, because these are not fundamentally different.[567] The separation seems artificial, especially when we consider that the 'infrastructure of care' permeates all social relationships, from the private to the public sphere. Care can 'spill over' from the private sphere to the public and *vice versa*. Care that a person experiences at home, for example, makes him more caring and attentive to people at his workplace.[568]

564 Clement, Grace: *Care, Autonomy, and Justice: Feminism and the Ethic of Care*. Westview Press: Boulder, Co. 1996, p. 67.

565 Slote admits that considering the incomplete character of care ethics, this statement can be subject to criticisms. Slote 2007, p. 2.

566 Ibid. 11.

567 For an overview of arguments, see Clement 1996, p. 69–75.

568 Kultgen 1995, p. 30.

5. Applications

5.1 Paternalism in the jurisprudence of the Hungarian Constitutional Court

5.1.1 Preliminary remarks

The expression 'paternalism' (i.e. its Hungarian equivalent, *paternalizmus*) appears only four times in the jurisprudence of the Hungarian Constitutional Court.[569] This does not mean that the Court did not have to deal with constitutional issues related to paternalism. Since it has started functioning in 1990, it had to examine the constitutionality of such 'typically' paternalistic cases like euthanasia, drug consumption, tobacco advertising, compulsory vaccination or seat-belt regulations.[570] My aim in this chapter is to analyse the most significant decisions related to paternalism, identify the 'strategy' of the Court in handling these cases and examine the arguments to see if there is a common ethical approach that informs the Court's decision-making. In my selection of cases, I focus mostly on classical 'harm-preventing' types of paternalism. It is also important to note that the Hungarian constitutional system has undergone significant changes since the writing of the main text of this book. As demonstrated by its preamble (the 'National Avowal'), the newly adopted Fundamental Law of Hungary takes a more 'value-saturated' approach to many constitutional issues, the effect of which still an open question with respect to the Court's jurisprudence on questions of paternalism.[571]

At first glance, the Court seems to adopt a deontology-based approach in most cases. When determining the justifiability of paternalism, the Court often

---

569 The decisions concerning sterilisation and registered partnership seem relevant from our perspective. The other two decisions related to hate speech and the operation of local governments use the word only in a rhetorical sense. Decisions 43/2005. (XI. 14) AB; 32/2010. (III. 25.) AB; 95/2008. (VII. 3.) AB, 18/2013. (VII. 3.), respectively.

570 Decisions 22/2003. (IV. 28) AB; 54/2004. (XII. 13.) AB; 37/2000. (X. 31.) AB; 39/2007. (VI.20) AB; 60/1993. (XI. 29.) AB, respectively. The judgments and their Engish translations are available at www.mkab.hu. I use these translations when quoting the decisions.

571 The Fundamental Law of Hungary was promulgated on 25 April 2011 and entered into force on 1 January 2012. My analysis mainly focuses on cases decided before 2012, most references are made to the country's previous constitution (Act XX of 1949).

stresses the voluntary decision-making capacity and the right to self-determination (i.e. autonomy) of the subject. As it was formulated in the so-called 'Rainbow-decision':

> "Everybody can harm him- or herself and can assume risks if he/she is capable of a free, informed and responsible decision. The law gives a wide range of possibilities for this by its noninterference, and the rights to self-definition and activity (Art. 54 of the Constitution) following from the general personality right, guarantee this possibility. The restrictive guardianship of the state is a matter of constitutional debates only in boundary cases (from the punishment of drug usage to euthanasia)."[572]

The legal basis for this autonomy-based approach is provided by the Court's jurisprudence which derives the right to self-determination (not explicitly mentioned in the Constitution) from the right to human dignity enshrined in Article 54 (1). The Court derived numerous fundamental rights (e.g. right to self-determination, right to privacy, right to bodily integrity, etc.) from human dignity by interpreting it as the basis of a 'general personality right'. As it was originally stated in one of the first decisions of the Court: "The general personality right is a 'mother right', i.e., a subsidiary fundamental right which may be relied upon at any time by both the Constitutional Court and other courts for the protection of an *individual's autonomy* when none of the concrete, named fundamental rights are applicable to a particular set of facts."[573] This extensive interpretation of human dignity can be criticized for its activism, although it is not unique in the practice of constitutional courts.[574] Some commentators attribute this extensive moral reading of the Constitution to the influence of Ronald Dworkin.[575] Dworkin claims that the clauses of the American Constitution that protect individual

---

572 21/1996. (V. 17.) AB, chapter III, section 2.

573 8/1990. (IV. 23.) AB, chapter III. Emphasis added.

574 The German *Bundesverfassungsgericht* and the US Supreme Court use similar interpretative methods to derive non-explicitly expressed fundamental rights from various constitutional regulations. The German court's method relies on human dignity, while the American uses the due process clauses of the Fifth and Fourteenth Amendments (cf. 'substantive' due process). See, e.g.: Catherine Dupré, *Importing Human Dignity from German Constitutional Case Law*, in Halmai, Gábor (ed.): *The Constitution Found?*. INDOK: Budapest 2000, p. 220; Tóth, Gábor Attila: *Túl a szövegen: Értekezés a magyar Alkotmányról*. Osiris: Budapest 2009.

575 Tóth, Gábor Attila: "Az eljárási alkotmányosság tartalma". *Fundamentum* 8 (3) (2004), pp. 5–33, p. 16. László Sólyom, the first President of the Court has also acknowledged Dworkin's influence on the Court's jurisprudence. He stated that "the moral perception of the justice plays a role in hard cases". See the interview with László Sólyom in Halmai 2000, p. 383.

and minority rights "are drafted in exceedingly abstract moral language. [...] According to the moral reading, these clauses must be understood in the way their language most naturally suggests: they refer to abstract moral principles and incorporate these by reference, as limits on government's power".[576] Following a similar reading of the Hungarian Constitution's human dignity clause, there must be certain 'unenumerated rights' rights that aim to protect moral values on which there are overlapping consensus in the society. Personal autonomy seems to be a value like that. A good example of the value attributed to autonomy appears in László Sólyom's concurring opinion in the case abolishing death penalty.[577] Adopting a Kantian reasoning, he claims that "[t]he right to human dignity means that the individual possesses a core of autonomy and self-determination beyond the reach of all others, whereby – according to the classic formulation – the human being remains a subject and cannot be transformed into an instrument or object".[578]

Despite the Court's seemingly anti-paternalistic starting point, there are quite few judgments with hard paternalistic outcome in its jurisprudence (cf. decisions on drug use and euthanasia). The Court generally avoids references to 'external' (i.e. non-legal) values because of the Constitution's alleged value neutrality since its amendment in 1990.[579] It especially tries to refrain from making moral judgments. Still, some judgments seem to take sides in questions of what constitutes a 'good' or 'valuable' life for citizens and seem to be informed by 'hidden' perfectionist considerations. A possible strategy for justifying these is to apply a sliding scale of voluntariness and transform the question to soft paternalism by raising the level of voluntariness required for valid consent (cf. decisions on sterilisation, drug use and vaccination).

---

576 Dworkin, Ronald: *Freedom's Law: The Moral Reading of the American Constitution*. Oxford University Press: Oxford 1996, p. 7.

577 23/1990 (X. 31.) AB.

578 Sólyom's formulation has been reiterated by the Court several times. For this exact quotation, see 39/2007. (VI. 20) AB, chapter IV, section 4.1. See also 64/1991 (XII. 17.) AB and 22/2003 (IV. 28.) AB.

579 Sólyom 2001, p. 689. As Sólyom explains, value neutrality had a stabilizing function after the political transition with respect to newly emerging ideologies, claims and interests. This neutrality was supported by the idea of the 'invisible constitution', according to which the jurisprudence of the Court constitutes a stable and coherent system independent from actual political or ideological influences. This concept appears in the concurring opinion of László Sólyom attached to the decision abolishing death penalty but it was not repeated in subsequent decisions of the Court. Gábor Halmai, *The End of Activism?*, in Halmai 2000, p. 15.

In constitutional law, paternalism generally appears as a limitation of the right to self-determination. The Hungarian Court applies the so-called 'necessity-proportionality test' to determine the constitutionality of restrictions on fundamental rights. Consequently, paternalistic restrictions are also subject to this test, which consists of three prongs: the limitation must be (1) necessary, (2) proportionate (i.e. the importance of the desired objective must be proportionate to the restriction of the fundamental right) and (3) suitable to reach a legitimate aim. These aims can be threefold:

> "In the permanent practice of the Constitutional Court, a regulation that restricts a fundamental right is only constitutional if it is suitable to achieve a legitimate objective of the legislator and also if it meets the requirement of proportionality and necessity. The individual fundamental rights of people may be restricted on the basis of the legitimate objective of protecting the fundamental rights of others, *the State's duty to institutionally (objectively) guarantee fundamental rights* [...] and the achievement of certain constitutional public objectives."[580]

Since paternalism generally does not restrict the rights of others, the typical legitimate objective invoked in defense of paternalistic limitations is the State's 'institutional' duty to guarantee fundamental rights. This duty, for example, implies a positive obligation on behalf of the State to provide "the highest possible level of physical and mental health to everyone living in the territory of the Republic of Hungary".[581] This argument regularly comes up in self-harming cases, though the content of this obligation is not entirely clear (i.e. if it suffices to provide the institutions for health care or it demands that the State takes active steps to protect the health of citizens).

5.1.2 Decisions concerning homosexuality

The Hungarian Constitutional Court has delivered five judgments concerning the constitutional rights of homosexuals. The first judgment dealt with the issue of homosexual marriage and cohabitation, the second one with the freedom of association, while the third and the fourth decisions annulled certain discriminatory provisions of the Criminal Code. The most recent decision ruled on the constitutionality of registered partnerships.

The first judgment of the Constitutional Court, although refused to declare the statutory definition of marriage (defining marriage as a partnership essentially between man and woman) unconstitutional, it annulled the regulation of the

580 39/2007. (VI. 20) AB, chapter V. Emphasis added.
581 Hungarian Constitution, Article 70/D.

Hungarian Civil Code which restricted the notion of 'cohabitation' merely to the cohabitation of opposite sexes.[582] The decision said no to homosexual marriages, but it established the possibility of legally recognized homosexual cohabitation, which was finally realized with the amendment of the Civil Code in 1996.[583] This made Hungary the first of the new EU member states to acknowledge homosexual cohabitation.[584] Although the Constitutional Court does not establish its decision explicitly on moral grounds, it gives a traditional interpretation of marriage that is based much more on moral than rational reasons. The concept of marriage was not constitutionally defined before the introduction of the Fundamental Law in 2012,[585] and it was the Constitutional Court that worked out its meaning as a 'partnership between man and woman with the purpose of giving life to children'. Childbirth is not a necessary element of valid marriages, but the abstract possibility is (i.e. a couple of opposite sexes). It is not discriminatory under Article 70/A to exclude homosexuals from marriages; the requirement of equal treatment applies to separate homogeneous groups of men and women. However, the cohabitation of two persons, regardless of their sexes, creates values which deserve legal protection. It would be unfair to exclude same-sex couples from the benefits (e.g. inheritance without will, refusal of testimony, widower's pension) provided by the legal recognition of cohabitation.

The Court's neutral approach and its reluctance to use explicit moral arguments in its reasoning became evident from the second homosexual decision, the so-called 'rainbow-decision' from 1996.[586] The Court emphasized that it did not wish to judge homosexuality from the viewpoint of morals. It observes that public morality plays less and less role in the decision of homosexual cases. Since the moral perception of homosexuality can significantly differ within a society, reference to a common moral standard is unreasonable. The Court also realizes that public morality can be present in the 'disguise' of other, easier defendable

---

582 14/1995. (III.13.) AB.

583 Article 578/G. of the previous Hungarian Civil Code (Polgári Törvénykönyvről szóló 1959. évi IV. Törvény).

584 Uitz, Renáta: "Melegházasságon innen és túl – A meleg párok esete a köztársasággal". *Fundamentum* 9 (2) (2005), pp. 73–83.

585 Article *L* of the Fundamental Law of Hungary declares that marriage is a union between a man and a woman established by voluntary decision.

586 21/1996. (V.17.) AB.

values and interests. Despite this rhetoric, a negative value judgment is also traceable in the Court's reasoning.[587]

The case before the Court involved the participation of persons under 18 in civil organizations protecting the interests of gay and lesbian people. Two fundamental rights had to be balanced against each other: freedom of association (Article 63 of the Constitution) and the right of children "to receive the protection and care of their family, and of the State and society, which is necessary for their satisfactory physical, mental and moral development" (Article 67 of the Constitution). The Court adopts a paternalistic reasoning, recognizing – following the traditional autonomy-based approach – the right of competent people to cause harm to themselves, while emphasizing the necessity of protection of minors:

> "Everybody can harm him- or herself and can assume risks if he/she is capable of a free, informed and responsible decision. […] But in the case of children, the Constitution itself and international treaties also compel the State to protect the development of the child from dangers and risks, exactly in order that the child can prepare for responsible and informed decisions once his/her maturity (supposed to correlate with age) renders him/her capable thereof."[588]

It claims that the Hungarian state has a positive obligation to protect the sound physical, mental and moral development of children. This obligation can justify a paternalistic restriction on freedom of association. The self-harm caused by participating in a homosexual organization is the harm related to admitting publicly one's homosexual orientation. The judges argue that the open declaration of homosexuality is an existentially challenging decision, which seriously affects the life of the individual.

> "The Constitutional Court does not qualify homosexuality from a moral point of view. […] In the present case, however, it cannot disregard either the peculiarities of homosexuality or the current social situation of homosexuals. […] Publicly assuming homosexuality, of any kind, is an existentially decisive decision also because of the current social reception of homosexuality by society; there is much to be assumed and later any change is difficult."[589]

According to the Court, a young person is definitely not mature enough to make such an important decision. Putting aside the question whether minors are really incapable of making this decision, the amount of harm suffered seems also

587 Halmai, Gábor: "Egy alkotmánybírósági (elő)ítélet nyomában". *Világosság* 37 (7) (1996), pp. 34–41.

588 21/1996. (V.17.) AB. chapter III, section 2.

589 Ibid.

debatable. The basis of the Court's paternalistic standpoint is the social harm related to the event of 'coming out'. However, as Gábor Halmai argues, reference to the majority's moral condemnation and to potential social harms is simply not enough to exclude young people from homosexual organizations.[590] It implies a hidden value judgment to refer to Article 67 (child's right to satisfactory physical, mental and moral development) because it suggests that homosexuality affects the moral development of the youth. Article 67 would not be applicable, if the judges themselves did not consider homosexuality as morally wrong. Therefore, the 'rainbow-decision' – despite all its rhetoric on the neutrality of the Court – seems to be morally biased against homosexuality.

The third judgment was delivered in 1999.[591] It concerned the constitutionality of incest, a crime enshrined in Article 203 of the Hungarian Criminal Code.[592] The Court acknowledges in the reasoning of the decision that incest is essentially a moral crime. The opinion of the society is so undivided on this issue that criminalization cannot be questioned. However, one of the applicants, based on the lack of actual harm to society, asked for full decriminalization and claimed that such acts should not be regulated by criminal law. They should be treated by medical, psychological and scientific means. This application was turned down. The second application was decided in favour of the applicant. The third paragraph of Article 203 punished the heterosexual intercourse and homosexual sodomy of siblings. Heterosexual sodomy of siblings was not criminalized. The Court found this regulation discriminatory under the non-discrimination clause of the Constitution (Article 70/A) and decriminalized the homosexual sodomy of siblings. As a consequence, incest between siblings can only take place via (heterosexual) intercourse; heterosexual and homosexual sodomy do not constitute a crime in such cases. This regulation is retained by the new Criminal Code presently in force.[593]

The fourth judgment concerning homosexual relations was delivered in 2002.[594] It is basically an 'age of consent' case. Article 199 of the Criminal Code called for a penalty of up to three years of imprisonment of a person over the age of 18 years who committed consensual sodomy with a person of the same

590 Halmai 1996.

591 20/1999. (VI.25.) AB.

592 Hungarian Criminal Code (1978. évi IV. Törvény a Büntető Törvénykönyvről).

593 Article 199 of the Hungarian Criminal Code (2012. évi C. Törvény a Büntető Törvénykönyvről).

594 37/2002. (IX.4.) AB.

sex between 14 and 18 (i.e. 'sodomy against nature').[595] However, there was no similar regulation with respect to heterosexual sodomy. The judgment, although basically ruled in favour of the applicants, had been criticized because the motive behind the decision was not a fundamental change in the Court's approach but rather external pressure from various international organizations. The European Parliament declared that the harmonization of heterosexual and homosexual ages of consent is a precondition for the EU accession.[596] The European Commission of Human Rights found a violation of Article 8 in conjunction with Article 14 of the ECHR in the Sutherland case, which was very similar to the present Hungarian case.[597] The dissenting opinion of Judge János Strausz represents a conservative (according to some commentators, openly homophobic) view on homosexuality that emphasizes the state's paternalistic duties to protect minors. He argues that the differentiation between the homosexual and heterosexual age limits is neither arbitrary nor irrational. Homosexuals and heterosexuals constitute two separate homogenous groups and treating two distinct groups differently is unproblematic. Judge Strausz considers homosexuality a 'biologically abnormal' sexual practice, which might have serious impact on the social life and sound mental development of young people. It is the obligation of the state to protect them from adult homosexuals and to take care of their 'healthy' moral and sexual development.

The Court examined the constitutionality of the law on registered partnership for same-sex couples in 2010.[598] The majority opinion reiterates that marriage is given special protection under Article 15 of the Constitution and according to the Court's established jurisprudence, marriage is a relationship 'between man and woman with the purpose of giving life to children'. However, the possibility of same-sex registered partnerships does not endanger or otherwise 'relativize' the value of marriage because married heterosexual couples are not affected

595 The expression 'sodomy against nature' (*'természet elleni fajtalanság'*) already implies moral condemnation.

596 Resolution on Hungary's application for membership of the European Union and the state of negotiations (5 September 2001) COM (2000) 705-C5-0605/2000-1997/2175 (COS), article 14.

597 Sutherland v United Kingdom, no. 25186/94, Commission decision of 21 May 1996; Commission report of 1 July 1997. The Sutherland case is discussed in the following chapter in more details.

598 32/2010. (III. 25.) AB.

adversely by granting similar rights to a different group.[599] In his concurring opinion, Judge András Bragyova agrees that the regulation is in line with the constitution but criticizes the majority for interpreting Article 15 as requiring the state to favour married couples (e.g. by providing financial benefits) to unmarried couples or singles. This is undue paternalism because it is not the state's business to decide between different conceptions of 'good life'. The majority opinion, however, suggests that marriage is the most valuable way of life and all other forms of cohabitation are permissible but not equal to marriage.

5.1.3 Drug policy and paternalism

The Constitutional Court delivered its (in)famous decision on the constitutionality of Hungarian drug regulation in 2004.[600] A complex, but often criticized decision,[601] it touches on different parts of the legislation, including problems of norm-clarity, compliance with international regulations but also on substantial issues related to the right to self-determination and paternalism.[602] Unconstitutionality was partially established with reference to the unclear character of certain expressions in the Criminal Code that violate the constitutional requirement of legal certainty, such as 'joint drug consumption' or 'without the licence of an authority'.[603] Putting aside the examination of these 'formal' questions, the following analysis focuses on the issues of self-determination and paternalism.

---

599 In a previous decision, the Constitutional Court found unconstitutional the proposed regulation of registered partnership on the grounds that it was also open to heterosexual couples. Since registered partnership is very similar to marriage, it is possible that they 'compete' with each other which violates the special protection afforded to marriage in the Constitution. Cf. 154/2008. (XII. 17.) AB.

600 54/2004. (XII. 13.) AB.

601 See, for example, Győrfi, Tamás: "Üzenet az elefántcsonttoronyból". *Fundamentum* 9 (1) (2005), pp. 73–85; Lévay, Miklós: "Paternalizmus és jogbizonytalanság". *Fundamentum* 9 (1) (2005), pp. 86–98; M. Tóth, Balázs: "Zavaros szigorúság". *Fundamentum* 9 (1) (2005), pp. 99–108; Dénes, Balázs: "Drog és jog". *Beszélő* 10 (1) (2005) (www.beszelo.c3.hu/cikkek/drog-es-jog); Küpper, Herbert: "A szocialista maradványok szerepe a magyar alkotmányban". *Fundamentum* 11 (4) (2007), pp. 53–60.

602 Győrfi 2005, p. 73.

603 The Court's problem with the term 'joint consumption' was that in the system of the Criminal Code, joint perpetration can be classified in various ways (i.e. co-offenders, contributors, or persons committing the offence in a group, in a criminal conspiracy or in a criminal organisation). As the Court remarks, "[…] it is not clear from the term 'joint consumption' what level of joint perpetration […] is meant by the joint

Petitions based on the right to self-determination, aiming for the decriminalization of drug consumption, were rejected by the Court. The Court makes it clear that there is no constitutional right to drug consumption:

> "The right to 'stupor' without restrictions does not follow even indirectly from Article 54 para. (1) of the Constitution, and it is not part of the right to have the highest possible level of physical and mental health, since self-narcotisation does not belong to the constitutionally guaranteed freedom of the individual's development of personality."[604]

However, the criminal punishment of drug consumption still seems to interfere with the right to self-determination and the general personality right derived from Article 54 (1) of the Constitution. "The general personality right [...] limits the State's punitive power [but] the tools of criminal law may [...] also restrict – within the limits of necessity and proportionality – the right to self-determination related to human dignity".[605] Consequently, the Court had to apply the 'necessity-proportionality test' to establish if the interference was legitimate or not.[606]

As for the legitimate aims of restricting drug use, two basic arguments are discernable in the Court's reasoning: (1) the protection from self-harm and (2) the

consumption of narcotic drugs" (chapter IV, section 10.3.1). The term 'without the licence of an authority' created exemptions from punishment but the Constitutional Court found that the obtaining such 'licence of an authority' was not clearly regulated, neither in the Criminal Code, nor in other complementary legal sources (chapter V). Apparently, removing these terms from the Criminal Code resulted in a stricter regulatory framework. The term 'joint consumption' (i.e. the consumption of drugs within a group) was introduced in 2003 in order to differentiate between acts of handing over drug fom one user to the other during consumption and acts of drug trading and trafficking. The former case was qualified less severely (with the possibility of exemption from criminal sanctions, under the condition of voluntarily undertaking medical or preventive treatment). Consequently, by removing 'joint consumption' from the Criminal Code, the Court created a more severe regulation for ordinary drug users. See Dénes 2005 and Győrfi 2005, p. 74. This 'negative legislation' seems unjustified activism on behalf of the Court and leads exactly to the sort of legal uncertainy that the Court tried to avoid. See Lévay 2005, p. 93; Győrfi 2005, p. 75; M. Tóth 2005, p. 105. See also section 1 of the dissenting opinion of Judge Mihály Bihari.

604 54/2004. (XII. 13.) AB, chapter IV, section 4.1.

605 Ibid. chapter IV. section 3.1.

606 Ibid. chapter IV. section 3.1. As Tamás Győrfi points out, the application of the necessity-proportionality test is not consequent in the Court's reasoning. There is an 'enumeration' of the possible legitimate aims that prohibition can serve but the application of the test is largely missing. Győrfi 2005, p. 78.

harm-to-others principle. (1) The paternalistic argument is quite straightforward – the Court includes in the concept of self-harm both the physical and mental harm caused by drugs and the harm caused by addiction to one's long-term autonomous decision-making capacity:

> "With regard to the consumer of drugs, this means that his or her positive right to self-determination is limited by his or her own rights to physical and mental health and the preservation of the freedom of action, *rather than by any other person's right.* Permitting the consumption of narcotic drugs would in fact eliminate the affected person's right to self-determination, as it would represent unconcern towards the limitation of the discretionary capacity of the person under the effect of and addicted to a narcotic substance."[607]

A sort of 'liberal perfectionist' argument appears here: autonomy is restricted for the sake of preserving autonomy in the long run. It is also similar to the argument from freedom maximization. According to the Court, the nature of addiction is such that "[p]aradoxically to the reference to the legality of 'free choice' stemming from the freedom of self-determination, the individual becomes increasingly subordinated to the use of drugs, i.e. the level of addiction is inversely proportional to the level of the freedom of action."[608] In order to avoid this, "the State must create for the members of the community, to the greatest extent possible, living conditions ensuring a *real, value-building freedom of action*".[609] As critics point out, the differentiation between "value-building" and "non-value building" freedom implies a moral judgment on behalf of the Court.[610] After all, who determines which freedom is value-building and which are the values that are worth being 'built'? The freedom to use drugs is certainly not such a freedom in the Court's interpretation. But actions that do not have a particular value still deserve to be respected; sitting before the television and eating potato chips, for example, is not a particularly valuable activity but it seems far-fetched to impose limits on it by legal means. On the other hand, it is possible to agree with the Court (and for that matter, with Mill, who argues the same in relation to slavery contracts) that freedom does not necessarily include the freedom to abdicate one's liberty.[611] A possible objection here can be that the Court does not differentiate between the addictive and harmful character of different drugs; it seems to have a stereotyped view of drug-consumers as addicted 'junkies' and does not

607 Ibid. chapter IV. section 3.1. Emphasis added.
608 Ibid. chapter IV, section 2.1.
609 Ibid. chapter IV, section 2.2. Emphasis added.
610 M. Tóth 2005, p. 99; Győrfi 2005, p. 77.
611 Mill 1975, p. 95.

consider recreational users who are aware of the risks and can use light drugs in a responsible way. It is hard to believe that someone who occasionally smokes marijuana gives away his freedom and becomes a total 'slave' of narcotics.

The physical and mental harm caused by drug consumption is another recurring argument in the Court's reasoning. As I mentioned in the introduction, Article 70/D of the Constitution imposes a positive obligation on the State to protect the health of its citizens. The State has a "constitutional duty to create an economic and legal environment, in line with the capacity of the national economy [...] that secures the most favourable conditions for the citizens' healthy lifestyle".[612] From here, the Court suddenly jumps to the conclusion that "to guarantee the enforcement of rights, in some cases it is necessary to set up rules limiting the possibility of action". However, if the institutional obligation of the state related to healthcare requires the prohibition of drugs, following this rationale, it would also require the prohibition of other unhealthy and no less dangerous substances (e.g. alcohol, tobacco or unhealthy food).

Citing the Rainbow-decision, the Court reiterates that everyone can harm him- or herself and can assume risks if he or she is capable of making a free, informed and responsible decision.[613] This anti-paternalistic starting point gradually changes with the examination of the decision-making capacity of drug users. There is an effort on the Court's part to avoid hard paternalism by turning the question to an issue of involuntary choice and soft-paternalism (cf. the soft paternalist strategy of Feinberg in chapter 2.2.1): "[...] the question is whether in the case of misusing drugs [...] the affected person's decision is in fact a free, informed and responsible one".[614] The Court's answer is a categorical no to this question. It depicts a quite horrifying picture of the effects of drugs and the nature of addiction, not differentiating between different substances that cause different levels of addictions. Addicted users cannot make free and informed decisions because "due to the damaging or elimination of chemical barriers, the affected person cannot control – or cannot fully control – his or her thoughts, behaviour, conduct and value judgements".[615] Even unaddicted users are unable to make a fully informed decision, because they have very little information about the potential consequences. This is partly due to the lack of 'tradition' of drug consumption in Hungary. "As there are no traditions of using narcotic drugs in Hungary, one cannot take it for granted that there is a high level of individual

612 54/2004. (XII. 13.) AB.
613 54/2004. (XII. 13.) AB, chapter IV, section 4.1.
614 Ibid.
615 Ibid.

experiences and knowledge in society about the consequences, effects and risks of the particular substances."[616]

Herbert Küpper also criticizes the decision for its paternalistic character which he attributes to a peculiar understanding of social rights characteristic to communist legal systems.[617] The Constitutional Court seems to follow this tradition when interpreting the protection of the right to health as requiring the restriction of other basic rights (i.e. the right to self-determination). The decision can only be understood against the backdrop of a 'paternalist-interventionist' state attitude that is the heritage of Hungary's socialist past.[618]

(2) The harm to others argument appears at various parts and in various forms of the Court's reasoning. The Court claims that "[t]he provisions of the Criminal Code on the misuse of drugs are aimed at protecting the whole population from the negative effects of drugs" and that "the legislator's action is justified by the need to eliminate both the abstract and concrete dangers for the purpose of safeguarding public interests".[619] But what could possibly be these abstract and concrete dangers?

One argument refers to public order and public security. According to the Court, drug consumption does not only affect individual consumers but also restricts the sense of security and freedom of action of others.[620] Crimes are related to obtaining money for drugs and to the uncontrolled behaviour of consumers.[621] Organized drug-dealing also poses a threat to society: "[t]hose distributing illicit drugs pose a threat to the health and welfare of the entire society, as well as to public safety and public peace."[622] In short, the crimes associated with illicit drug trade, both on the sides of supply and demand, seem to be a good reason for criminal prohibition. However, it is not a clearly established fact that criminalization necessarily decreases the number of related crimes. To accept such consequentialist reasoning, the Court would need to provide empirical proofs

---

616 Ibid.

617 Küpper 2007.

618 Ibid. 55.

619 Ibid. chapter IV, sections 3.2 and 3.3.

620 Ibid. chapter IV, section 2.2.

621 In section 2.2., the Court argues the following way: "[...] the narcotic effect causes an altered state of consciousness characterised [...] by the affected person's inability to control his or her own behaviour. Thus there is a real danger that he or she re-evaluates or disregards the restraints preventing persons of full capacity from endangering others."

622 Ibid. chapter IV, section 2.2.

in support of its position but researchers' opinions seem to be divided over this issue.

The other harm-to-others argument refers to the additional social costs connected to the treatment of drug consumers. The Court establishes that there is a positive duty for the State to provide at least symptomatic or 'palliative' care for those, who cannot take care of themselves, "even if such incapability is the result of their own choice".[623] The price has to be paid by non-users, which justifies the application of criminal law for preventive reasons. Reference to social costs, however, seems somewhat hypocritical here. The medical costs associated with smoking and alcohol use are much higher than the costs of treating drug addicts. Following the Court's rationale implies the prohibition of these substances as well.

To sum up, it is possible to say that under the veil of proclaimed value neutrality, the majority of the Court takes a firm stand on issues of drug policy and has certain hidden preconceptions about drugs and drug users.[624] The Court endorses a prohibitionist approach to promote full abstinence and claims that "[t]he 'eradication of drugs' is an acknowledged aim of the State [...], which is inseparably connected to the prevention of crime as well." It has a vision of a fully drug-free society but omits to consider the possibility of other, less coercive policies that emphasize, for instance, harm reduction instead of prohibition.[625] While condemning drugs, the Court suggests that smoking or drinking is less dangerous because they are less addictive and because "European culture has 'learnt' to live together with alcohol, nicotine and coffee, as they have been used for centuries".[626] The claim that Hungarian society has learned to live with alcohol and nicotine is unfortunately not supported by statistical facts. In the past three decades, 10.4 per cent and 19.6 per cent of the total mortality was caused by alcohol and smoking and in 2003 the number of alcoholics was estimated at nearly one million.[627]

5.1.4 Decision on sterilisation

The petitioners of the case challenged the constitutionality of the regulation concerning human sterilisation as contained in Section 187 of the Act on

623 Ibid. chapter IV, section 2.2.
624 Lévay 2005, p. 88.
625 Ibid. 89.
626 54/2004. (XII. 13.) AB, chapter IV, section 6.2.
627 Dissenting opinion of Judge István Kukorelli, section 2.1.

Healthcare.[628] The second paragraph of this section states that "sterilisation for family planning purposes may be performed on a person over the age of 35 years, or a person having three blood children." The petitioners claimed (inter alia) that this provision violates their right to self-determination and includes arbitrary and discriminative conditions. The question is basically if such 'hard' paternalism (i.e. prescribing an age limit or minimum number of children for competent adults to decide about their own reproductive capacities) can be justified or not. Even though the judges found the regulation unconstitutional, the decision does not categorically rule out the possibility of paternalism. Prescribing a higher age limit for sterilisation than the age limit of general competence, for example, remains permissible.

Three questions seem to play a central role in the Court's decision. (1) Does the right to self-determination cover the choice of sterilisation? (2) Do the paternalistic requirements of the Act on Healthcare violate the right to self-determination based on the autonomy and human dignity of individuals? (3) If yes, are these restrictions justifiable or is the right to self-determination an absolute right? The Court answers the first two questions in the affirmative and says partially 'yes' to the third one.

As to the *first question*, the Court, referring to its previous jurisprudence, reiterates that the right to self-determination provides a wide scale of protection for "persons capable of making free, informed and responsible decisions about their own bodies and lives."[629] This includes, for example, the issues of marriage, abortion or euthanasia.[630] Consequently, the Court establishes that self-determination also extends to the questions of contraception and sterilisation: "What is important in the present case is that on the basis of the right to self-determination, people may decide freely – within the limits set by statutes in accordance with the Constitution – on issues related to family life, marriage and having a child."[631]

The Court's answer to the *second question* is also affirmative. Following an anti-perfectionist reasoning, the Court states:

> "The Constitutional Court considers these two provisions [i.e. that the applicant must either be older than 35 years or have three blood children] to be restrictions of the right to self-determination stemming from the right to human dignity. In respect of those who can make *responsible and reasonable informed decisions* on their family lives, sexual

628 Act CLIV of 1997 on Healthcare.

629 43/2005. (XI. 14) AB, chapter II, section 3.

630 Decisions 22/1992. (IV.10.) AB; 64/1991. (XII.17.) AB and 22/2003. (IV.28.) AB, respectively.

631 43/2005. (XI. 14) AB, chapter II, section 3.

> lives, and on contraception and having children, the State may not prohibit sterilisation aimed at preventing the birth of children or further children in line with their *own views of life, or on the basis of their social and financial circumstances*. It follows from the right to self-determination that the State may not take over from the people the responsibility of choosing between methods and means of contraception and that of assessing advantages and disadvantages; that would be *unjustified paternalism*."[632]

Two explicit arguments appear against paternalistic intervention in this passage. There is the idea of a pluralist, ideologically neutral state that should refrain from imposing a uniform conception of the good on its citizens. The number of children somebody wants to have, is predominantly one's private business; making sterilisation dependant on this implies a perfectionist approach on behalf of the state. Secondly, the Court makes reference to the voluntary character of self-harm as 'responsible and reasonable informed decisions'. The perfectionist argument is a strong reason to eliminate the 'three children' requirement of the regulation, but it is not clear that the voluntariness standard in the present case can or should be connected to age of general competence (i.e. 18 years).

The *final question* is what kind of paternalistic limitations can be justified in the case of sterilisation. The right to self-determination and the right to personal integrity are not absolute, non-qualifiable rights, therefore the necessity-proportionality test applies. As mentioned before, there are three legitimate objectives for limiting fundamental rights: protecting the fundamental rights of others, the State's duty to institutionally guarantee certain rights and the achievement of constitutional public objectives.

The first aim does not seem to come into play since paternalistic regulations are directed towards primarily self-regarding actions. Utilitarian considerations, such as increasing the population, can serve as legitimate public objectives. "It is well known that the population of Hungary is decreasing and the age composition is becoming less and less favourable. The termination of unfavourable processes is a legitimate aim of the legislator."[633] However, "[…] in democratic states, the expedient tools for improving demographic statistics are […] regulations on sharing public burdens and social policy as well as the development of the culture of birth control, rather than the restriction of the right to self-determination."[634] The restriction in question fails the necessity-proportionality test because it is not suitable (i.e. disproportional) for the realization of otherwise legitimate objectives of population policy.

---

632 Ibid. section 4. Emphasis added.

633 Ibid. chapter III, section 2.

634 Ibid.

The third possibility to limit one's fundamental rights is connected to the State's positive duty to institutionally guarantee certain basic rights. In the present case, the right to self-determination can conflict with the state's obligation to provide protection for children (Article 67 of the Constitution) and its public duties concerning the protection of health (Article 70/D). Somewhat paradoxically, the Court also had to take into account the possibility of a conflict *within* the right to self-determination. Since sterilisation is mostly irreversible, it has a long-term effect on people's life. Short-term preferences, however, can clash with long-term ones: it is possible that the person choosing sterilisation changes his or her mind later. Consequently, appropriate legal guarantees are needed to protect the 'substantive' autonomy of citizens. In the words of the Court: "Article 54 (1) requiring institutional guarantees for self-determination and Article 67 (3) on the protection of the young require that the rules of sterilisation contain limitations and conditions."[635]

The Act on Healthcare contains several guarantees aimed at ensuring that the applicant for sterilisation makes an informed and free decision. The physician, for example, "shall provide information to the applicant [...] on other possibilities of contraception, as well as on the nature of the intervention and the possible risks."[636] The Act also prescribes a 'cooling off' period: sterilisation can be performed only three months after submitting the application.[637] In addition, the consent can be verbally withdrawn anytime before the operation.

Besides these rules, another guarantee can be to raise the age of consent necessary for sterilisation. This method is similar to Feinberg's sliding scale of voluntariness (cf. chapter 2.2.1), which requires higher standards of voluntariness in cases having serious or irreversible consequences. Self-mutilation seems irrational in most cases and therefore it requires that the subject shows that it is performed voluntarily and with a reasonable objective. The Court establishes that the age required for making a decision about sterilisation is not necessarily the same as the age of general competence (i.e. 18 years). The explanation is the following: "The basic assumption can be [....] that the persons affected by the restriction do not have the discretionary capacity required for sterilisation, as they cannot assess the *extraordinary consequences* of their decision."[638] Keeping in mind that the age of legal competence was set originally as a precondition for the validity of declarations related to property rights, deviating from it is

635 43/2005. (XI. 14) AB, chapter III, section 3.2.

636 Act on Healthcare, Section 187, para. 5.

637 Ibid. para. 4.

638 43/2005. (XI. 14) AB, chapter III, section 3.2. Emphasis added.

not unconstitutional *per se*. The Court declared that "[i]t is primarily up to the legislator to decide whether it is justified to apply, in determining the conditions of sterilisation, an age limit different from that of general disposing capacity".[639]

Prescribing a minimum number of children as a condition for sterilisation was found unconstitutional by the Court. This prescription seems to serve demographic aims, which is a legitimate governmental objective but may not be enforced by disproportionately restricting the right to self-determination. Also, reference to a 'minimally required' number of children suggests, in a perfectionist manner, the number of children that individuals must have in order to lead a good and satisfying life.

To sum up, the Court found unconstitutional the 'having three blood children' but not the age requirement to undergo medical sterilisation. However, due to the fact these are alternative rather than conjunctive conditions, the regulation would be more restrictive if the 'three blood children' requirement was simply removed from the statute.[640] Hence, both requirements were annulled, even though the Court emphasized that the legislator may (and with the *pro futuro* annulment, even encouraged that it should) define age limits different to the ones in the Civil Code. The legislator did not implement new regulations until 2014, which meant basically that anyone over the age of 18 could ask for sterilisation in this period. The Act on Healthcare was amended in 2013 prescribing a new minimum age (40 years) and reintroducing the 'three blood children' requirement necessary for the intervention.

Judge Attila Harmathy, in his dissenting opinion, refers to the European Court's judgment in the Laskey, Jaggard and Brown v United Kingdom case.[641] The applicants of this case, even though consented to cause injuries to each other during their sado-masochistic activities, were sentenced to imprisonment by domestic courts. The criminal punishment of the applicants constituted an interference with their rights to privacy and self-determination but the European Court, taking the protection of health into account, held that the interference did not qualify as a violation of Article 8 of the European Convention. Similarly in the present case, the state's duty to protect health (in the form of preventing permanent impairment to it, i.e. irreversible sterilisation) overrides the right to self-determination, especially that there are other means of contraception besides permanent sterilisation.

---

639 Ibid. section 4.1.

640 Ibid. section 4.2.3.

641 For a more thorough analysis, see chapter 5.2.

The dissenting opinion of Judge Éva Tersztyánszky-Vasadi goes one step further in paternalistic reasoning. She argues that sterilisation for family planning purposes is nothing else than arbitrary self-mutilation. Sterilisation performed for reasons other than medical ones causes *disability* which is contrary to human dignity. Therefore, sterilisation is unprotected by the right to self-determination. It seems that she considers surgical sterilisation as a harm-to-others issue, where the consent of the subject is irrelevant. She explicitly rejects the harm principle in her reasoning but, quite paradoxically, denies that her approach is paternalistic:

> "The statement that 'everyone may harm him- or herself' is not of general and unconditional applicability, and it cannot be applied in the present case, either. [...] The State's commitment to constitutional values – such as life, human dignity, or the highest possible level of physical and mental health – *does not constitute paternalism in relation to individuals*. In my opinion, it is a question to be specifically examined whether the right to self-determination can theoretically include cases where the person harms him- or herself with the active participation of another person (medical institution, physician) *without a due reason* – e.g. a medical one."[642]

In spite of her categorical approach in this passage, she argues later that the problem with the majority decision is that it fails to provide adequate guarantees for the voluntariness of sterilisation. After removing the objective criteria (being over the age of 35 or having three blood children), no adequate guarantees are left in the statute (the obligation of information and the compulsory waiting time cannot be considered as such). It may not be ignored that even persons with full capacity can temporarily find themselves in helpless situations where they cannot actually make free and informed decisions.

5.1.5 Euthanasia

According to the current regulations, active voluntary euthanasia and physician assisted suicide are not allowed in Hungary. The Act on Healthcare permits passive euthanasia (i.e. the possibility to refuse medical treatment) if the patient has full decision-making capacity and "suffers from an incurable disease that will inevitably lead to death within a short period of time".[643] A commission of three physicians must also examine the patient and state in writing that his or request is based on a "considered decision". The patient must reconfirm his or her intention before two witnesses after three days of the commission's report.

642 43/2005. (XI. 14) AB, dissenting opinion of Éva Tersztyánszky-Vasadi. Emphasis added.

643 Act CLIV of 1997 on Healthcare, Article 20.

The Constitutional Court examined the constitutionality of this regulation in its Decision 22/2003 (IV.28) AB. The petitioners argued that the requirements prescribed by the Act on Healthcare are disproportional limitations on the right to self-determination. They also claimed that the prohibition of active euthanasia and the fact that the Criminal Code did not distinguish assisted suicide from homicide were unconstitutional. All of the petitioners' claims were rejected.

The Court first establishes that neither the right to self-determination nor the right to human dignity is unrestrictable in the present case. The right to self-determination, a subsidiary right derived from human dignity, just like most other fundamental rights, can be restricted following the 'necessity-proportionality' test. Human dignity is only unlimited when manifesting itself in unity with human life. However, "the right to die with dignity [...] does not manifest itself in unity with the right to life; on the contrary: human dignity is violated by forcing a terminally ill patient to live".[644] This means that the exercise of one of these rights may push the other into the background and *vice versa*. In the reasoning, the Court refers to the principle of neutrality and tries to avoid perfectionist arguments. "A legal system based on ideologically neutral constitutional foundations may not reflect either a supporting or a condemning view about one's decision to end one's life; this is a sphere where, as a general rule, the State has to refrain from interference."[645] The dilemma, however, is that non-interference necessarily implies taking a 'pro-life' side in the case of euthanasia (cf. the argument of impossibility in chapter 3.4).

As for the refusal of treatment, we see that the Act on Healthcare is busy with ensuring the full voluntariness of the patient's refusal which is in line with the Court's general autonomy-based approach towards paternalism. Consequently, the Court did not find the requirements of the Act disproportionate with the objective of protecting the right to life. The petitioners challenged, *inter alia*, the requirement that the illness must lead to death within a *short* period of time established by a commission of physicians.[646] The petitioners argue that this may lead to arbitrary decision making. The Court states that the medical commission's decision is not subjective, but it is based on objective facts: the illness must be terminal and be expected to lead to death within a short period of time "according to the state of medical knowledge at the given time".[647] The petitioners also complained of the requirements that patients have to undergo an additional

644 Decision 22/2003 (IV.28) AB, chapter V.
645 Decision 22/2003 (IV.28) AB, chapter IV, section 6.1.
646 Decision 22/2003 (IV.28) AB, chapter IX. section 1.
647 Ibid.

medical examination and compulsory assessment of mental capacity. These, taken together with the requirement of reconfirming the refusal of treatment after three days, create an overly complicated procedure that violates the exercise of one's right to self-determination. The patient is required to express his consent to the refusal of treatment at least three times during the procedure, which is unnecessarily demanding according to some commentators.[648] For the Court, these prescriptions are necessary to ensure 'informed consent', especially that the state has a positive obligation to protect the right to life. "The committee, and in particular its psychiatrist member must interview the patient to verify that the patient suffers from a terminal illness and that the patient's will of refusing the intervention is clear and unambiguous".[649] Clearly, both the Act and the Constitutional Court focus on the 'consent to harm' question. However, from the aspect of care, it is hard to see how such regulation exhibits emphatic concern to the patient, especially that the voluntariness of consent could be established by less complicated means.

5.1.6 The compulsory vaccination of children

Another conflicting case of autonomy and state paternalism was the case when the Constitutional Court had to examine the constitutionality of the regulation that prescribed the compulsory vaccination of children.[650] The petitioners were parents who refused to vaccinate their children because it offended their religious convictions to "keep the body healthy by injecting antigenic materials into the veins". They argued that "the State acts as an unwanted guardian and makes decisions about the citizens [...] for its own objectives without providing an opportunity for deliberation."[651] It seems that the main question in this case was not if children can be paternalistically treated but rather who has the right to exercise paternalism over them.

The first question is which (and whose) right does compulsory vaccination violate. From the viewpoint of children, compulsory vaccination is a form of benefit-promoting paternalism that qualifies as soft paternalism, since children seem to lack the capacity to decide on issues with such serious and long-lasting consequences. Hence, in the deontological framework, such intervention is

648 Kis, János / Sajó, András: "Amicus Curiae az Alkotmánybírósághoz". *Fundamentum* 1 (2003), pp. 134–141, p. 135.
649 Act on Health Care, Article 23 (1).
650 39/2007. (VI.20) AB.
651 Ibid. chapter I, paragraph 4.

non-problematic because it does not interfere with autonomy. This accords well with the Court's assessment of the case: the right to self-determination is not violated by compulsory vaccination, since children are not in the position to exercise this right on their own. As it was already demonstrated in the case of sterilisation, exercising the right to self-determination in healthcare cases is not necessarily related to the age of competence prescribed in the Civil Code. In principle, minors are not excluded from making medical decisions on their own. However, the required standard of voluntariness seems to increase with the seriousness of the decision's consequences. Citing the Rainbow-judgment, the Court establishes that where laws do not regulate minors' and juveniles' exercise of rights, it has to be determined on a case-by-case basis which fundamental rights the child can exercise, or who should exercise these on his or her behalf. "The possibility of the child's exercise of fundamental rights – including the right personally to exercise them – gradually widens by age and by the development of an ability of decision considering the consequences of exercising a right."[652] In the present case, the Court ruled that minors do not have the capacity necessary for exercising the right to self-determination because they are unable to assess the long-term advantages and disadvantages of vaccinations.

In sum, compulsory vaccination does not interfere with the minor's right to self-determination. It does, however, interfere with the minor's right to bodily integrity and with the parents' right "to take care of their children in accordance with their ideological beliefs and conscience".[653] A person is entitled to the right to physical integrity regardless of his or her decision-making capacity.[654]

The Court's examination whether these interferences can be justified follows its established jurisprudence. The legitimate objectives of interference are the State's constitutional duty to protect children and its epidemiological tasks related to the protection of public health.[655] Concerning the necessity of compulsory vaccinations, the Court admits that "several democratic countries do not regard compulsory vaccination as the method to improve the immunization rate of society" and that the World Health Organization suggests that "the key to effective public health measures is cooperation between the authorities and the people" instead of coercion. Nevertheless, the Court rules that the present system

---

652 39/2007. (VI.20) AB, chapter IV, section 3.2. (with reference to 21/1996 (V. 17.) AB).

653 As jointly defined by Article 60 (1) and 67 (2) of the Constitution. See chapter IV, section 6.2.

654 39/2007. (VI.20) AB, chapter IV, section 4.2.

655 Articles 67 (1) and 70/D of the Constitution, respectively.

of vaccinations is 'not unnecessary' to protect children and the whole society against infections and epidemics.[656]

A delicate question is raised by the tension between parents' right to exempt their children from vaccination with reference to their religious conviction and the state's positive duty to provide protection and care for the satisfactory physical, mental and moral development of children. The state can grant exemptions from certain obligations when issues of conscience or religious conviction are at stake. However, such exemptions must be the result of a careful balancing procedure (the Court's so-called 'comparative test of burdens') that takes into account value pluralism against the equal rights and obligations of all citizens and the specific circumstances of each case (e.g. how closely the requested exception is related to the religious dogma of the applicant).[657] The Court, in the present case, found that compulsory vaccination did not violate parental rights, mainly for two reasons. Firstly, the debated issue was not whether competent adults are allowed to refuse vaccinations on religious grounds but whether they may refuse this on behalf of their children. Secondly, the regulation complies with the requirement of state neutrality because the contested provisions are not based on accepting the truth of ideologies or dogmas (i.e. they do not favour one dogma

656 39/2007. (VI.20) AB, chapter IV, section 3.6.

657 The Court describes the 'comparative test of burdens' in chapter 5.1. of the reasoning: "In constitutional democracies it is a frequently debated issue whether citizens may be exempted based on their conscience and religious beliefs from statutes that prescribe general obligations. [...] When considering the proportionality of the fundamental right restriction in this type of regulation, the Constitutional Court applies a different, so-called 'comparative test of burdens' for those whose conscience and religious freedoms are also violated by the regulations. On the one hand, one should take into consideration the basic principle of a state under the rule of law which says that everybody has rights and obligations in the same legal system, and therefore the statutes apply to all in such a way that the law treats everybody as equals [...] On the other hand, it should not be ignored that the fundamental values of a constitutional democracy include variety within the political [...] Due to the various and sometimes contradicting constitutionality criteria, the constitutionality issue of whether an exception should be made from the general laws due to the freedom of religion may only be decided case by case. The decision is largely influenced by, for example, the question of whether the requested exception is closely related to a dogma, religious ceremony and also whether the exception violates the rights of non-members of the religious community."

over the other) but they are based on scientific facts that apply to everyone, regardless of their beliefs.[658]

To sum up, the Constitutional Court did not find the system of compulsory vaccination unconstitutional in general. Some minor parts of the regulation were found unconstitutional, namely that information affecting the rights and obligations of citizens (e.g. the exact age and method of receiving the vaccination) was not communicated satisfactorily and that the right to an efficient legal remedy was violated by the Act on Healthcare when prescribing that vaccination is 'enforceable without delay' regardless of the outcome of the appeal procedure.

5.2 Moral paternalism and the European Court of Human Rights

5.2.1 Legal moralism

5.2.1.1 The historical progress of the debate on legal moralism

As discussed in chapter 3.2 in details, the harm principle in its pure form radically limits the boundaries of state intervention, allowing the limitation of individual liberty only if it is necessary to prevent harm to others. All measures of legal paternalism and moralism are excluded from the sphere of legitimate state interventions.

Mill was adamant that the enforcement of morals should not be the subject of criminal law.[659] James Fitzjames Stephen challenged Mill's position in his book *Liberty, Equality, Fraternity* published in 1873. Stephen claims that "[...] there are acts of wickedness so gross and outrageous, [...] that they must be prevented at any cost to the offender and punished if they occur with exemplary severity."[660] Feinberg categorizes Stephen as a 'pure legal moralist in the strict sense',[661] because he is concerned with inherently immoral evils and does not refer to some kind of indirect social harm caused by immoral actions. In fact, the attractiveness of Stephen's argument lies in its simplicity. It is difficult to dispute such simple claim but the 'burden of proof' seems to be on Stephen to show that such 'inherently immoral' evils actually exist.[662] He asserts that the prevention of immorality

---

658 39/2007. (VI.20) AB, chapter IV, section 5.2.

659 Lee, Simon: *Law and Morals: Warnock, Gillick, and Beyond*. Oxford University Press: New York 1986, p. 23.

660 Stephen 1993, p. 102. See also Feinberg 1990, p. 44.

661 Feinberg 1990, p. 9.

662 Feinberg tries to give examples of such evils. Ibid. 128.

is a proper end in itself for coercion and immorality can be determined by reference to the moral code of the majority. However, as mentioned in chapter 3.2.2, Stephen was a utilitarian himself and tried to justify the enforcement of morals on utilitarian grounds.[663] Thus, there seems to be a contradiction between the allegedly 'pure' character of Stephen's moralism asserted by Feinberg and Stephen's utilitarianism that takes into account the harmful (i.e. utility decreasing) character of immoral actions.

In the twentieth century, the issue of legal moralism came into the forefront of public attention with the publication of the Wolfenden Report, examining the law and practice relating to homosexual offences and prostitution.[664] The Report moved away from the traditional moralist approach of criminal law, when concluding that "unless [...] the sphere of crime [can be equated] with that of sin, there must remain a realm of private morality and immorality which is, in brief and crude terms, not the law's business".[665] The committee accordingly recommended that homosexual behaviour between consenting adults in private and prostitution itself should not be a criminal offence, though related harmful or offensive public acts (e.g. soliciting in the street for the purposes of prostitution, brothel-keeping, homosexual contact with an under-aged person, etc.) must remain criminalized. The Wolfenden Report was a clear step towards abandoning Stephen's strict moralism. The recommendation of the Report (i.e. the decriminalization of homosexual acts between persons over 21) was implemented in England only ten years later, in the 1967 Sexual Offences Act.[666]

Shortly after the publication of the Wolfenden Report, Sir Patrick Devlin delivered the British Academy's second Maccabean Lecture in Jurisprudence. This lecture formed the basis of his 1965 book called 'The Enforcement of Morals'.[667] As the title of the book suggests, Devlin disagreed with the conclusions of the

---

663 It is interesting that Stephen and Mill, both using the utilitarian method, come to completely opposite conclusions. The reason for this, according to Ten, is that Stephen takes into account 'pleasures of malevolence' (i.e. pleasure derived from punishing immoral behavior). Häyry claims that there is a difference between the general happiness of mankind and personal utility in Stephen's theory. Coercion (even in self-regarding matters) is a necessary element of social life because it is the only instrument to motivate people to advance the good of mankind. Ten 1980, p. 35. Häyry 1991, p. 85.

664 Report of the Committee on Homosexual Offences and Prostitution (London: HMSO) Cmnd 247 (1957).

665 Ibid. para. 61.

666 Riddall, J.G.: *Jurisprudence*. Butterwoths: London 1999, p. 305.

667 Devlin, Patrick: *The Enforcement of Morals*. Oxford University Press: Oxford 1965.

Wolfenden Report. His theory represents a 'softer' form of moralism compared to Stephen's, because he makes an effort to bring legal moralism under the harm principle. Following Feinberg, he can be qualified as an 'impure moralist in the strict sense'.[668]

Devlin's line of reasoning follows three main questions. The first question is whether society as a whole has the right to pass judgments on moral matters. An affirmative answer suggests the existence of a shared public morality and the rejection of 'subjective' moral standards determined by private judgments. For Devlin, morality is necessarily public morality. What makes a number of individuals into a society is that they are bound together by shared moral norms. Consequently, the Wolfenden Committee's reference to a 'realm of private morality' seems ill-founded. Objective moral standards are the essence, the foundations of community: "society is not something that is kept together physically; it is held by the invisible bonds of common thought".[669] Therefore, society does have the right to pass judgments on moral issues.[670]

The second question of Devlin follows from the first one: if society has the right to judge moral matters, does it also have the right to use the 'weapon' of law to enforce it? Devlin's answer is that society has such right because "a recognized morality is as necessary to society as, say, a recognized government" and "society may use the law to preserve morality in the same way as it uses it to safeguard anything else that is essential for its existence".[671] According to Devlin's 'social disintegration thesis', immorality, just as treason, is capable of destroying the fabric of society. Moralism that focuses on the prevention of such 'indirect' harm might be compatible with Mill's harm principle and, in theory, with liberal ideology.[672] Of course, this is if and only if the social disintegration thesis is true.

The third question deals with the scope of enforcement, whether the 'weapon' of (criminal) law should be used in all or only in some cases. Devlin's 'moderate' approach does not demand that every immorality should be punished by law: individual rights can limit the scope of the state's intervention. A fair balance

668 Feinberg 1990, p. 133.
669 Devlin 1965, p. 10.
670 Feinberg argues that Devlin's first question is badly formulated and misleading. No one, not even liberal thinkers deny that society has the right to pass judgment on *certain* moral matters (e.g. immoral actions that harm others). Devlin, however, seems to draw a wrong conclusion, namely that individuals must share all moral beliefs to constitute a functioning society. Feinberg 1990, p. 135.
671 Devlin 1965, p. 11.
672 Ten 1980, p. 91.

must be struck between the interests of society and the rights of individuals but there are no clear-cut rules how to perform such balancing. There are certain 'elastic' principles that determine when to resort to legal coercion.[673] As a rule of thumb, there should be toleration of "the maximum individual freedom that is consistent with the integrity of society".[674]

Let us return to the social disintegration thesis for a moment. Even if we accept that deviations from the shared morality undermine social life, the question still remains how to identify the standards that constitute public morality. According to Devlin, public morality consists of moral judgments with which a substantial number of 'ordinary persons' would agree. The feeling of disgust is a clear sign of immorality; when a typical 'right-minded' person is filled with loathing at the very thought of a behaviour (e.g. homosexuality), then that behaviour can be considered as immoral.[675]

The most influential critique of Devlin's theory was given by H.L.A. Hart in his book entitled 'Law, Liberty and Morality'.[676] Hart, both as a legal positivist and as a liberal thinker, supports the separation of law and morals and criticizes legal moralism as an unjustifiable method to limit personal freedom.

Before examining Hart's critique in details, it is important to discuss his separation of 'positive' and 'critical' morality.[677] For Hart, moralism poses the 'meta-ethical' question whether it is morally permissible to legally enforce morality as such. To answer this, Hart distinguishes between positive morality (the moral rules actually accepted and shared by a given social group) and critical morality (the general principles and ideals used in the critique of actual social institutions including positive morality).[678] It is from the viewpoint of critical morality that the legal enforcement of the currently accepted moral standards can be criticized.

673 Ibid.

674 Devlin 1965, p. 16.

675 Feinberg 1990, p. 137.

676 Hart 1963.

677 This distinction is by no means new. As Hart admits, it is rooted in the utilitarian thinking of the nineteenth century. Somewhat similarly, Lon Fuller distinguishes between the morality of duty (the minimum rules which are necessary to preserve a well-ordered society) and the morality of aspiration (the 'perfectionist' morality of Good Life and excellence). Moral and legal judgments depend on which aspect of morality is applied. Gambling, for example, would be probably forbidden by the morality of duty but not by the morality of aspiration, which perceives gambling as a lack of excellence and not as a violation of a distinct moral obligation. Fuller, Lon L.: *The Morality of Law*. Yale University Press: New Haven 1964, pp. 5–7.

678 Hart 1963, p. 20.

These critical ideals are central to all societies such as that human misery or the restriction of freedom is evil.[679] Therefore, there are two arguments against legal moralism. First, legal coercion always calls for a good justification because it limits individual liberties, which goes against the fundamental principles of critical morality. Second, positive morals protected by legal coercion must be assessed in the light of the above mentioned critical moral principles. If an existing moral standard goes against these 'higher' principles (e.g. ancient or medieval moral standards that exclude certain social groups from society), it should not be reinforced by the legal system. Hart, by introducing the distinction between positive and critical morality, establishes the possibility of rejecting legal moralism that aims to enforce the positive moral standards of a specific society.

Hart's critique of Devlin is based on the separation of public and private immoral acts. He raises no objection to laws prohibiting immoral acts on the ground that the action, committed in public, causes offence to others and turns the matter into a public nuisance. Public immorality which offends other people is within the law's proper scope. Hart introduces the offense principle and by doing so, he extends the sphere of legitimate state intervention to the category of public offenses.

It is much easier to defend liberty in the private sphere. Hart is mainly occupied with the morality of private homosexual conducts in this respect. Corresponding to Devlin's previously discussed three questions, he has three possibilities to attack legal moralism: (1) to refute the presupposition that private immorality causes harm to society (i.e. to attack the social disintegration thesis); (2) to show that society does not have the right to pass judgment on all moral matters because there are other forms of morality (i.e. critical morality) besides positive morality; (3) to show that criminal law is unsuitable to enforce moral rules.

As for the first point, Hart argues that the bare knowledge of private immoral acts is simply not offensive enough to justify the limitation of individual liberty.[680] According to Hart, "to punish people for causing this form of distress would be tantamount to punishing them simply because others object to what they do".[681] Thus, private immorality does not cause direct harm to others. It is neither sure that it causes indirect harm to society. It seems merely a speculation that deviation from a particular 'positive' moral standard necessarily threatens social order.

679 This brings Hart's position close to natural law arguments. MacCormick, Neil: *H.L.A. Hart*. Stanford University Press: Stanford 1981, p. 149.

680 The offense principle applies only to public immoralities. The fact that 'immoral' acts are potentially performed in private does not qualify as an offense.

681 Hart 1963, p. 47.

Devlin tends to regard morality as a single seamless web of interconnected rules, so that those who deviate from any part are likely to deviate from the whole.[682] This view seems incorrect because there is no evidence that those, for example, who deviate from conventional sexual morality, are predisposed to act immorally in other ways. All in all, in Hart's opinion, Devlin's social disintegration thesis lacks empirical evidence. Without going into a detailed empirical analysis, Hart offers two types of potential evidence that might support the validity of Devlin's thesis.[683] First, he suggests examining societies which have 'disintegrated' during the course of history and exploring whether a causal relation can be detected between a country's decline and a previous 'malignant change' in its common morality. Second, he refers to social psychology that can potentially establish a connection between moral decay and increase in antisocial behaviour such as violence, disrespect for property and dishonesty.

Hart's second argument is directed against Devlin's first point described earlier. Hart criticizes Devlin for moving from the acceptable proposition that some shared morality is "essential to the existence of any society to the unacceptable proposition that a society is identical with its morality as that is at any given moment of its history".[684] Hart thinks that society cannot pass judgments on all moral questions, since morality is not identical with a set of positive moral rules. The source of Devlin's mistake is that he does not distinguish between positive and critical morality. However, it seems impossible to explain the evolution of moral rules without introducing the concept of critical morality: strictly taken, whenever the morals of a specific society change, one would have to say that the given society disappeared and another one has taken its place.[685]

Even if we disregard these problems, the question remains how to identify the shared positive morality of a society. Hart disagrees with Devlin's criterion of disgust because it can give rise to oppression by the majority.

> "Certainly there is a special risk in a democracy that the majority may dictate how all should live. [...] But loyalty to democratic principles does not require us to maximize this risk: yet this is what we shall do if we mount the man in the street on the top of the Clapham omnibus and tell him that only if he feels sick enough about what other people

682 Ibid. 51.

683 H.L.A. Hart, *Social Solidarity and the Enforcement of Morality*, in *Essays in Jurisprudence and Philosophy*. Clarendon Press: Oxford 1983, pp.260–261. See also Bretter, Zoltán: *Politika a határon*. Kalligram: Pozsony 2004, p. 103.

684 Hart 1963, p. 51.

685 Ibid.

do in private to demand its suppression by law no theoretical criticism can be made of his demand."[686]

Ronald Dworkin's main concern is also the way Devlin establishes what a positive moral rule is.[687] He has no principled objection to the legal enforcement of genuine moral convictions; the problem is that the legislator is not always able to assess the 'genuinity' of moral standards. When people build their moral convictions on prejudices, rationalizations, allergic aversions (i.e. the disgust of people on the Clapham omnibus) or "faithful parrotings of authority", they do not argue morally.[688] These factors especially emotions like disgust or hatred are susceptible to distortion.[689] Dworkin thinks that one should be very careful when assessing 'majority morality' and must distinguish between real moral arguments supporting the majority opinion and unreliable non-moral arguments.

Hart's last argument is directed against Devlin's third point, the legal enforcement of moral rules. While Devlin does not claim that all moral standards should be regulated by criminal law, he does believe in legal coercion in certain cases. Hart rejects this idea. He thinks that moral standards should be promoted through public discussion and education. If moral rules are enforced by criminal law, there is a chance that the fear of punishment may remain the sole motive for conformity. If moral standards are not 'internalized', external compulsion is useless in the long run.

It is possible to defend Devlin by interpreting his theory as being concealed utilitarian. Devlin is not trying to protect some kind of God-given, absolute moral rule, but the well-being of the society and through society, the well-being of the individuals. This also explains the rejection of categorical prohibition of the harm principle. "Viewed in this way, Devlin is not challenging liberalism but is rather exploiting a tension within liberalism itself – the tension between the value of individual liberty, on the one hand, and the value of democratic rule toward utilitarian ends on the other".[690]

---

686 H.L.A. Hart, *Immorality and Treason,* in The Listener, 30 July 1959, pp. 162–163. Reprinted in Dworkin, Ronald (ed.): *The Philosophy of Law*. Oxford University Press: Oxford 1977b, pp. 83–88.

687 Dworkin, Ronald: "Lord Devlin and the Enforcement of Morals". *Yale Law Journal* 75 (1966), pp. 986–1005 (reprinted as chapter 10 of *Taking Rights Seriously*).

688 Feinberg 1990, p. 142.

689 Stanton-Ife, John: "The Limits of Law". In: Zalta, Edward N. (ed.): *The Stanford Encyclopedia of Philosophy.* Winter 2014. (http://plato.stanford.edu/entries/law-limits/).

690 Murphy, Jeffrie G.: "Legal Moralism and Liberalism". *Arizona Law Review* 37 (1995), pp. 73–93, p. 76.

The debate between Devlin and Hart generated widespread public discussion from academic journals to the popular press.[691] The work of Joel Feinberg must be mentioned because his conceptual distinctions seem to contribute to a better understanding of moralism and its relation to the harm principle. He distinguishes between four categories of legal moralism, two of which do not come under the scope of the harm and/or offense principles.[692] Impure moralism makes an appeal to some form of indirect harm or offense caused by immoral behaviour. Pure moralism does not require the existence of harm or offence for criminalization. Strict (narrow) moralism only refers to the inherently evil character of immorality; moralism in the broad sense refers to 'other forms of free-floating evils' that are not inherently immoral. These categories cut across each other, generating four subcategories:

	Narrow (strict)	Broad
Pure	Pure strict moralism (Stephen)	Pure broad moralism (moral conservatives)
Impure	Impure strict moralism (Devlin)	Impure broad moralism (perfectionists)

Pure legal moralists in the strict sense like James Fitzjames Stephen demand that the law punish inherent immoralities even when they are harmless and inoffensive. Pure broad moralism requires the criminalization of harmless free-floating evils (cf. chapter 3.3). Representatives of this approach are called moral conservatives. They argue, for example, that "[...] drastic social change is an evil in itself even when it occurs in such a way or at such a pace that no one is harmed and few are offended by it".[693] Finally, impure broad moralism argues for intervention to prevent a free-floating evil on the basis that it may incidentally harm or offend others.[694] It is clear that liberals can oppose both impure strict and impure broad moralism under the harm and offense principles. But what about its pure forms? Feinberg admits that a 'bold' form of liberalism, which accepts only the harm and offense principles as legitimate is inadequate for the regulation of morality.

691 Devlin includes references to these repercussions in the bibliography of *The Enforcement of Morals*. Devlin 1965, p. xiii.

692 Feinberg 1990, pp. 8–9.

693 Ibid.

694 Ibid.

5.2.1.2 *Legal moralism in the context of political philosophy*

The discussion on legal moralism extended beyond the Hart-Devlin debate. A revival of the debate took place in the form of a symposium held in 1988 at the Berkeley campus of the University of California with such participants as Ronald Dworkin, Bernard Williams, Jeremy Waldron and Michael Sandel.[695] The immediate reason of the conference was provided by the U.S. Supreme Court's decision in the Bowers v Hardwick case, in which the Court upheld Georgia's sodomy regulations and the criminalization of consensual homosexual conduct. Another symposium held at the University of Arizona in 1995 provided additional 'fuel' to the debate.[696]

The central issue no longer concerns whether legal moralism can somehow be subsumed under the harm principle. The question is, if the state, through moralistic coercion, has a right to impose a particular conception of the good life on its citizens. Thus, the debate gradually transforms to a debate between liberalism and communitarianism, in which the heritage of John Stuart Mill seems less and less appealing for liberals as they are put increasingly on the defence by communitarian authors.[697] It is possible to notice that the debate about moralism becomes very similar to the debate about paternalism in the context of political philosophy.

Ronald Dworkin argues against moralism on the basis of neutrality, which he derives from the general value of treating all persons with equal concern and respect (cf. chapter 3.4). Governments must be neutral on what constitutes a good life, not because neutrality is *per se* valuable, but for the sake of equality. "Political decisions must be, so far as [is] possible, independent of any particular conception of the good life, or of what gives value to life. Since the citizens of a society differ in their conceptions, the government does not treat them as equals if it prefers one conception to another."[698]

Dworkin, in his contribution to the California debate, seeks new ways to defend the idea of a liberal community. (1) He starts by criticizing the majoritarian idea, which basically asserts that the moral preferences of the majority should determine political decisions. Dworkin argues that the community's ethical

---

695 Bretter 2004, p. 170.

696 The materials of the symposiums can be found in 77 California Law Review 479 (1989) and 37 Arizona Law Review 73 (1995).

697 Bretter 2004, p. 171.

698 Dworkin, Ronald: *A Matter of Principle*. Harvard University Press: Cambridge, Mass. 1985, p. 191.

environment, analogously to its economic environment, should not be determined in a winner-take-all fashion; rather, both of them should be the product of the choices individual people make.[699] The dictatorship of the majority may lead to grave injustices (e.g. the majority of citizens could decide to assign all economic resources to themselves). (2) Dworkin proceeds by examining the possibility of paternalism in a liberal community. His argument builds on the distinction between critical and volitional well-being. I have already discussed Dworkin's views on paternalism in chapter 3.4. (3) Another frequent communitarian criticism is that a liberal community is less able to serve the 'intellectual needs' of its members. Tolerance and pluralism destroys the ability of the individual to identify himself in the light of the community to which he belongs. Dworkin agrees that it is impossible for someone to detach himself completely from the community when identifying himself. However, this does not mean that he cannot detach himself from one aspect of the community while holding others in place (i.e. to detach himself from the common sexual morality like in Bowers v Hardwick). (4) According to the argument from integration, if we accept that the lives of individual people are integrated to the community, people will necessarily care for the community, because their own well-being is derived from the community's well-being.[700] Moral 'health' is one element of the community's overall health. Dworkin claims that such an organic view of the community is erroneous. Following Rawls' example, he likens society to an orchestra, which constitutes a separate entity independent of its members. The life of the orchestra is limited to producing music and it does not entail the integration of the musicians' private life into the orchestra's communal life:

> "The musicians treat their performances together as the performance of their orchestra personified, and they share in its triumphs and failures as their own. But they do not suppose that the orchestra also has a sex life, in some way composed of the sexual activities of its members."[701]

This example of Dworkin, though quite convincing, does not offer too much new. It is a common liberal approach to narrow the public life of the community to political questions and bring sexual morality under the protection of the private sphere.

---

699 Dworkin, Ronald: "Liberal Community". *California Law Review* 77 (1989), pp. 479–504, p. 482.
700 Ibid. 491.
701 Ibid. 495.

Communitarian authors are generally more tolerant towards moralistic interventions than liberals. The idea of moral perfectionism is rooted in ancient Greek philosophy. As Hart observes:

> "It is possible to extract from Plato's Republic and Laws, and perhaps from Aristotle's Ethics and Politics, the following thesis about the role of law in relation to the enforcement of morality: the law of the city-state exists not merely to secure that men have the opportunity to lead a morally good life, but to see that they do. [...] This theory is strongly associated with a specific conception of morality as a uniquely true or correct set of principles – not man-made, but either awaiting man's discovery by the use of his reason or (in a theological setting) awaiting its disclosure by revelation."[702]

This form of moralism is different from Devlin's social disintegration thesis. For Devlin, morality is an instrument that keeps society together; for the ancients, it is society that helps people to lead a virtuous life. Consequently, Devlin's approach allows for moral relativism, while perfectionists presuppose the existence of objective moral standards. The "classical thesis" or "central tradition" rejects Devlin's relativism. The "public interest served by moral laws consists in the maintenance of a cultural context conducive to *genuine* virtue and inhospitable to *genuine* vice".[703] Moral standards are not instrumentally valuable (for the sake of preventing social disintegration) but they are intrinsically worthwhile. After all, a decline of moral standards does not necessarily affect social cohesion. Other things are capable of supporting social order and people may continue to live in proximity to each other without constituting a real community.

An easier way for communitarians is to attack the idea of liberal neutrality. According to the argument from incoherence (cf. chapter 3.4), liberalism itself can be regarded as a morality among other moralities. It is possible to argue that liberals want the law to enforce their own morality, the 'morality of freedom'.[704] Sandel also warns us that liberalism contains moral presuppositions, even its 'minimalist' Rawlsian version.[705] Sandel's objection to Rawls' approach is that 'bracketing' a particular moral controversy may partly depend on an implicit answer to the controversy it purports to bracket. Acting neutrally may not always preclude taking sides in the moral debate and bracketing moral issues may help to get rid of unwanted arguments. The Court in Roe v Wade, as Sandel shows, by

702 Hart, H.L.A.: "Social Solidarity and the Enforcement of Morality". *University of Chicago Law Review* 35 (1967).

703 George 1995, p. 79.

704 Lee 1986, p. 15–16.

705 Sandel, Michael J.: "Moral Argument and Liberal Toleration: Abortion and Homosexuality". *California Law Review* 77 (3) (1989), pp. 521–538, p. 531.

declaring that it does not want to rule on the human character of foetuses, rejects the idea that life begins with conception.[706] At the same time, despite its professed neutrality, it attaches moral weight to the viability of the foetus. Murphy draws attention to two other examples in which the neutral state seems to be morally biased.[707] While liberals oppose the criminalization of immoral acts, most of them, including Mill and Hart, endorse the retributivist approach to punishment: they see no problem in punishing particularly vicious criminals more severely than those of greater virtue. This implies that 'additional' punishment is given for vicious moral character and not for the crime committed. The other inconsistency relates to the protection of fundamental rights in liberal societies. It seems impossible to create an acceptable list of civil liberties without drawing on a specific account of human good. For sure, some liberties may be defended as fundamental because they are instrumental to free and democratic political institutions (e.g. freedom of political speech). Other liberties, such as freedom of religion or sexual liberty must refer to some account of the good.

5.2.2 The protection of morals in the European Court of Human Rights

The following chapter examines some typical issues related to 'moral paternalism'. It is focused on the case law of the European Court of Human Rights, although cases from other jurisdictions also appear. The investigation is divided in two parts: the first part deals with privacy issues (homosexuality, prostitution), while the second one with freedom of expression cases (obscenity and blasphemy).

5.2.2.1 The issue of morals in the European Convention

The European Convention makes reference to the concept of morals in connection to the rights enshrined in Articles 8, 9, 10 and 11 of the Convention and in Article 2 of the Fourth Protocol.[708] These Articles guarantee basic civil liberties (the right to respect private and family life, freedom of religion, freedom of expression, freedom of peaceful assembly and association, freedom of movement and residence, respectively). The Convention, after having defined the fundamental right in the first paragraph, contains an almost identical limitation

706 Ibid. 532.

707 Murphy 1995.

708 The European Convention for the Protection of Human Rights and Fundamental Freedoms (1950).

clause in the second paragraph of each Article.[709] Take, for example, the second paragraph of Article 8:

> "There shall be no interference by a public authority with the exercise of this right except such as is in accordance with law and is necessary in a democratic society in the interests of national security, public safety or the economic well-being of the country, for the prevention of disorder or crime, *for the protection of health or morals,* or for the protection of the rights and freedoms of others."

The protection of morals is mentioned as a legitimate aim to restrict fundamental freedoms. This exception, together with the extensive interpretation of the margin of appreciation doctrine, can serve as a tool for the justification of moralistic interventions of Member States.

The main instrument to balance the sovereignty of Member States with their obligations under the Convention is the doctrine of margin of appreciation.[710] It provides an area of discretion for Member States to decide the justifiability of human rights limitations.[711] From the perspective of legal moralism, the decisive breakthrough in the evolution of the doctrine was the Handyside case.[712] Certain factors, for example moral considerations, have the capacity to 'broaden' the margin of appreciation. This wider discretion in case of moral issues is justified by two reasons. First, national authorities are considered to be better suited than international courts to assess domestic moral standards. Second, moral standards vary from country to country and change over the course of time. As it is stated in paragraph 48 of the Handyside case, there is no 'European uniform

---

709 Arai-Takahashi, Yutaka: *The Margin of Appreciation Doctrine and the Principle of Proportionality in the Jurisprudence of the ECHR*. Intersentia: Antwerp 2002, p. 9.

710 St. J. Macdonald, Ronald / Matscher, Franz / Petzold, Herbert (eds.): *The European System for the Protection of Human Rights*. Martinus Nijhoff: Dordrecht 1993, p. 123.

711 The scheme of the European Court of Human Rights to determine the acceptability of human rights limitations is the following. (1) The Court examines whether the right laid down in the first paragraph of Articles 8–11 has been interfered with. (2) The Court examines whether the limitation was 'prescribed by law'. (3) The limitation must pursue a legitimate aim. These aims are exhaustively listed in the limitation clauses. (4) The assessment of the merits is concerned mostly with the 'necessary in a democratic society' condition which implies, in the Court's terminology a 'pressing social need'. On the one hand, the interference of the State must be proportionate to the legitimate aim pursued. On the other hand, in evaluating whether a 'pressing social need' exists, national courts are allowed a certain 'margin of appreciation'. van Dijk, Pieter /van Hoof, Godefridus: *Theory and Practice of the European Convention on Human Rights*. Kluwer Law and Taxation Publishers: Deventer 1990, p. 771.

712 Handyside v United Kingdom, Judgment of 7 December 1976.

conception of morals'. The 'fuzziness' of morals is caused by a time factor (old moral standards deteriorate over a certain period of time, as in the Dudgeon case) and a space factor (morals vary from one state to another or within one specific state, as in Handyside).[713] But is it really impossible that there are no common values shared throughout Europe? Are national authorities always in a better position to assess domestic moral standards? It seems that the Strasbourg organs are "not always at such a disadvantage [regarding the establishment of facts] as compared with the national authorities".[714] An international court with a comparative perspective has a more detached view and might be more successful in the impartial assessment of moral standards. Critics also argue that the doctrine creates legally uncertain situations and provides an 'escape route' for the Court.[715] If the Court is unwilling to examine the substance of a 'delicate' matter, it can always hide behind the doctrine of margin of appreciation. As Lord Lester points out:

> "Too often [...] the margin of appreciation is used to obviate the need for the Court to discern and explain the criteria appropriate to particular problems. This can result in a variable geometry and unequal protection of human rights. [...] The concept of the margin of appreciation has become as slippery and elusive as an eel."[716]

5.2.2.2 Privacy cases

5.2.2.2.1 Homosexuality

The moral character of homosexuality has significantly changed throughout the course of history. In ancient Greece, homosexuality was regarded as natural behaviour: the gender of the partner had far less importance than it does in our present society.[717] In Plato's *Symposium*, homosexuality appears as a virtuous trait by which couples have the potential to make a valuable civic contribution.[718]

---

713 Delmas-Marty, Mireille (ed.): *The European Convention for the Protection of Human Rights: International Protection versus National Restrictions*. Kluwer Academic: Dordrecht 1992, p. 85.

714 van Dijk / van Hoof 1990, p. 585.

715 Arai-Takahashi 2002, p. 231.

716 Lord Lester of Herne Hill: "Universality versus Subsidiarity: A Reply". *European Human Rights Law Review* 1 (1998), p. 76.

717 Nussbaum, Martha: *Sex and Social Justice*. Oxford University Press: New York 1999, p. 305.

718 It must be noted that opinions are divided about the interpretation of Plato's text, and more generally on the moral character of homosexuality in ancient Greece. John Finnis and Robert P. George claim that homosexual conduct was regarded by Plato as

Aristophanes' speech describes the intimacy and joy connected to both homosexual and heterosexual intercourse.[719]

Presently, those who oppose homosexuality focus on its 'abnormal' or 'atypical', rather than its immoral character. Homosexuality is non-desirable because it is likely to lead to unhappiness due to its 'abnormal' character.[720] An activity is abnormal whenever it involves using an organ for purposes for which it was not intended.[721] To identify the purpose of an organ, one needs to examine if this function explains the organ's existence in an evolutionary framework: teeth are intended for chewing and to help digestion; the penis is intended to be inserted into the vagina and thereby facilitate human reproduction. The problematic part of this approach is the connection made between the 'proper' use of an organ and the happiness of the subject. "Human beings have ears because the ability to hear helped our ancestors to detect approaching predators [...], but it does not follow that it will make us unhappy to use them to sport earrings, to listen to music, or to keep our eyeglasses from slipping off our noses."[722] What is more, empirical evidence does not seem to support that homosexual couples are unhappier than heterosexual ones; homosexuals engage in homosexual relations exactly because these relations make them happy. Homosexuality can facilitate the same goods as heterosexual, non-procreative relations. "It can be an avenue of intimacy, of pleasure, and of lasting interpersonal fulfillment. [...] These bonds enrich human life and can make us better people – happier, more secure, more sensitive and more generous."[723] Sexual intercourse is valuable, but not only because of its role in the reproduction of children, but also because it manifests and enhances intimacy between persons.

John Finnis, a representative of modern natural law, argues that there is a certain basic good (other than 'happiness', 'lasting interpersonal fulfillment' or 'pleasure') that can only be realized in married heterosexual relations. The

---

intrinsically shameful, immoral and depraving. See Finnis, John: "Law, Morality and 'Sexual Orientation'". *Notre Dame Law Review* 69 (5) (1994), pp. 1049–1076, p. 1056.

719 Consider the following excerpt from Aristophanes' speech in the *Symposium*: "But they who are a section of the male follow the male, and while they are young, being slices of the original man, they hang about men and embrace them, and they are themselves the best of boys and youths, because they have the most manly nature. Some indeed assert that they are shameless, but this is not true."

720 Michael Levin, *Why Homosexuality is Abnormal?* in LaFollette 2002, p. 233.

721 John Corvino, *Homosexuality and the Moral Relevance of Experience,* in ibid. 244.

722 Ibid. 246.

723 Ibid. 243.

'marital good' is intrinsically valuable and cannot be reduced to other goods.[724] It realizes two important values, but it cannot be reduced to either of them: procreation and friendship. Marital intercourse has an instrumental value because it furthers procreation and friendship between the spouses. However, it is also intrinsically valuable. Non-marital intercourse, either in homosexual or heterosexual relations, may aim to realize one of these instrumental values, yet it can never achieve the intrinsic good achievable in marital intercourse. Consequently, it is wrong to engage in sexual activity as a means to either of these goods, for to do so would be to treat one's body merely as an instrument.[725]

The criminalization of consensual homosexual conduct is a field where the European Court of Human Rights takes firm position against domestic legal moralism. The Dudgeon case is a landmark case in this respect.[726] Private homosexual acts between consenting males over 21 were decriminalized in England and Wales by the Sexual Offences Act in 1967 and in Scotland in 1980 (cf. the Wolfenden Report and the Hart-Devlin debate). The government of the United Kingdom proposed similar legislation for Northern Ireland, but the draft was withdrawn due to its unpopularity. The applicant, a homosexual activist appealed to the European Court of Human Rights, which found that the contested legislation and threat of prosecution violated the applicant's privacy rights as protected by Article 8 (1) of the Convention. As the Court states in paragraph 41, the maintenance of the contested legislation constitutes an interference with the applicant's right to privacy; "[…] the very existence of this legislation continuously and directly affects his private life". Concerning the justification of the interference, the judges are satisfied that it was both prescribed by law (by two Acts of 1861 and 1885) and served a legitimate aim (i.e. the protection of morals). The

---

724 Consider the following excerpt that explains the concept of 'marital good': "sexual union [of married couples] therefore can *actualize* and allow them to *experience* their *real common good – their marriage* with the two goods, parenthood and friendship, which (leaving aside the order of grace) are the parts of its wholeness as an intelligible common good even if, independently of what the spouses will, their capacity for biological parenthood will not be fulfilled by that act of genital union." Finnis 1994, p. 1066.

725 LaFollette 2002, p. 248.

726 Dudgeon v United Kingdom, Judgment of 22 October 1981. See also Norris v Ireland, Judgment of 26 October 1988 and Modynos v Cyprus, Judgment of 22 April 1993. According to Chief Justice O'Higgins, the Norris case can be considered different from Dudgeon because the Irish Constitution adopts a religious, hostile view towards homosexuality. The European Court, however, ruled that Norris in essence was no different than Dudgeon.

term 'necessary in a democratic society' implies the existence of a 'pressing social need', the assessment of which is left to discretion of Member States. However, the Court narrows the Member States' margin of appreciation by two means. First, the nature of the activity in the present case involves the most intimate aspects of private life; therefore only particularly serious reasons may justify criminalization. Second, the restriction must be proportionate to the legitimate aim pursued. To prove the disproportionality of the legislation, the Court starts a lengthy comparative interpretation, looking at the development of morals in Northern Ireland and the relevant practice of other Member States.[727] The Court comes to the conclusion that there seems to be a better understanding, and in consequence an increased tolerance, of homosexual behaviour in Europe. Such European consensus narrows the discretion of nation states, leaving the decision to the Court, which finally establishes that the contested regulations violate the applicant's privacy rights. Simply put, the Court seems to conclude that homosexuality is not immoral and therefore its limitation is not appropriate. But even if it were immoral would restriction be right? While overemphasizing the existence of a common European moral standard, the Court, although referring to it in paragraphs 17 and 49, seems to neglect the examination of the Wolfenden Report and the main theoretical arguments presented by Hart.

Ironically enough, it is one of the dissenting judges, Judge Walsh, who makes a reference to the Hart-Devlin debate.[728] The Irish judge takes a conservative position and argues that private consensual homosexual activities can be harmful to some homosexuals:

> "A distinction must be drawn between homosexuals who are such because of some kind of innate instinct or pathological constitution judged to be incurable and those whose tendency comes from a lack of normal sexual development or from habit or from experience or from other similar causes but whose tendency is not incurable. [...] Even assuming one of the two persons involved has the incurable tendency, the other may not."[729]

The criminalization of homosexuality is therefore acceptable in order to protect 'curable' homosexuals from harm caused by their 'incurable' partners. Besides direct harm, Judge Walsh is also concerned with the 'damaging effects of decriminalization on moral attitudes', by which he comes close to the social disintegration thesis of Devlin. He seems to rely on the harm-to-others principle

727 St. J. Macdonald / Matscher / Petzold 1993, p. 69.
728 Partially dissenting opinion of Judge Walsh, para. 9.
729 Ibid. para. 13.

in his reasoning, both in a direct and an indirect way. Judge Zekia, the Cypriot judge, adopts a similar view. He compares the privacy rights of homosexuals with the majority's right to respect for their religious and moral beliefs. Contrary to Hart's opinion in *Law, Liberty and Morality*, Judge Zekia seems to imply that the mere knowledge of homosexuality is so offensive for the majority that it warrants criminalization.

According to Finnis, the standard modern European position on homosexuality has two 'limbs'. The Dudgeon case represents the first limb, namely that "[...] the state is not authorized to, and does not make it a punishable offence for adult consenting persons to engage, in private, in immoral sexual acts."[730] The second limb, however, allows states to discourage homosexual conduct by means of legal regulations, e.g. by discriminating between heterosexual and homosexual conducts. This observation of Finnis seems to be supported by the jurisprudence of the European Court of Human Rights. The Court has a much more cautious attitude in homosexual age of consent or adoption cases (i.e. regulations that aim to discourage homosexual conduct) than in the Dudgeon case (i.e. explicit criminalization of consensual homosexual conduct). Up until 1977, the Commission ruled all 'age of consent' applications inadmissible. In X v Germany, the Commission decision of inadmissibility relied on sociological studies which referred to "a specific social danger in the case of masculine homosexuals [who] often constitute a distinct socio-cultural group with a clear tendency to proselytize adolescents".[731] The first 'age of consent' case found admissible was the X v UK case in 1977, but this case never made it to the Court, as the Commission found no violation a year later. The admission of the case represented the Commission's willingness to alter its views in the light of changing social circumstances and to "take into account the development of moral opinion in recent years".[732] The Commission finally changed its position in the Sutherland case in 1996 and established that fixing the age of consent for homosexual relations at 18 rather than 16, as in the case of heterosexual activities, was discriminatory. The results of new medical research suggested that "sexual orientation was usually established before the age of puberty in both boys and girls [...] and reducing the age of

730 Finnis 1994, p. 1049.

731 X v Germany, Decision of 30 September 1975. See Richard Nunan, *Legal Moralism and the European Court of Human Rights*, in Leiser M., Burton / Campbell D., Tom (eds.): *Human Rights in Philosophy and Practice*. Ashgate: Dartmouth 2001, p. 539.

732 X v United Kingdom, Decision of 7 July 1977.

consent would be unlikely to affect the majority of men engaging in homosexual activity".[733]

The decriminalization of homosexuality was a longer procedure in the United States. Five years after the Dudgeon judgment, the Supreme Court in the Bowers v Hardwick decision refused to invalidate sodomy laws of the type considered in Dudgeon.[734] There is no explicit provision protecting privacy in the United States Constitution. Nevertheless, the Supreme Court derived certain privacy rights from the 'due process' clauses of the Fifth and the Fourteenth Amendment.[735] Although Justice White, writing for the majority, acknowledges that "the cases are legion in which those clauses [the due process clauses] have been interpreted to have substantive content", homosexuality is not one of them. The majority came to an openly moralistic conclusion. Justice White states, that "the law [...] is constantly based on notions of morality, and if all laws representing essentially moral choices are to be invalidated [...], the courts will be very busy indeed". The dissenting opinion of Justice Blackmun refers to Hart's reasoning and distinguishes between private and public immoral acts to apply the offense principle. He accepts that "statutes banning public sexual activity are entirely consistent with protecting the individual's liberty" but this does not mean that "states can regulate intimate behavior that occurs in intimate places".[736]

---

733 Sutherland v United Kingdom, no. 25186/94, Commission decision of 21 May 1996; Commission Report of 1 July 1997, para. 59. The case was later struck out from the list by the Court due to the coming into force of the Sexual Offences Act (2000) in the UK. Two recent cases concerning the discharge of homosexual men from the military show the Court's increasing willingness to intervene into the discriminatory practices of Member States concerning homosexuals. Smith and Grady v United Kingdom, Judgment of 27 September 1999; Lustig-Prean and Beckett v United Kingdom, Judgment of 27 September 1999.

734 Bowers v Hardwick 478 U.S. 186 (1986).

735 Griswold v Connecticut 381 U.S. 479 (1965).

736 Although Bowers v Hardwick established that there is no fundamental right to engage in consensual homosexual activity, the equal protection clause of the Fourteenth Amendment was used to challenge state sodomy statutes. In Romer v Evans, the Supreme Court held that an amendment to the Colorado Constitution prohibiting measures forbidding discrimination on the basis of sexual orientation was discriminatory against homosexuals. It was the Lawrence v Texas decision that finally and explicitly overruled Bowers. The Court established that consensual and private homosexual relations are protected by the due process clause of the Constitution: "it is a promise of the Constitution that there is a realm of personal liberty which the government may not enter". These words are similar to the reasoning of the Wolfenden Committee. Both the Wolfenden Report and the Dudgeon case are explicitly

5.2.2.2.2 *Prostitution*

Sticking consequently to liberal principles, it is hard to see why prostitution would be morally objectionable. The mutual agreement of two competent persons which neither causes harm nor offense to others shall not be interfered with. The contractarian defence of prostitution builds on the idea that prostitution is a service occupation and should be treated as a contract between a seller (i.e. the prostitute) and a buyer (i.e. the client).[737] On the other hand, it is clear that non-voluntary forms of prostitution are morally wrong; they come under the harm-to-others principle and can legitimately be criminalized.

Prostitution can be opposed on both paternalistic and moralistic grounds. The 'paternalistic charge' refers mainly to the occupational hazards connected with prostitution. The prostitute is subject to certain risks both physically and mentally (e.g. sexually transmitted diseases, depression, alcohol and drug abuse, etc.). However, the voluntariness of the consent negates the paternalistic charge in the eyes of most liberals. Representatives of the contract theory also point out that prostitution is not the only potentially harmful profession.[738] Miners, for example, have a dangerous job, yet people do not think that mining should be prohibited just because it is dangerous.

The moralistic arguments against prostitution may take different forms. Overt moralism is increasingly substituted by covert moralistic legislation, hidden behind the 'nuisance' rhetoric of the offense principle.[739] Impure forms of moralist arguments refer to the socially harmful character of prostitution. They emphasize, for example, the threat that prostitution poses to families and to monogamous marriage. Pure moralist arguments are even 'worse' because they terminate the possibility of any rational discussion: "[t]o say that prostitution is intrinsically immoral is in a way to refuse to give any arguments".[740] Moralists can also appeal to perfectionist ideals and ask how prostitution contributes to the development of human nature. Presumably, it does not develop human nature: sex between a client and a prostitute is much more impoverished and impersonal than sex between a couple in love. But does this necessarily mean that prostitution is

---

mentioned in the majority opinion. Romer v Evans 517 U.S. 620 (1996); Lawrence v Texas, 539 U.S. 558 (2003).

737 Fabre, Cécile: *Whose Body is it Anyway?*. Clarendon Press: Oxford 2006, p. 158.

738 Ericsson, Lars O.: "Charges Against Prostitution". *Ethics* 90 (3) (1980), pp. 335–366, p. 343.

739 Shaver, Francis M.: "The Regulation of Prostitution: Avoiding the Morality Traps". *Canadian Journal of Law and Society* 9 (1) (1994), pp. 123–145, p. 124.

740 Ericsson 1980, p. 339.

undesirable or immoral? "That would be like contending that because 1955 Ch. Mouton-Rotschild is a much better wine than ordinary claret, we should condemn the act of drinking the latter". Another perfectionist-like argument is the 'charge of commercialization of society', which builds on the idea that there are certain areas of life that cannot be commercialized.[741]

Feminists oppose prostitution on the ground that women who provide sexual services for money "submit to sexual domination by men, and suffer degradation by being treated as sexual commodities".[742] Radical feminists criticize the contract theory of liberals by trying to show that prostitution is not similar to other forms of work. First of all, they claim that it is bodies, not only services or products, which are being sold in the case of prostitution.[743] Normally, an employer is primarily interested in the commodities produced or the service provided by his employees. The factory owner is interested in the products produced by physical work. Even if we consider services that are closely related to the body of the service provider, there is a fundamental difference. For example, the clients of a masseuse are indifferent how they acquire refreshment and relief from pain: if they would be able to get what they want by other means (e.g. a particularly good massage robot), they would be willing to do so.[744] By contrast, in the case of prostitution, it is inherent that the client seeks sexual pleasure from his interaction with the prostitute; this cannot be substituted with other means. Prostitution is also different from other occupations because it involves an element of distancing: prostitutes employ different techniques to maintain an impersonal attitude during the intercourse.[745] Distancing strategies, however, are not unique to sex work. Doctors and nurses also distance themselves from their patients; either to emotionally protect themselves or to comply with the code of their professional ethics.

Overall, moral arguments seem unnecessary for an adequate regulation of prostitution. It is possible to reconcile our moral concerns with personal liberty and restrict lawful prostitution to a thin line of cases that satisfy the requirements of the harm and offense principles. Consider the following application of liberty-limiting principles to the case of prostitution. (1) The offense principle prohibits prostitution if it takes place in public and offends other people. (2) Involuntary

---

741 Ibid. 355.

742 Shrage, Laurie: "Should Feminists Oppose Prostitution?". *Ethics* 99 (2) (1989), pp. 347–361, p. 347.

743 Shaver 1994, p. 135.

744 Fabre 2006, p. 158.

745 Shaver 1994, p. 137.

prostitution with a coercive element is unacceptable and shall be criminalized. Pimps who terrorize vulnerable individuals into prostituting themselves by physically or sexually abusing them or clients who themselves abuse and rape prostitutes should not be tolerated. (3) The harm principle prohibits prostitution if it causes harm to external 'third' parties. Such harm can be psychical harm caused by adultery to the spouse of the client or physical harm caused by sexually transmitted diseases. (4) Additional 'services' (extortion, pimping, etc.) connected to prostitution should be criminalized, if they harm, exploit or coerce the prostitute. However, Fabre argues that pimping *per se* is not necessarily immoral: pimps do actually provide services for their prostitutes, for instance they protect them from abusive clients.[746] (5) Prostitution is a risky conduct that may involve many different forms of harm to both parties. Prostitutes are subject to sexually transmitted diseases, abuse, drug or alcohol addiction, and psychological harm. However, due to the *volenti non fit iniuria* principle, the harm principle cannot be invoked to tackle these problems.

The European Court of Justice discussed the issue of prostitution related to the free movement of persons in two cases. In Adoui and Cornuaille, two French nationals complained about the refusal of their residence permit by Belgian authorities on the basis that their work (i.e. prostitution) was suspect from a moral viewpoint.[747] The Belgian authorities tried to justify the derogation from the principle of free movement of persons on public policy arguments. The Court refrained from ruling on the morality of prostitution and stated that "[...] community law does not impose upon the Member States a uniform scale of values as regards the assessment of conduct which may be considered as contrary to public policy".[748] However, a conduct cannot be considered to go against public policy, if the Member State does not adopt on the part of its own nationals the same repressive or other measures intended to combat such conduct. Since prostitution is not prohibited in Belgium, the conduct of the applicants cannot be considered to go against public policy and it was unlawful to deny them permission to reside in Belgium. A similar issue was brought before the Court with the Jany case, in which Polish and Czech nationals complained about the refusal of residence permits that would have enabled them to work as self-employed prostitutes in the Netherlands.[749] The main question was whether prostitution comes within the notion of 'economic activities of self-employed persons' or it is excluded either

746 Fabre 2006, p. 155.

747 Joined Cases C-115/81 and C-116/81, *Adoui and Cornuaille* [1982] ECR 1665.

748 Ibid. para. 8.

749 Case C-268/99, *Jany* [2001] ECR-I 8615.

for moral reasons or on the ground that it gives rise to problems concerning the 'independence' of prostitutes. Concerning the immorality of prostitution, the Court has already held that it is not for the Court to substitute its own moral judgment for that of the legislatures of the Member States where an allegedly immoral activity is practiced legally.[750] Prostitution is tolerated, even regulated in certain Member States, including the Netherlands. Therefore, the Court – reiterating the Adoui and Cornuaille case – claims that public policy cannot serve as a basis for derogation. The Court establishes three criteria for prostitution to qualify as 'self-employed economic activity'. It should be carried on by the service provider (1) outside any relationship of subordination (2) under his or her own responsibility (3) in return for remuneration paid directly and in full.

The European Court of Human Rights refused to deal with prostitution under Article 8 of the Convention. The applicant of F. v. Switzerland complained that her conviction for having engaged professionally in homosexual relations constitutes an interference with her privacy rights.[751] The Commission notes that the right to respect for private life guarantees the individual a sphere within which he or she can pursue freely the development and fulfilment of his or her personality, including the establishment of sexual relations as well. However, it also observes that in the particular case the sexual relations that caused the conviction of the applicant were established professionally and in exchange of remuneration. Prostitution does not belong to the sphere of private life protected by Article 8 of the Convention and the complaint is incompatible *ratione materiae* with the provisions of the Convention.

The case of Laskey, Jaggard and Brown involved a group of homosexual men inflicting minor bodily injuries to each other with the purpose of achieving sexual gratification.[752] The activities were consensual and were conducted in private. None of the injuries required hospital treatment. The applicants were sentenced for assault and wounding under the Offences against the Person Act 1861. The European Court resolved the case from the perspective of the protection of health and did not find it necessary to deal with moral issues.[753] It found no violation of the applicants' privacy rights under Article 8 of the Convention. The punishment was necessary to prevent the applicants from the harm caused to each other during their sadomasochistic sexual activities.

---

750 Ibid. para. 56. See also Case C-159/90 *Society for the Protection of Unborn Children Ireland* [1991] ECR I-4685, para. 20.

751 F. v Switzerland, Decision of 10 March 1988.

752 Laskey, Jaggard and Brown v United Kingdom, Judgment of 19 February 1997.

753 Ibid. para. 51.

Since the Court refused to examine the moral implications of the case and the offense principle is also inapplicable (the contested acts were committed in private), the question becomes a question of paternalism. The Court overlooked the fact that the element of consent transforms the 'harm to others' to a 'harm to self' issue. It claims that the inflicted injuries make the case essentially different from 'simple' homosexuality, which is permissible according to the previous jurisprudence of the Court (Dudgeon v United Kingdom). The reasoning reinterprets the *volenti non fit iniuria* principle; it claims that consent is not always capable of transforming other-regarding acts to self-regarding. The consent of the victim should not be a defence for inflicting serious bodily harm.[754] Lord Templeman also points out that common law does not recognize consent as a defence. Member States are left with a wide margin of appreciation in this matter. "The determination of the level of harm that should be tolerated by the law in situations where the victim consents is in the first instance a matter for the State concerned".[755] There are certain exceptions, such as lawful sports or surgery. These exceptions are permitted because a countervailing value overrides the interest of society to protect its members from their own folly. However, it could also be argued that individual self-fulfilment (e.g. by means of 'alternative' sexual practices) is more important than the prevention of minor physical wounds.

5.2.2.3 Freedom of expression cases

5.2.2.3.1 The Court's approach to freedom of expression

The margin of appreciation provided for Member States is changeable in freedom of expression cases. The European Court of Human Rights has been criticized for delivering seemingly inconsistent judgments under Article 10 of the Convention. As Paul Mahoney explains, cases concerning the 'cultural' aspect of freedom of expression were granted a wide margin of appreciation, while Member

754 The seriousness of injuries is an open question. Although none of the injuries required hospital treatment, the committed acts seem quite serious. The acts consisted of the maltreatment of the genitalia (with, for example, hot wax, sandpaper, fish hooks and needles) and ritualistic beatings either with the assailant's bare hands or a variety of implements, including stinging nettles, spiked belts and a cat-o'-nine tails. There were instances of branding and infliction of injuries, which resulted in the flow of blood and which left scarring. Ibid. para. 8.

755 Ibid. para. 44.

States were given less discretion to decide cases with 'political' aspects.[756] The Court found no violation of Article 10 in cases concerned with artistic freedom (Wingrove v UK and Otto Preminger Institut v Austria). In other cases, such as Jersild v Denmark or Goodwin v UK (cases concerned with the dissemination of racist statements and disclosing the identity of a journalist's source), the Court has been more active in the protection of free speech.[757] This is why some commentators accuse the Court of an inconsistent approach to the protection of free speech, "one day blowing hot, the next day blowing cold".[758] Mahoney argues that this inconsistency stems from two different purposes of free speech: enabling participation in decision-making by all members of society and ensuring individual and group self-fulfilment. Hence the Court's strict approach in political cases and the permissive approach in cultural cases. Lord Lester, in his reply to Mahoney criticizes this distinction as arbitrary and unworkable.[759] Artistic freedom deserves no less protection than the freedom to express political ideas. Artistic expression can have, besides self-fulfilment, political functions as well. The Court observed in the Müller case, that:

> "Through his creative work the artist expresses not only a personal vision of the world but also his view of the society in which he lives. To that extent art not only helps shape public opinion but is also an expression of it and can confront the public with the major issues of the day."[760]

Making the margin of appreciation doctrine contingent on the distinction between 'political' and 'cultural' aspects of freedom of expression can lead to uncertainties in the case law. It can also be dangerous, because the passivity of the Strasbourg Court can give way to the moralism of Member States when it comes to cultural aspects of freedom of expression.

5.2.2.3.2 Pornography and obscenity

In Müller v Switzerland, the Swiss cantonal authorities had prosecuted an artist and the promoters of an art show for display of obscene materials. The paintings

---

756 Mahoney, Paul: "Universality and Subsidiarity in the Strasbourg Case Law on Free Speech: Explaining Some Recent Judgments". *European Human Rights Law Review* 4 (1997), pp. 364–379, p. 364.

757 Jersild v Denmark, Judgment of 23 September 1994; Goodwin v UK, Judgment of 27 March 1996.

758 Mahoney 1997, p. 366.

759 Lord Lester of Herne Hill 1998, p. 75.

760 Müller v Switzerland, Judgment of 24 May 1988, para. 95.

at issue depicted an orgy of unnatural sexual practices and were found to violate Article 204 of the Swiss Criminal Code, which prohibited obscene publications. The applicants were sentenced to a fine of 300 Swiss francs and the paintings were confiscated. The general public had free access to the exhibition, as the organizers had not imposed any admission charge or any age limit. The Court found no violation of Article 10. The interference was sufficiently prescribed by law (the Criminal Code) and served a legitimate aim (the protection of morals). The analysis of the judges focused on the terms 'necessary in a democratic society' and 'existence of a pressing social need'. The Member State's margin of appreciation is modified by two factors. First, the nature of the right narrows the discretion of domestic authorities. Freedom of expression "constitutes one of the essential foundations of a democratic society [...] and it is applicable not only to information or ideas that are favourably received [...], but also to those that offend, shock and disturb." Second, the aim pursued by the interference provides more discretion to Switzerland, since it is not possible to find a uniform European conception of morals in this matter. It is the task of the domestic authorities to assess the sensitivity of the Swiss society, but the Court generally agrees that the paintings were capable of offending "the sense of sexual propriety of persons of ordinary sensitivity".[761]

This case can be regarded as an example of the application of the offense principle. Society definitely has the right to regulate immoral public activities that may offend the feelings of others. However, the punishment must be proportionate to the offense suffered. The organizers should have ensured that only those, who are genuinely interested, attend the exhibition. This could have been accomplished by providing prior information on the content of the exhibition and imposing an age limit on visitors. Such regulations are acceptable to protect individuals from unnecessary moral offences, but the confiscation of the paintings was clearly disproportionate. As Judge Spielmann points it out in his dissenting opinion, the notion of obscenity is relative and subject to quick change. Flaubert was prosecuted for his novel 'Madame Bovary' and Baudelaire for the 'Les Fleurs du Mal'. Both works are considered today as fine pieces of art. By confiscating the paintings of Mr. Müller, the authorities deprived those who had different notions about obscenity of the possibility to visit the exhibition.

761 Ibid. paras. 18 and 36.

5.2.2.3.3 *Blasphemy*

The case of Otto Preminger Institut v Austria is largely similar to Müller, except for the fact that freedom of expression here was not limited for moral reasons, but for the protection of religious feelings of others.[762] The legal basis for intervention was a fairly standard blasphemy regulation of the Austrian Penal Code, traditionally adopted for the protection of the Roman Catholic Church. The European Court upheld a ban on the film *Das Liebeskonzil* (Council in Heaven), which ridiculed central figures of Catholicism, i.e. God, Jesus and the Virgin Mary. The film was scheduled for screening in Innsbruck's Otto Preminger Institut, a non-profit association and art cinema. The Institut made particular steps to avoid public offense. It advertised the film with an explicit warning and prescribed a minimum admission age of seventeen. The majority ruling provided Austria a wide margin of appreciation on the basis that "[…] as in the case of morals, it is not possible to discern throughout Europe a uniform conception of the significance of religion in society".[763] Despite the efforts of the applicant, the Court found that the proposed screening was sufficiently 'public' to offend the religious feelings of Austrian people.

The dissenting opinion of Judges Palm, Pekkanen and Makarczyk points out the weaknesses of the majority reasoning. The only liberty-limiting principle applicable, since neither direct nor indirect harm occurred, is the offense principle. However, unlike in Müller, it can be argued in this case that the measures taken by the organizers were sufficient to prevent those who did not wish to watch the movie from attending the shows. Even if we accept that the screening constituted a public offense, the measures taken must be proportionate to the legitimate aim pursued. The majority opinion, just as in Müller, neglected the examination of proportionality. In paragraph 7, the dissenters refer to the 'less restrictive means' doctrine and state that "the complete prevention of the exercise of freedom of expression can only be accepted if the behaviour concerned reaches so high a level of abuse […] as to forfeit for itself the right to be tolerated by society".

The judgment of Otto Preminger Institut was confirmed in Wingrove v UK.[764] The Court was called upon to review the English law of blasphemy. The source of offense in Wingrove was not public screening, but the intended distribution of a blasphemous video material based on the visions of St. Teresa of Avila. The applicants argued that the video entitled 'Visions of Ecstasy' would have reached

762 Otto Preminger Institut v Austria, Judgment of 20 September 1994.

763 Ibid. para. 50.

764 Wingrove v United Kingdom, Judgment of 25 November 1996.

a considerably smaller audience than the film in the Otto Preminger Institut case. However, the Court, bearing in mind the huge explosion of the video industry at the time, held that it was possible that the video reached an audience who would have found it offensive. Both the Otto Preminger Institut and Wingrove cases have been widely criticized for upholding domestic blasphemy regulations. The original rationale behind these laws, adopted centuries ago, had been the protection of the authority of Christian doctrines and institutions.[765] Most European states have abolished or have not recently applied blasphemy laws. Even in the United Kingdom, where the offense of blasphemy still exists in common law, there had only been one 'modern' prosecution before the Wingrove case.[766] Apart from their outdated character, blasphemy laws can also be criticized for being discriminatory to non-Christian religions. Lord Justice Watkins declared in R. v Chief Metropolitan Stipendiary Magistrate, ex parte Choudhory that "[…] we have no doubt that as the law stands it does not extend to religions other than Christianity".[767] This was confirmed in Choudhory v United Kingdom: the European Commission held that the fact that blasphemy protected only the Christian religion was not a breach of Article 9. The Court has moved away from the Commission's view in Otto Preminger Institut.[768]

765 Unsworth, Clive: "Blasphemy, Cultural Divergence and Legal Relativism". *Modern Law Review* 58 (5) (1995), pp. 658–677.

766 R. v Lemon, R. v Gay News Ltd (1979) 1 All E.R. 898.

767 R v Chief Metropolitan Stipendiary Magistrate, ex parte Choudhory (1991) 1 All E.R. 306 at 318.

768 Heinze, Eric: "Viewpoint Absolutism and Hate Speech". *Modern Law Review* 69 (4) (2006), pp. 543–582, p. 554.

6. Conclusion

6.1 At the intersection of two conflicting principles

6.1.1 Autonomy

> "If a man does not keep pace with his companions, perhaps it is because he hears a different drummer. Let him step to the music which he hears, however measured or far away."[769]

Throughout this book, the problem of paternalism emerges as the tension of two fundamental principles: autonomy and benevolence. Autonomy appears as a central notion of paternalism both from a definitional and a justificatory aspect. Most definitions consider interference with autonomy as an essential characteristic of paternalistic regulations. They term the 'element of interference' in different ways which seems to cause some conceptual uncertainty as to what exactly qualifies as paternalism.

Autonomy-based justificatory theories seem to be rather one-sided. The distinction between hard and soft paternalism, for example, focuses solely on the voluntary character of self-harming decisions. However, it is not always easy to establish the voluntariness of a decision. At first glance, it is tempting to equate voluntariness with rationality. Some forms of self-harming behaviour seem so irrational that most of us would deny that they were taken voluntarily. There are people who jump off 400 meter high buildings with small parachutes. Others find pleasure in drinking and smoking excessively, while knowing that these harmful passions considerably decrease life expectancy. It is possible to claim that these choices are irrational and therefore paternalistic intervention is justified in such cases. However, there are seemingly unreasonable decisions that are delivered autonomously. Evaluative choices, even if not in line with the values of the majority, are completely 'sensible' for the individual who makes them. Some of us may value a short but adventurous life to a long and passive one. Others value artificial pleasures derived from dangerous substances. Some people may sacrifice their lives rather than violate the commands of their religion. It seems unfair to say that these people act involuntarily: they are following different values, which are incommensurable with each other.

769 Thoreau, Henry David: *Walden*. Houghton Mifflin Harcourt: New York 1995, p. 317.

6.1.2 Benevolence and interconnectedness

> "All mankind is of one author, and is one volume; when one man dies, one chapter is not torn out of the book, but translated into a better language; ... No man is an island, entire of itself ... and therefore never send to know for whom the bell tolls; it tolls for thee."[770]

The principle of benevolence provides the motivational element behind paternalism. It is the wish to protect others from self-harm or to promote their benefit that calls paternalism into being. Thus, benevolence seems to be an integral element of the concept and it has a strong normative force as well. This does not imply that benevolence unconditionally justifies paternalism, irrespective of consequences or the violation of autonomy. It rather seems to be a necessary precondition for the justification of paternalistic acts, even if it is not always easy to determine benevolent motivations. Genuine benevolence develops from a feeling of interconnectedness and empathy. In cases of private paternalism, the paternalistic actor does not see self-harm primarily in terms of 'reduction of utility' but in terms of anticipated pain for the actor himself. "If others hurt themselves, you are hurt" – this seems to be one of the basic experiences behind paternalistic interventions.[771]

The potential justificatory force of benevolence becomes more apparent if we connect it to the virtue of care. Benevolent care is valuable because it improves the character of the actor, even if the intervention seems unjustified from the subject's perspective. Care is an essential element of good life and personal happiness. In Kultgen's words "real contentment and lasting satisfaction are only blossoms on the sturdy plant of an existence that reaches maturity through caring and being cared for."[772] Nevertheless, care does not sanction unlimited violation of autonomy. The feeling of interconnectedness and empathy (i.e. being 'engrossed' in the other) guarantees that „someone who cares deeply and genuinly about someone else is open and receptive to the reality of the other human being."[773]

770 John Donne: *Meditation XVII.*
771 Kennedy 1982, p. 639.
772 Kultgen 1995, p. 7.
773 Slote 2007, p. 12.

6.2 The changing interpretation of the harm principle

The harm principle, from its very inception, was an enterprise for a principle that is able to "govern absolutely the dealings of society with the individual in the way of compulsion or control".[774] Mill argues that absolute respect for freedom will maximize social utility and individual well-being in the long run. Partly because empirical evidence suggests that Mill's presupposition is not always right, the utilitarian justification of the harm principle was gradually replaced by deontological ethics. As I tried to demonstrate, this interpretational change is already implicit in Mill's theory. Arguably, there is a second interpretational shift in the philosophy of Joseph Raz which makes a move from deontology to the direction of 'liberal perfectionism'. Parallel and somewhat contrary to these developments, a gradual 'softening' of the principle also takes place. The soft-paternalistic strategy of Feinberg aims to requalify hard paternalistic interventions as soft paternalism by showing that the self-harming action was not taken voluntarily. The introduction of the offense principle, as a legitimate liberty-limiting principle, facilitates the prohibition of non-harmful, but universally disliked, unpleasant or offensive behaviour (public nuisances, public immorality, etc.). These developments also demonstrate that it is probably illusory that a single moral principle can comprehensively regulate all dilemmas created by paternalism.

6.3 Liberal neutrality

Since citizens in modern pluralistic societies hold different views about what constitutes a valuable life, it is a common liberal claim that the state should be neutral towards the competing conceptions of the moral good, while enforcing the 'right' (i.e. the basic rules that maintain the integrity society together). It seems to me that the key question is how to determine which acts belong to the sphere of the right and which to the sphere of the good. The common answer is that claims about the good are essentially controversial while the "principles of justice [the sphere of the right] are objective and interpersonally recognizable" and they extend only to constitutional essentials and to principles that regulate the basic structure of society.[775] The harm principle seems to belong to the realm of the 'right' and reflect the requirements of neutrality. Paternalism is excluded by

774 Mill 1975, p. 10.

775 Arneson, Richard: "Liberal Neutrality on the Good: An Autopsy". In: Wall, Steven / Klosko, George (eds.): Perfectionism and Neutrality: Essays in Liberal Theory. Rowman & Littlefield Publishers: Lanham, Md. 2003, pp. 191–218, p. 195, 206.

the harm principle because there seems to be no overlapping consensus in most cases of paternalism.

6.4 Lessons learned from case law

The aims of my empirical research were twofold. Firstly, I wanted to provide vivid examples of paternalism that demonstrate the potential discrepancy between one's moral intuitions and moral principles. The evaluative decisions mentioned in chapter 3.3 (e.g. active voluntary euthanasia in *Pretty v UK,* dwarf-tossing in *Wackenheim v France,* shooting-game prohibition in *Omega*, crash-helmet regulation in *Chahal*, etc.) present dilemmas that are 'hard nuts to crack' for autonomy-based theories, because, if the harm principle and the soft-hard distinction were taken seriously, the actions in these cases should not have been prohibited. They are based on perfectly voluntary choices and cause no harm to others. Still, our moral intuition tells us that some of these self-harming actions are just 'not right' and should be restricted (or at least, there is nothing wrong with restricting them). These intuitions are reflected in the court rulings as well. Obviously, these 'stubborn counterexamples' are not conclusive counterarguments, but they raise serious doubts about the adequacy of some of the traditional approaches.

The second aim of the empirical investigation was to explore what moral arguments and presuppositions determine court decisions and how the problem of paternalism is transformed to a legal question. The Hungarian constitutional jurisprudence seems to reveal a predominantly value neutral approach. The principle of state neutrality, i.e. that the state has no right to impose particular moral standards on its citizens is reiterated in numerous cases.[776] Following Kantian inspiration, the Court attributes an inherent value to autonomy that is derived from the right to human dignity: "the right to human dignity means that the individual possesses a core of autonomy and self-determination beyond the reach of all others, whereby [...] the human being remains a subject and cannot be transformed into an instrument or object".[777] Correspondingly, the Court seems to approach paternalism primarily from a deontological perspective. It emphasizes voluntariness as being decisive in paternalistic cases.[778] Of course, autonomy-based arguments are complemented with consequentialist considerations (e.g. the possible social effects of permitting certain self-harming conducts, like drug consumption, voluntary sterilization, euthanasia, etc.). As for the 'legal

776 Cf. 21/1996. (V.17.) AB.
777 See, e.g. 39/2007. (VI. 20) AB, chapter IV, section 4.1.
778 Cf. 521/1996. (V.17.) AB; 4/2004. (XII. 13.) AB; 43/2005. (XI. 14) AB.

transformation' of paternalism, generally two constitutional requirements clash in the examined cases: the right to self-determination (an 'unenumerated' right derived from human dignity) and the State's 'institutional' duty to guarantee certain rights, for example, "the highest possible level of physical and mental health to everyone living in the territory of the Republic of Hungary".[779]

The case law of the European Court of Human Rights is particularly rich when it comes to the protection of morals, but there is no clearly discernible tendency in the jurisprudence. The Court sometimes upholds Member States' moralistic regulations,[780] but sometimes rejects them.[781] State regulations aimed at the protection of morals appear in the Convention's framework as interferences with the right to privacy (e.g. the issue of homosexuality) or the right to freedom of expression (e.g. obscenity). The margin of appreciation doctrine seems to give a wide discretion to Member States for moralistic interventions, especially in freedom of expression cases. The Court tries to refrain from intervention in cases where there is no 'European uniform conception of morals'. But non-interference can represent a biased commitment here as well: it leaves perfectionism to Member States, but it is not sure that they are in a better position to assess positive morality than the Court.

6.5 Beyond principles

From a critical perspective, if the state is conceived as an instrument of domination, legal paternalism that lacks the element of care is nothing else than a mask for exploitation. "The distant and impersonal relations of bureaucracies foster the opposite of sincerely cooperative [i.e. caring] paternalism, that is, conflictful paternalism – exploitative relations in the guise of paternalism."[782] Thus, paternalism, especially its benefit-promoting version, can have an 'ideological' function. Even if this view is a bit exaggerated, it is true that oppressive state interventions can be disguised by benevolence, hence the distinguished value of autonomy and the negative connotations attached to paternalism in modern times.

779 Article 70/D of the Hungarian Constitution (Act XX of 1949). Article XX of the Fundamental Law of Hungary guarantees similar rights.

780 Cf. Müller v Switzerland; Otto Preminger Institute v Austria; Laskey, Jaggard and Brown v UK.

781 Cf. Dudgeon v UK.

782 Jack D. Douglas, *Cooperative vs. Conflictful Paternalism*, in Sartorius, Rolf E.: Paternalism. University of Minnesota Press: 1983, p. 197.

Caring paternalism prevails predominantly in direct personal relations. It would be a mistake to "assume that justified forms of public paternalism exactly parallel those of personal paternalism".[783] Law treats people under abstract descriptions and presupposes a certain degree of standardization. Nevertheless, care can find its way through the barrier of abstraction by the 'infrastructure of care'. If benevolent paternalism is a manifestation of care and care is a virtue, then the state has a task to develop the 'infrastructure of care', that is, the institutions, organizations, practices and shared beliefs by which a society nurtures mutual care among its members.[784] Consequently, the task of legal paternalism can be conceived as developing this 'infrastructure' rather than directly coercing people to their 'own' good. Since generalized paternalistic regulations are insensitive to the context in which paternalism takes place, it might be more promising to foster the virtue of care in people who, if the assumption of virtue ethics is right, will find the appropriate way to respond to particular dilemmas of paternalism through the application of 'practical wisdom'.

783 Kultgen 1995, p. 161.
784 Ibid. 30.

Bibliography

Abbey, Ruth: *Charles Taylor*. Acumen: Teddington 2000.

Ackerman, Bruce: *Social Justice in the Liberal State*. Yale University Press: New Haven 1980.

Ackermann, Thomas: "Case Law Review – C-36/02 Omega Spielhallen und Automatenaufstellungs GmbH v Oberbürgermeisterin der Bundesstadt Bonn". *Common Market Law Review* 42 (4) (2005), pp. 1107–1120.

Annas, Julia: *Intelligent Virtue*. Oxford University Press: Oxford 2011.

Anscombe, Elizabeth: "Modern Moral Philosophy". *Philosophy* 33 (124) (1958), pp. 1–19.

Arai-Takahashi, Yutaka: *The Margin of Appreciation Doctrine and the Principle of Proportionality in the Jurisprudence of the ECHR*. Intersentia: Antwerp 2002.

Archard, David: "Paternalism Defined". *Analysis* 50 (1) (1990), pp. 36–42.

Aristotle: *Nicomachean Ethics*. Hackett Publishing: Indianapolis, Ind. 1999.

Aristotle: *Politics*. Hackett Publishing: Indianapolis, Ind. 1998.

Aristotle / Ross, W. D. / Brown, Lesley: *The Nicomachean Ethics*. Oxford University Press: Oxford 2009.

Arneson, Richard: "Joel Feinberg and the Justification of Hard Paternalism". *Legal Theory* 11 (03) (2005), pp. 259–284.

Arneson, Richard: "Liberal Neutrality on the Good: An Autopsy". In: Wall, Steven / Klosko, George (eds.): *Perfectionism and Neutrality: Essays in Liberal Theory*. Rowman & Littlefield Publishers: Lanham, Md. 2003, pp. 191–218.

Arneson, Richard: "Mill versus Paternalism". *Ethics* 90 (4) (1980), pp. 470–489.

Arneson, Richard: "Paternalism, Utility and Fairness". In: Dworkin, Gerald (ed.): *Mill's On Liberty: Critical Essays*. Rowman & Littlefield Publishers: Lanham, Md. 1997.

Arneson, Richard J.: "Perfectionism and Politics". *Ethics* 111 (1) (2000), pp. 37–63.

Baron, Marcia / Pettit, Philip / Slote, Michael: *Three Methods of Ethics: A Debate*. Wiley-Blackwell: Cambridge, Mass. 1997.

Beauchamp, Tom L.: "Paternalism and Bio-Behavioral Control". *The Monist* 62 (1976).

Beauchamp, Tom L. / Childress, James F.: *Principles of Biomedical Ethics*. 6th edition. Oxford University Press: New York 2009.

Behaviour Change. Report of the Science and Technology Select Committee. House of Lords: London 2011 (http://www.publications.parliament.uk).

Bennett, Frederick Joseph: The Virtuoso Human: A Virtue Ethics Model Based on Care, University of South Florida: 2011.

Benson, Peter (ed.): *The Theory of Contract Law: New Essays*. Cambridge University Press: Cambridge 2001.

Bentham, Jeremy: *An Introduction to the Principles of Morals and Legislation*. Clarendon Press: Oxford 1907.

Bergelson, Vera: "The Right to Be Hurt: Testing the Boundaries of Consent". *The George Washington Law Review* 75 (2007), p. 165.

Berlin, Isaiah: "Two Concepts of Liberty". In: *Four Essays on Liberty*. Oxford University Press: Oxford 1969.

Bretter, Zoltán: *Politika a határon*. Kalligram: Pozsony 2004.

Christman, John / Anderson, Joel (eds.): *Autonomy and the Challenges to Liberalism: New Essays*. Cambridge University Press: Cambridge 2005.

Clarke, Simon: "Debate: State Paternalism, Neutrality and Perfectionism". *Journal of Political Philosophy* 14 (2006), pp. 111–121.

Clement, Grace: *Care, Autonomy, and Justice: Feminism and the Ethic of Care*. Westview Press: Boulder, Co. 1996.

Coons, Christian / Weber, Michael (eds.): *Paternalism: Theory and Practice*. Cambridge University Press: Cambridge 2013.

Cornell, Nicholas: "A Third Theory of Paternalism". *Michigan Law Review* 113 (2015), forthcoming.

Crisp, Roger / Slote, Michael (eds.): *Virtue Ethics*. Oxford University Press: Oxford 1997.

Cserne, Péter: *Freedom of Contract and Paternalism: Prospects and Limits of an Economic Approach*. Palgrave Macmillan: New York 2012.

Davidson, Donald: "Actions, Reasons, and Causes". *The Journal of Philosophy* 60 (23) (1963), pp. 685–700.

Davidson, Donald: *Essays on Actions and Events*. Oxford University Press: Oxford 1980.

Delmas-Marty, Mireille (ed.): *The European Convention for the Protection of Human Rights: International Protection versus National Restrictions*. Kluwer Academic: Dordrecht 1992.

Dénes, Balázs: "Drog és jog". *Beszélő* 10 (1) (2005) (www.beszelo.c3.hu/cikkek/drog-es-jog).

Devlin, Patrick: *The Enforcement of Morals*. Oxford University Press: Oxford 1965.

van Dijk, Pieter / van Hoof, Godefridus: *Theory and Practice of the European Convention on Human Rights*. Kluwer Law and Taxation Publishers: Deventer 1990.

Duff, Antony: "Harms and Wrongs". *Buffalo Criminal Law Review* 5 (1) (2001), pp. 13–45.

Dworkin, Gerald (ed.): *Mill's On Liberty: Critical Essays*. Rowman & Littlefield Publishers: Lanham, Md. 1997.

Dworkin, Gerald: "Moral Paternalism". *Law and Philosophy* 24 (3) (2005), pp. 305–319.

Dworkin, Gerald: "Paternalism". *The Monist* 56 (1) (1972), pp. 64–84.

Dworkin, Gerald: *The Theory and Practice of Autonomy*. Cambridge University Press: Cambridge 1988.

Dworkin, Ronald: *A Matter of Principle*. Harvard University Press: Cambridge, Mass. 1985.

Dworkin, Ronald: *Freedom's Law: The Moral Reading of the American Constitution*. Oxford University Press: Oxford 1996.

Dworkin, Ronald: "Liberal Community". *California Law Review* 77 (1989), pp. 479–504.

Dworkin, Ronald: *Life's Dominion*. HarperCollins: London 1993.

Dworkin, Ronald: "Lord Devlin and the Enforcement of Morals". *Yale Law Journal* 75 (1966), pp. 986–1005

Dworkin, Ronald: *Sovereign Virtue: The Theory and Practice of Equality*. Harvard University Press: Cambridge, Mass. 2000.

Dworkin, Ronald: *Taking Rights Seriously*. Harvard University Press: Cambridge, Mass. 1977a.

Dworkin, Ronald (ed.): *The Philosophy of Law*. Oxford University Press: Oxford 1977b.

Ericsson, Lars O.: "Charges Against Prostitution". *Ethics* 90 (3) (1980), pp. 335–366.

Fabre, Cécile: *Whose Body is it Anyway?*. Clarendon Press: Oxford 2006.

Feinberg, Joel: *Harmless Wrongdoing*. (= The Moral Limits of the Criminal Law), Oxford University Press: New York 1990.

Feinberg, Joel: *Harm to Others*. (= The Moral Limits of the Criminal Law), Oxford University Press: New York 1984.

Feinberg, Joel: *Harm to Self*. (= The Moral Limits of the Criminal Law), Oxford University Press: New York 1989.

Feinberg, Joel: "Legal Paternalism". *Canadian Journal of Philosophy* 1 (1) (1971), pp. 105–124.

Feinberg, Joel: "Legal Paternalism". In: *Rights, Justice and the Bounds of Liberty*. Princeton University Press: Princeton, NJ 1980.

Feinberg, Joel: *Social Philosophy*. Prentice-Hall: Englewood Cliffs 1973.

Feinberg, Joel / Coleman, Jules (eds.): *Philosophy of Law*. Cengage Learning: Belmont, Calif. 2008.

Feinberg, Joel / Gross, Hyman (eds.): *Philosophy of Law*. Wadsworth Publishing Co: Belmont 1991.

Filmer, Robert: *Patriarcha and Other Writings*. Cambridge University Press: Cambridge 1991.

Finnis, John: "Law, Morality and "Sexual Orientation"". *Notre Dame Law Review* 69 (5) (1994), pp. 1049–1076.

Foot, Philippa: "Euthanasia". *Philosophy & Public Affairs* 6 (2) (1977), pp. 85–112.

Frankfurt, Harry G.: *Necessity, Volition, and Love*. Cambridge University Press: Cambridge 1999.

Fuller, Lon L.: *The Morality of Law*. Yale University Press: New Haven 1964.

Garren, David J.: "Paternalism, Part I". *Philosophical Books* 47 (4) (2006), pp. 334–341.

Gaus, Gerald F.: *Social Philosophy*. M.E. Sharpe Inc.: Armonk, NY 1999.

George, Robert P.: *Making Men Moral – Civil Liberties and Public Morality*. Clarendon Press: Oxford 1995.

Gert, Bernard / Culver, Charles M.: "Paternalistic Behavior". *Philosophy & Public Affairs* 6 (1) (1976), pp. 45–57.

Gert, Bernard / Culver, Charles M.: "The Justification of Paternalism". 89 (2) (1979), pp. 199–210.

Gert, Bernard / Culver, Charles M. / Clouser, K. Danner: *Bioethics: a Return to Fundamentals*. Oxford University Press: New York 1997.

Gilligan, Carol: *In a Different Voice: Psychological Theory and Women's Development*. Harvard University Press: Cambridge, Mass. 1982.

Grill, Kalle: "The Normative Core of Paternalism". *Res Publica* 13 (4) (2007), pp. 441–458.

Győrfi, Tamás: "Üzenet az elefántcsonttoronyból". *Fundamentum* 9 (1) (2005), pp. 73–85.

Haksar, Vinit: *Equality, Liberty and Perfectionism*. Oxford University Press: Oxford 1979.

Halmai, Gábor: "Egy alkotmánybírósági (elő)ítélet nyomában". *Világosság* 37 (7) (1996), pp. 34–41.

Halmai, Gábor (ed.): *The Constitution Found?*. INDOK: Budapest 2000.

Halwani, Raja: "Care Ethics and Virtue Ethics". *Hypatia* 18 (3) (2003), pp. 161–192.

Hampton, Jean: *Political Philosophy*. Westview Press: Boulder, Co. 1997.

Hart, H.L.A.: *Essays in Jurisprudence and Philosophy*. Clarendon Press: Oxford 1983.

Hart, H.L.A.: *Law, Liberty and Morality*. Stanford University Press: Stanford 1963.

Hart, H.L.A.: "Social Solidarity and the Enforcement of Morality". *University of Chicago Law Review* 35 (1967).

Häyry, Heta: *The Limits of Medical Paternalism*. Routledge: London, New York 1991.

Heidegger, Martin: *Being and Time*. Blackwell: Oxford 1962.

Heinze, Eric: "Viewpoint Absolutism and Hate Speech". *Modern Law Review* 69 (4) (2006), pp. 543–582.

Held, Virginia (ed.): *Justice and Care: Essential Readings in Feminist Ethics*. Westview Press: Boulder, Co. 1995.

Heller, Ágnes: *Általános etika*. Cserépfalvi: Budapest 1994.

Herring, Jonathan: *Caring and the Law*. Hart Publishing: Oxford 2013.

Van Hoecke, Mark: *Law as Communication*. Hart Publishing: Oxford 2002.

Holroyd, Jules: "Relational Autonomy and Paternalistic Interventions". *Res Publica* 15 (4) (2009), pp. 321–336.

Horkheimer, Max: *Eclipse of Reason*. Continuum: London; New York 2004.

Horkheimer, Max / Adorno, Theodor W.: *Dialectic of Enlightenment*. Verso: London 1992.

Hospers, John: "Libertarianism and Legal Paternalism". *Journal of Libertarian Studies* 4 (3) (1980), pp. 255–265.

Hurka, Thomas: *Perfectionism*. Oxford University Press: New York 1993.

Hurley, Patrick J.: *A Concise Introduction to Logic*. 9th ed. Thomson/Wadsworth: Belmont, CA 2006.

Hursthouse, Rosalind: *On Virtue Ethics*. Oxford University Press: Oxford 1999.

Husak, Douglas N.: "Paternalism and autonomy". *Philosophy & Public Affairs* 10 (1981), pp. 27–46.

Husson, Céline: "“Lancer de nain” ou “lancer de nains”? Variations sur un thème". *Revue l'Europe des Libertés* 4 (11) (2003) (http://leuropedeslibertes.u-strasbg.fr/).

St. J. Macdonald, Ronald / Matscher, Franz / Petzold, Herbert (eds.): *The European System for the Protection of Human Rights*. Martinus Nijhoff: Dordrecht 1993.

Kant, Immanuel: *Groundwork of the Metaphysics of Morals*. (= Cambridge Texts in the History of Philosophy), Cambridge University Press: Cambridge 1998.

Kant, Immanuel: *Kant Selections*. Macmillan: New York, London 1988.

Kant, Immanuel: *On the Old Saw: That May be Right in Theory But It Won't Work in Practice*. University of Pennsylvania Press: Philadelphia 1974.

Kennedy, Duncan: "Distributive and Paternalist Motives in Contract and Tort Law, with Special Reference to Compulsory Terms and Unequal Bargaining Power". *Maryland Law Review* 41 (1982), pp. 563–658.

Kierkegaard, Soren: *Either/Or – A Fragment of Life*. Penguin Books: London 1992.

Kis, János: *Az állam semlegessége*. Atlantisz: Budapest 1997.

Kis, János / Sajó, András: "Amicus Curiae az Alkotmánybírósághoz". *Fundamentum* 1 (2003), pp. 134–141.

Kleinig, John: *Paternalism*. Manchester University Press: Manchester 1983.

Klosko, George / Wall, Steven (eds.): *Perfectionism and Neutrality: Essays in Liberal Theory*. Rowman & Littlefield Publishers: Lanham, Md 2003.

Knight, Kelvin (ed.): *The Macintyre Reader*. University of Notre Dame Press: Notre Dame, Ind. 1998.

Kommers, Donald P.: *The Constitutional Jurisprudence of the Federal Republic of Germany*. Second edition. Duke University Press: Durham, N.C. 1997.

Korsgaard, Christine M.: *The Sources of Normativity*. Cambridge University Press: Cambridge 1996.

Kuhn, Thomas S.: *A tudományos forradalmak szerkezete*. Osiris: Budapest 2000.

Kultgen, John: *Autonomy and Intervention: Parentalism in the Caring Life*. Oxford University Press: New York 1995.

Küpper, Herbert: "A szocialista maradványok szerepe a magyar alkotmányban". *Fundamentum* 11 (4) (2007), pp. 53–60.

Kymlicka, Will: *Contemporary Political Philosophy*. Oxford University Press: Oxford 1992.

Kymlicka, Will: *Contemporary Political Philosophy: an Introduction*. 2nd edition. Oxford University Press: Oxford 2002.

Kymlicka, Will: "Liberal Individualism and Liberal Neutrality". *Ethics* 99 (4) (1989), pp. 883–905.

LaFollette, Hugh (ed.): *Ethics in Practice: an Anthology*. Blackwell: Malden, Mass. 2002.

Lee, Simon: *Law and Morals: Warnock, Gillick, and Beyond*. Oxford University Press: New York 1986.

Leiser M., Burton / Campbell D., Tom (eds.): *Human Rights in Philosophy and Practice*. Ashgate: Dartmouth 2001.

Lévay, Miklós: "Paternalizmus és jogbizonytalanság". *Fundamentum* 9 (1) (2005), pp. 86–98.

Locke, John: *Second Treatise of Government*. Hackett Publishing: Indianapolis, Ind. 1980.

Lónyai, Mária (ed.): *Tények és értékek – A modern angolszász etika irodalmából*. Gondolat: Budapest 1981.

Lord Lester of Herne Hill: "Universality versus Subsidiarity: A Reply". *European Human Rights Law Review* 1 (1998), p. 73.

Lyons, David: *Ethics and the Rule of Law*. Cambridge University Press: Cambridge 1984.

Lyons, David (ed.): *Mill's Utilitarianism*. Rowman & Littlefield Publishers: Lanham, Md. 1997.

MacCormick, Neil: *H.L.A. Hart*. Stanford University Press: Stanford 1981.

MacIntyre, Alasdair C.: *After Virtue: a Study in Moral Theory*. University of Notre Dame Press: Notre Dame, Ind. 2007.

MacIntyre, Alasdair C: *A Short History of Ethics – A History of Moral Philosophy from the Homeric Age to the Twentieth Century*. Routledge: London 1998.

Mahlmann, Matthias: "Heidegger's Political Philosophy and the Theory of the Liberal State". *Law and Critique* 14 (3) (2003), pp. 229–252.

Mahoney, Paul: "Universality and Subsidiarity in the Strasbourg Case Law on Free Speech: Explaining Some Recent Judgments". *European Human Rights Law Review* 4 (1997), pp. 364–379.

Malm, Heidi M.: "Bad Samaritan Laws: Harm, Help, or Hype?". *Law and Philosophy* (2000), pp. 707–750.

Malm, Heidi M.: "Malm – Liberalism, Bad Samaritan Law and Legal Paternalism". *Ethics* 106 (1) (1995), pp. 4–31.

Marcuse, Herbert: *One-Dimensional Man: Studies in the Ideology of Advanced Industrial Society*. Routledge: London 2002.

Matravers, Derek / Pike, Jonathan / Warburton, Nigel: *Reading Political Philosophy: Machiavelli to Mill*. Routledge in association with the Open University: London 2000.

McCabe, David: "Joseph Raz and the Contextual Argument for Liberal Perfectionism". *Ethics* 111 (2001), pp. 493–522.

Mele, Alfred (ed.): *The Philosophy of Action*. Oxford University Press: Oxford 1997.

Ménard, Jean-Frédérick: "A "Nudge" for Public Health Ethics: Libertarian Paternalism as a Framework for Ethical Analysis of Public Health Interventions?". *Public Health Ethics* 3 (3) (2010), pp. 229–238.

Mill, John Stuart: *On Liberty*. Norton: New York 1975.

Mill, John Stuart: *On Liberty*. Penguin Books: London 1985.

Mill, John Stuart: *Utilitarianism*. Collins: London 1962.

M. Tóth, Balázs: "Zavaros szigorúság". *Fundamentum* 9 (1) (2005), pp. 99–108.

Murphy, Jeffrie G.: "Incompetence and Paternalism". *Archiv für Rechts- und Sozialphilosophie* 60 (4) (1974), pp. 465–486.

Murphy, Jeffrie G.: "Legal Moralism and Liberalism". *Arizona Law Review* 37 (1995), pp. 73–93.

New, Bill: "Paternalism and Public Policy". *Economics and Philosophy* 15 (1) (1999), pp. 63–83.

Nietzsche, Friedrich: *The Antichrist*. Noontide Press: Costa Mesa, CA 1980.

Nietzsche, Friedrich: *The Gay Science*. Cambridge University Press: Cambridge 2001.

Nussbaum, Martha C.: "Perfectionist Liberalism and Political Liberalism". *Philosophy & Public Affairs* 39 (1) (2011), pp. 3–45.

Nussbaum, Martha C.: *Sex and Social Justice*. Oxford University Press: New York 1999.

Nussbaum, Martha C.: *Women and Human Development: The Capabilities Approach*. Cambridge University Press: Cambridge 2000.

Oshana, Marina: *Personal Autonomy in Society*. Ashgate: Aldershot 2006.

Paley, John: "Heidegger and the Ethics of Care". *Nursing Philosophy* 1 (1) (2000), pp. 64–75.

Parfit, Derek: *Reasons and Persons*. Clarendon Press: Oxford 1984.

Peczenik, Aleksander: *On Law and Reason*. Springer: New York 2008.

Pennock, J. Roland / Chapman, John W. (eds.): *Nomos XV: The Limits of Law*. Lieber-Atherton: New York 1974.

Pfordten, Dietmar Von der: "Paternalismus und die Berücksichtigung des Anderen". In: Anderheiden, Michael et al. (eds.): *Paternalismus und Recht: in memoriam Angela Augustin (1968–2004)*. Mohr Siebeck: Tübingen 2006.

Pieper, Annemarie: *Van -e feminista etika?*. Áron Kiadó: Budapest 2004.

Plato: *The Republic*. Penguin Books: Harmondsworth 1955.

Pope, Thaddeus Mason: "Balancing Public Health Against Individual Liberty: the Ethics of Smoking Regulations". *University of Pittsburgh Law Review* 61 (2) (2000).

Pope, Thaddeus Mason: "Counting the Dragon's Teeth and Claws: The Definition of Hard Paternalism". *Georgia State University Law Review* 20 (3) (2004), pp. 659–722.

Pope, Thaddeus Mason: "Is Public Health Paternalism Really Never Justified? A Response to Joel Feinberg". *Oklahoma City University Law Review* 30 (1) (2005)(a), pp. 121–207.

Pope, Thaddeus Mason: "Monstrous Impersonation: A Critique of Consent-based Justifications for Hard Paternalism". *University of Missouri-Kansas City Law Review* 73 (2005)(b), pp. 681–713.

Rawls, John: *A Theory of Justice*. Revised edition. Belknap Press of Harvard University Press: Cambridge, Mass. 1999.

Rawls, John: "Justice as Fairness: Political not Metaphysical". *Philosophy & Public Affairs* 14 (3) (1985), pp. 223–251.

Rawls, John: "The Priority of Right and Ideas of the Good". *Philosophy & Public Affairs* 17 (4) (1988), pp. 251–276.

Rawls, John: "Two Concepts of Rules". *The Philosophical Review* 64 (1) (1955), pp. 3–32.

Raz, Joseph: "Facing up: A Reply". *Southern California Law Review* 62 (1989), pp. 1153–1235.

Raz, Joseph: *The Morality of Freedom*. Clarendon Press: Oxford 1986.

Riddall, J.G.: *Jurisprudence*. Butterwoths: London 1999.

Riley, Jonathan: *Mill on Liberty*. Routledge: London ; New York 1998.

Ross, David: *Aristotle*. Routledge: London, New York 1995.

Sadurski, Wojciech: "Joseph Raz on Liberal Neutrality and the Harm Principle". *Oxford Journal of Legal Studies* 10 (1990)(a), pp. 122–133.

Sadurski, Wojciech: *Moral Pluralism and Legal Neutrality*. (= Law and Philosophy Library), Springer Netherlands: Dordrecht 1990b.

Sadurski, Wojciech: "The Right, the Good and the Jurisprude". *Law and Philosophy* 7 (1) (1988), pp. 35–66.

Sandel, Michael J.: *Justice: What's the Right Thing to Do?*. Allen Lane: London 2009.

Sandel, Michael J.: *Liberalism and the Limits of Justice*. Cambridge University Press: Cambridge 1982.

Sandel, Michael J.: "Moral Argument and Liberal Toleration: Abortion and Homosexuality". *California Law Review* 77 (3) (1989), pp. 521–538.

Sartorius, Rolf E.: *Paternalism*. University of Minnesota Press: 1983.

Schneewind, Jerome B.: *The Invention of Autonomy*. Cambridge University Press: Cambridge 1998.

Scoccia, Danny: "In Defense of Hard Paternalism". *Law and Philosophy* 27 (4) (2008), pp. 351–381.

Scoccia, Danny: "Moral Paternalism, Virtue and Autonomy". *Australasian Journal of Philosophy* 78 (2000), pp. 53–71.

Shafer-Landau, Russ (ed.): *Ethical Theory: an Anthology*. (= Blackwell philosophy anthologies), 2nd ed. Wiley-Blackwell: Chichester, West Sussex ; Malden, MA 2013.

Shaver, Francis M.: "The Regulation of Prostitution: Avoiding the Morality Traps". *Canadian Journal of Law and Society* 9 (1) (1994), pp. 123–145.

Sher, George: *Beyond Neutrality: Perfectionism and Politics*. Cambridge University Press: Cambridge 1997.

Shiffrin, Seana: "Paternalism, Unconscionability Doctrine, and Accommodation". *Philosophy & Public Affairs* 29 (3) (2000), pp. 205–250.

Shrage, Laurie: "Should Feminists Oppose Prostitution?". *Ethics* 99 (2) (1989), pp. 347–361.

Singer, Peter: *Practical Ethics*. Cambridge University Press: Cambridge 1993.

Slote, Michael: *The Ethics of Care and Empathy*. Routledge: London, New York 2007.

Smart, J.J.C. / Williams, Bernard: *Utilitarianism: For and Against*. Cambridge University Press: Cambridge 1973.

Smith, Paul: *Moral and Political Philosophy: Key Issues, Concepts and Theories*. Palgrave Macmillan: Basingstoke 2008.

Smith, Peter / Jones, O.R.: *The Philosophy of Mind: An Introduction*. Cambridge University Press: Cambridge 1986.

Sólyom, László: *Az alkotmánybíráskodás kezdetei Magyarországon*. Osiris: Budapest 2001.

Stephen, James Fitzjames: *Law, Equality, Fraternity*. Liberty Fund: Indianapolis, Ind 1993.

Stewart, Hamish: "Harms, Wrongs, and Set-Backs in Feinberg's Moral Limits of the Criminal Law". *Buffalo Criminal Law Review* 5 (1) (2001), pp. 47–67.

Sunstein, Cass R.: *Why Nudge? – The Politics of Libertarian Paternalism*. Yale University Press: New Haven 2014.

Sunstein, Cass R. / Thaler, Richard H.: "Libertarian Paternalism is not an Oxymoron". *University of Chicago Law Review* 70 (2003), p. 1159.

Takács, Péter: *Nehéz jogi esetek*. Napvilág Kiadó: Budapest 2002.

Taylor, Charles: *Sources of the Self: The Making of the Modern Identity*. Harvard University Press: Cambridge, Mass. 1989.

Taylor, Charles: *The Ethics of Authenticity*. Harvard University Press: Cambridge, Mass 1992.

Ten, C. L.: *Mill on Liberty*. Clarendon Press: Oxford 1980.

Ten, C. L.: *Mill's On Liberty – A Critical Guide*. Cambridge University Press: Cambridge 2009.

Tengelyi, László: "A cselekvés narratív értelmezése". *Aspecto* 1 (1) (2008), pp. 149–164.

Thaler, Richard H. / Sunstein, Cass R.: *Nudge: Improving Decisions About Health, Wealth, and Happiness*. Revised & Expanded edition. Penguin Books: New York 2009.

Thomas, Matthew / Buckmaster, Luke: *Paternalism in Social Policy – When It Is Justifiable?*. Parliament of Australia, Department of Parliamentary Services: 2010.

Tóth, Gábor Attila: "Az eljárási alkotmányosság tartalma". *Fundamentum* 8 (3) (2004), pp. 5–33.

Tóth, Gábor Attila: *Túl a szövegen: Értekezés a magyar Alkotmányról*. Osiris: Budapest 2009.

Tversky, Amos / Kahneman, Daniel: "Judgment under Uncertainty: Heuristics and Biases". *Science* 185 (1974), pp. 1124–1131.

Uitz, Renáta: "Melegházasságon innen és túl – A meleg párok esete a köztársasággal". *Fundamentum* 9 (2) (2005), pp. 73–83.

Unsworth, Clive: "Blasphemy, Cultural Divergence and Legal Relativism". *Modern Law Review* 58 (5) (1995), pp. 658–677.

Valdés, Ernesto Garzón: "On Justifying Legal Paternalism". *Ratio Juris* 3 (1990), pp. 173–184.

VanDeVeer, Donald: *Paternalistic Intervention: The Moral Bounds of Benevolence*. Princeton University Press: Princeton, NJ 1986.

Veitch, Scott: *Moral Conflict and Legal Reasoning*. Hart Publishing: Oxford 1999.

Waldron, Jeremy: "Autonomy and Perfectionism in Raz's Morality of Freedom". *Southern California Law Review* 62 (1989), pp. 1097–1152.

Westlund, Andrea C.: "Rethinking Relational Autonomy". *Hypatia* 24 (4) (2009), pp. 26–49.

Wittgenstein, Ludwig: *Philosophical Investigations*. Basil Blackwell: Oxford 1968.

Wolfe, Christopher: "Liberalism and Paternalism: A Critique of Ronald Dworkin". *The Review of Politics* 56 (4) (1994), pp. 615–640.

Zamir, Eyal: "The Efficiency of Paternalism". *Virginia Law Review* 84 (2) (1998), pp. 229–286.

Zwolinski, Matt: "The Ethics of Price Gouging". *Business Ethics Quarterly* 18 (03) (2008), pp. 347–378.

Internet resources

Ashley, Viv: *Philosophical Models of Autonomy*. (= Essex Autonomy Project Green Paper Report), 2012. (In: http://autonomy.essex.ac.uk/philosophical-models-of-autonomy).

Athanassoulis, Nafsika: "Virtue Ethics". In: *Internet Encyclopedia of Philosophy*. (In: http://www.iep.utm.edu/virtue/).

Beauchamp, Tom: "The Principle of Beneficence in Applied Ethics". In: Zalta, Edward N. (ed.): *The Stanford Encyclopedia of Philosophy*. Winter 2013. (In: http://plato.stanford.edu/archives/win2013/entries/principle-beneficence/).

Bird, Alexander / Tobin, Emma: "Natural Kinds". In: Zalta, Edward N. (ed.): *The Stanford Encyclopedia of Philosophy*. 2012 Winter. (In: http://plato.stanford.edu/entries/natural-kinds/).

Brink, David: "Mill's Moral and Political Philosophy". In: Zalta, Edward N. (ed.): *The Stanford Encyclopedia of Philosophy*. Fall 2014. (In: http://plato.stanford.edu/entries/mill-moral-political/).

Carter, Ian: "Positive and Negative Liberty". In: Zalta, Edward N. (ed.): *The Stanford Encyclopedia of Philosophy*. Spring 2012. (In: http://plato.stanford.edu/entries/liberty-positive-negative/).

Chappell, Sophie Grace: "Bernard Williams". In: Zalta, Edward N. (ed.): *The Stanford Encyclopedia of Philosophy*. 2015 Spring. (In: http://plato.stanford.edu/entries/williams-bernard/).

Christman, John: "Autonomy in Moral and Political Philosophy". In: Zalta, Edward N. (ed.): *The Stanford Encyclopedia of Philosophy*. Spring 2015. (In: http://plato.stanford.edu/entries/autonomy-moral/).

Hooker, Brad: "Rule Consequentialism". In: Zalta, Edward N. (ed.): *The Stanford Encyclopedia of Philosophy*. Spring 2011. (In: http://plato.stanford.edu/archives/spr2011/entries/consequentialism-rule/).

Hursthouse, Rosalind: "Virtue Ethics". In: Zalta, Edward N. (ed.): *The Stanford Encyclopedia of Philosophy*. Fall 2013. (In: http://plato.stanford.edu/entries/ethics-virtue/).

Johnson, Robert: "Kant's Moral Philosophy". In: Zalta, Edward N. (ed.): *The Stanford Encyclopedia of Philosophy*. Summer 2014. (In: http://plato.stanford.edu/entries/kant-moral/).

O'Shea, Tom: *Critics of Autonomy*. (= Essex Autonomy Project Green Paper Report), University of Essex: 2012. (In: http://autonomy.essex.ac.uk/critics-of-autonomy).

Paternalism, Oxford English Dictionary (Oxford University Press: June 2015) (http://www.oed.com/).

Sander-Staudt, Maureen: "Care Ethics". In: *Internet Encyclopedia of Philosophy*. (In: http://www.iep.utm.edu/care-eth/).

Shor, Mikhael: "Game of Chicken". In: *Dictionary of Game Theory Terms*. (In: http://www.gametheory.net/Dictionary/Games/GameofChicken.html).

Sinnott-Armstrong, Walter: "Consequentialism". In: Zalta, Edward N. (ed.): *The Stanford Encyclopedia of Philosophy*. Spring 2014. (In: http://plato.stanford.edu/entries/consequentialism).

Stanton-Ife, John: "The Limits of Law". In: Zalta, Edward N. (ed.): *The Stanford Encyclopedia of Philosophy*. Winter 2014. (In: http://plato.stanford.edu/en tries/law-limits/).

Stoljar, Natalie: "Feminist Perspectives on Autonomy". In: Zalta, Edward N. (ed.): *The Stanford Encyclopedia of Philosophy*. Spring 2014. (In: http://plato.stan ford.edu/entries/feminism-autonomy/).

Sussman, David: Is Agent-Regret Rational? (Working paper, 47th Chapel Hill Colloquium in Philosophy, University of Illinois at Urbana-Champaign) (http://philosophy.unc.edu/files/2014/07/Sussman_colloquium-.pdf) (06.06.2015).

Thompson, Lindsay: Paternalism. Encyclopedia Britannica Online, 2015. (http://www.britannica.com/topic/paternalism).

Wilson, George / Shpall, Samuel: "Action". In: Zalta, Edward N. (ed.): *Stanford Encyclopedia of Philosophy*. Summer 2012. (In: http://plato.stanford.edu/entries/action).

Wall, Steven: "Perfectionism in Moral and Political Philosophy". In: Zalta, Edward N. (ed.): *The Stanford Encyclopedia of Philosophy*. Winter 2012. (http://plato.stanford.edu/entries/perfectionism-moral/).

Wenar, Leif: "John Rawls". In: Zalta, Edward N. (ed.): *The Stanford Encyclopedia of Philosophy*. Winter 2013. (In: http://plato.stanford.edu/entries/rawls/).

Index of cases

European Court of Human Rights

Hungarian Constitutional Court

Decision 8/1990. (IV. 23.) AB

Decision 23/1990 (X. 31.) AB

Decision 64/1991 (XII. 17.) AB

Decision 22/1992. (IV.10.) AB

Decision 60/1993. (XI. 29.) AB

Decision 14/1995. (III.13.) AB

Decision 21/1996. (V. 17.) AB

Decision 20/1999. (VI.25.) AB

Decision 37/2000. (X. 31.) AB

Decision 37/2002. (IX.4.) AB

Decision 22/2003. (IV. 28) AB

Decision 54/2004. (XII. 13.) AB

Decision 43/2005. (XI. 14) AB

Decision 39/2007. (VI.20) AB

Decision 95/2008. (VII. 3.) AB

Decision 32/2010. (III. 25.) AB

Decision 18/2013. (VII. 3.) AB

European Court of Justice

Adoui and Cornuaille [1982] ECR 1665, Joined Cases C-115/81 and C-116/81

Germany v Parliament and Council, [2000] ECR I-8419, C-376/98

Jany and others v Staatssecretaris van Justitie [2001] ECR-I 8615, C-268/99

Liga Portuguesa de Futebol Profissional v Departamento de Jogos da Santa Casa da Misericórdia de Lisboa, C-42/07

Omega Spielhallen und Automatenaufstellungs GmbH v Oberbürgermeisterin der Bundesstadt Bonn, 2004 I-9609, C-36/02

Rewe-Zentral AG v Bundesmonopolverwaltung für Branntwein, [1979] ECR 649, C-120/78

Society for the Protection of Unborn Children Ireland [1991] ECR I-4685, C-159/90

The Netherlands v European Parliament and the Council, [2001] ECR I-7079, C-377/98

Supreme Court of the United States

Bowers v Hardwick 478 U.S. 186 (1986)

Griswold v Connecticut 381 U.S. 479 (1965)

Lawrence v Texas, 539 U.S. 558 (2003)

Miller v California 413 U.S. 15 (1973)

Romer v Evans 517 U.S. 620 (1996)

Stanley v Georgia 394 U.S. 557 (1969)

Other jurisdictions

R v Butler (1992) 1. S.C.R. 452.

R v Chief Metropolitan Stipendiary Magistrate, ex parte Choudhory (1991) 1 All E.R. 306 at 318

R v Crown Court at Aylesbury, ex parte Chahal [1976]

R v Lemon, R. v Gay News Ltd (1979) 1 All E.R. 898.

R (G) v Nottinghamshire Healthcare NHS Trust [2008] EWHC 1096

Wackenheim v France CCPR/C/75/D/854/1999;

Wackenheim v France, Conseil d'Etat, 27 Octobre 1995, N° 136727, Commune de Morsang-sur-Orge.

Warsaw Studies in Philosophy and Social Sciences

Edited by Tadeusz Szawiel and Jakub Kloc-Konkołowicz

Vol. 1 Paweł Skuczyński: The Status of Legal Ethics. 2013.

Vol. 2 Szymon Wróbel: Grammar and Glamour of Cooperation. Lectures on the Philosophy of Mind, Language and Action. 2014.

Vol. 3 Zbigniew Drozdowicz: Cartesian Rationalism. Understanding Descartes. 2015.

Vol. 4 Daria Lebedeva: Quaternion of the Examples of a Philosophical Influence: Schopenhauer-Dostoevsky-Nietzsche-Cioran. 2015.

Vol. 5 Antal Szerletics: Paternalism. Moral Theory and Legal Practice. 2015.

www.peterlang.com

www.ingramcontent.com/pod-product-compliance
Ingram Content Group UK Ltd.
Pitfield, Milton Keynes, MK11 3LW, UK
UKHW041827100926
8556IPUK00002B/62

9 783631 668009